W9-AWQ-975

DATE		

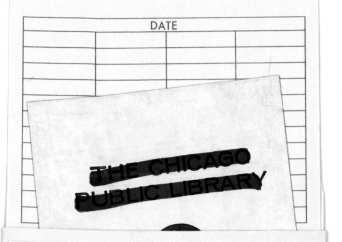

THE CHICAGO
PUBLIC LIBRARY

Dedication

This volume is fittingly dedicated to the memory of

GERALD G. SOMERS

*a member of the Committee on Evaluation of
Employment and Training Programs, whose untimely
death in December 1977 was a great loss to us all.
Dr. Somers, a professor of economics at the University
of Wisconsin, brought to the Committee not only
skill in human resources research and professional
objectivity, but also a compassionate view of the
problems of the disadvantaged. His influence is
reflected in the recommendations of the Committee.*

v

SURVEY AREAS AND FIELD RESEARCH ASSOCIATES

ARIZONA

Phoenix–Maricopa County Consortium
Balance of Arizona
    Edmund V. Mech, Professor, School of Social Work, Arizona State
University

CALIFORNIA

Long Beach
Orange County Consortium
    Paul Bullock, Research Economist, Institute of Industrial Relations,
University of California, Los Angeles

San Joaquin Consortium
    John J. Mitchell, Research Associate, Center for Applied Manpower
Research

Stanislaus County
    Richard R. Kropp, Research Assistant, Center for Applied Manpower
Research

FLORIDA

Pasco County
Pinellas County–St. Petersburg Consortium
    Emil Bie, former Deputy Director, Office of Technical Support, U.S.
Employment Service

ILLINOIS

Cook County
    Douglas Windham, Associate Professor, Department of Education,
University of Chicago

INDIANA

Gary
    William S. Griffith, Associate Professor, Department of Education,
University of Chicago

Kansas City–Wyandotte County Consortium
Joseph A. Pichler, Dean, School of Business, University of Kansas

Topeka–Shawnee County Consortium
Charles E. Krider, Associate Professor, School of Business, University of Kansas

MAINE

Balance of Maine
Roderick A. Forsgren, Professor and Associate Dean, Graduate School, University of Maine

MICHIGAN

Calhoun County
E. Earl Wright, Director, W. E. Upjohn Institute for Employment Research

Lansing Tri-County Regional Manpower Consortium
Steven M. Director, Assistant Professor, School of Labor and Industrial Relations, Michigan State University

MINNESOTA

St. Paul
Ramsey County
James E. Jernberg, Associate Director for Administration, School of Public Affairs, University of Minnesota

NEW JERSEY

Middlesex County
Union County
Jack Chernick, Professor, Institute of Management and Labor Relations, Rutgers University

NEW YORK

New York City
Lois Blume, Professor, New School for Social Research

NORTH CAROLINA

Raleigh Consortium
Robert M. Fearn, Professor, North Carolina State University

Balance of North Carolina
Alvin M. Cruze, Director, Center for the Study of Social Behavior, Research Triangle Institute

OHIO

Cleveland Area–Western Reserve Consortium
Lorain County
Jan P. Muczyk, Associate Professor, Department of Management and Labor, Cleveland State University

PENNSYLVANIA

Chester County
Philadelphia
David R. Zimmerman, Assistant Professor, Department of Management, Temple University

TEXAS

Capital Area Consortium
Balance of Texas
Robert W. Glover, Associate Director, Center for the Study of Human Resources, University of Texas

Preface

The need for federal programs to assist persons who are at a disadvantage in the labor market was recognized early in the 1960s with the passage of the Manpower Development and Training Act (MDTA). A score of categorical programs, all designed to deal with the problems of the disadvantaged, was launched during the decade, each with its own protective statute and institutions. By 1973, the federal government was spending over $2 billion a year on employment and training programs, most of them administered directly by federal officials. In that year the Comprehensive Employment and Training Act (CETA) changed, in a very fundamental way, responsibility for employment and training programs and the status of the categorical programs. Control was entrusted to state and local officials; most separate, categorical programs were eliminated as independent entities.

The act's passage was widely acclaimed. Department of Labor officials, frustrated by a maze of uncoordinated programs, welcomed the decategorization of overlapping programs as a major reform that promised to bring order into the manpower system. The Nixon Administration, philosophically committed to decentralization, saw CETA as constraining the federal role and placing greater control at the grass roots. Local elected officials, who for a decade had been passive observers of the manpower scene, embraced the opportunity to incorporate employment and training programs into the structure of local government. Decentralization, it was assumed, would enable them to establish control over local manpower programs; decategorization would permit the flexibility necessary to put together combinations of programs most responsive to local needs.

To test the extent to which these expectations have been realized and to assess the economic, social, and political impact of CETA, the National Research Council established the Committee on Evaluation of Employment and Training Programs in 1974.

The evaluation study of the Committee was conducted in two phases. The first, completed in 1976, dealt mainly with the implementation and operation of CETA in its first year. The focus was on CETA programs dealing with the problems of structural unemployment (Title I), with particular attention to changes in methods of allocating resources, planning, types of manpower programs, systems for delivering services, and the types of people served. Three reports were produced: *The Comprehensive Employment and Training Act: Impact on People, Places and Programs;* a volume of case studies, *Transition to Decentralized Manpower Programs;* and *The Comprehensive Employment and Training Act: Abstracts of Selected Studies.*

The second phase of the study was a follow-up on the subsequent year's experiences under CETA. Soon after its enactment, CETA was engulfed by a recession. In response, a new title designed as a countercyclical measure was added. Title VI added a new public service employment program and radically changed the nature and objectives of CETA. In order to explore the issues and effects associated with this public service employment title, the original study design was broadened and the project extended.

This volume, the final report of the study, examines the differences between CETA Title I programs and their predecessors and compares legislative goals with results. It also examines the impact of public service employment programs on the structurally oriented programs of Title I and the degree to which the primary objective of Title VI—creation of new jobs—is achieved.

The last chapter incorporates the recommendations of the Committee on Evaluation of Employment and Training Programs. These proposals should be useful in suggesting legislative initiatives, developing Department of Labor policy, and improving local operations.

As this report is issued, Congress is considering bills to reauthorize CETA and extend it for 4 years, to September 1982. The reauthorization bills in the House and Senate differ in some respects but have these features in common: the targeting of most programs to persons in low-income families who meet unemployment eligibility criteria; a continuing public service employment program; limitation on the duration of participation in any CETA program; limitation on supplementation of wages above the limits set for public service employment; incorporation of new youth programs, including the Young Adult Conservation Corps; a separate title to encourage private sector initiatives; and simplification of the grant application process.

The information for the study was obtained from 28 prime sponsors, the designated units of government responsible for CETA programs. The study covers the range of CETA programs administered by local officials, but not those administered directly by the national office of CETA, such as the Job Corps (Title IV) or special programs for Indians and migrants. The sample of 28 prime sponsors, stratified by type of sponsor (6 cities, 9 counties, 9 consortia, and 4 states) and by variations in population and degree of unemployment, was drawn from the universe of more than 400 prime sponsors. In each of the 28 sites, resident field-research associates interviewed key officials, as well as other knowledgeable persons. The information they collected was supplemented by data from the national reporting system of the Employment and Training Administration of the Department of Labor and by other sources.

This study is part of the program of the Assembly of Behavioral and Social Sciences of the National Research Council. William Mirengoff, who originated the project, was the study director. He was assisted by Lester Rindler, senior research associate. Dr. Claire K. Lipsman, on loan from the Department of Labor, made an invaluable contribution to the design of the second phase of the survey and to the analysis and drafting of chapters dealing with manpower planning, Title I programs, delivery of services, and public service employment, as well as in formulating recommendations for consideration by the Committee. The Committee is indebted to the resident field-research associates, whose diligence and expertise made this study possible. Bernard Offerman and Robert Ferrar, assistant professors, Department of Management and Labor, Cleveland State University, contributed to the reports for the Cleveland and Lorain areas, respectively. The Committee is especially grateful to the prime sponsors and local respondents who patiently responded to lengthy questionnaires and provided statistical information above and beyond normal reporting requirements. Research assistance for the project was provided by Richard C. Piper and Scott S. Seablom. Mark Kendall was a consultant for the econometric model in the public service employment chapter. Phyllis Groom McCreary was the editor; Marian D. Miller, Rose Gunn, Diane Goldman, and Ingrid C. Larsen furnished the support services.

I am grateful to the members of the Committee on Evaluation of Employment and Training Programs, who provided advice and guidance throughout the project and reviewed a succession of drafts of this report.

This study was prepared under a grant from the Ford Foundation. Supplementary funding was provided by the Department of Labor. Robert Schrank of the Ford Foundation contributed to the formulation of the study objectives and to the case study design. Stanley Brezenoff, also of the Ford Foundation, has been a constant source of encouragement and support. The authors wish to acknowledge the cooperation of the many persons in the national and regional offices of the Employment and Training Administration who provided data and commented on the drafts of the staff report and of Howard Rosen, Director, Office of Research and Development, and Seymour Brandwein, Director, Office of Program Evaluation for helpful technical advice and encouragement.

PHILIP J. RUTLEDGE, *Chairman*
Committee on Evaluation of
  Employment and Training Programs

Contents

xiii

APPENDIXES

List of Figures

List of Tables

CETA:
Manpower
Programs
Under
Local
Control

1 Overview

BACKGROUND

The Comprehensive Employment and Training Act of 1973[1] can be viewed against the backdrop of changes in manpower policy over several decades. There has been growing acceptance of government intervention in the processes of the labor market to minimize dislocations and to protect individuals from hazards over which they have little control. Legislation to set up a network of public employment offices, to establish minimum standards of wages and hours of work, and to provide income support during periods of joblessness date back to the 1930s. Federal subsidies for vocational education to help prepare youth for the job market were authorized even earlier. The Employment Act of 1946, which acknowledged federal responsibility to promote maximum employment, is landmark legislation.

In the 1960s manpower policy entered a new phase. Emphasis was on development of human resources, equal opportunity for minority groups and others who faced special barriers to employment, and the elimination of poverty. There was recognition that, even in periods of rapid economic growth, there are persons who, because of inadequate education, lack of skills, or structural impediments in the labor market, have a particularly hard time in entering and competing in the labor market.

[1]See page 4 for a summary of the act.

The specific design of manpower programs has, from the beginning, been shaped by the prevailing economic, social, and political climate. In the 1960s, the climate was conducive to manpower programs focused on the problems of those most in need of assistance in obtaining employment. The disadvantaged were "discovered"; the civil rights movement was at a peak; the administration was committed to a "war on poverty"; and the economy was in a position to absorb additional workers, even those at the margin of the labor market.

In this propitious setting, a host of manpower programs for special groups and places was initiated. The primary legislative vehicles were the Manpower Development and Training Act of 1962 and the Economic Opportunity Act of 1964. Their major components were work experience for disadvantaged youth and ski'l training for adults. Smaller programs were designed for older workers and other special groups and for inner cities. These programs were designed and controlled at the federal level and operated locally by the employment services, vocational education agencies, and various community organizations that were usually outside the local governmental unit.

Dissatisfaction with the tangle of separate programs that evolved, plus the drive of the Nixon Administration towards decentralization of federal programs, laid the foundation for a basic reform of the nation's manpower system.

In December 1973, after several years of legislative gestation, the Comprehensive Employment and Training Act (CETA) was passed. Program control shifted from the federal level to more than 400 state and local units of government, and programs lost their separate identities and funding. These changes were expected to permit greater flexibility in fashioning programs to local circumstances. This reform of the manpower system appealed to pragmatic administrators seeking a more rational way to conduct employment and training activities, to those attracted by the features of grass roots participation, and to those committed to a reduction of the federal role.

The 1970s were marked by sluggish economic growth and diminished social activism. The number of people seeking help as a result of the recession increased sharply as job opportunities grew more scarce. Rising unemployment stimulated interest in job creation programs that had been dormant since the 1930s and changed the size, objectives, and designs of manpower programs. The Emergency Employment Act of 1971, known as PEP, authorized $2.25 billion over a 2-year period to employ jobless persons in essential public service activities. By 1973, when CETA was enacted, the economy had improved significantly except in lingering pockets of high unemployment. These were addressed by a modest public service employment program under Title II of CETA. Before this program could be fairly launched, however, unemployment rose precipitously, and in late 1974 Congress passed the Emergency Jobs and Unemployment Assistance Act, adding a new public service employment component (Title VI) to CETA and authorizing $2.5 billion for it for 1 year.

As the recession persisted, the Title VI public service employment program grew and soon overshadowed the Title I programs, which were designed to deal essentially with persons at a disadvantage in seeking employment. In 1976, Congress extended Title VI and in 1977 authorized its expansion from 300,000 to 600,000 jobs. By 1978, Titles II and VI, the public service employment programs, accounted for 58 percent of the CETA appropriation, compared with 34 percent in 1975. CETA was now addressing two major dysfunctions of the labor market— structural and cyclical.

CETA OBJECTIVES

The major objective of CETA is to provide training and improve employment opportunities for the economically disadvantaged and for the unemployed and underemployed. The means for accomplishing this end, the strategic objective, is to place the administration of manpower programs with local authorities and permit them to select programs appropriate to their needs.

STRATEGIC OBJECTIVES

The first and central strategic objective of CETA, decentralization, has been achieved. Now, for the first time, manpower programs in each community are built into the local government structures under the authority of elected officials. But the shift from federal to local control occurred without abdication of federal oversight responsibilities and the degree of federal presence continues to be a controversial issue. Although 90 percent of the fiscal 1978 CETA funds are in programs under local control, there are increasing federal constraints on programs arising out of new legislation and from emphasis on Department of Labor accountability that limits local autonomy. Moreover, after the Nixon Administration there was less of an ideological commitment to decentralization.

SUMMARY OF THE COMPREHENSIVE
EMPLOYMENT AND TRAINING ACT (CETA)

The Comprehensive Employment and Training Act of 1973 (PL 93-203), as amended by the Emergency Jobs and Unemployment Assistance Act of 1974 (PL 93-567), by the Emergency Jobs Programs Extension Act of 1976 (PL 94-444), by the Comprehensive Employment and Training Act Amendments of 1977 (PL 95-44), and by the Youth Employment and Demonstration Projects Act of 1977 (PL 95-93), has eight titles:

Title I authorizes comprehensive manpower services for the unemployed, underemployed, and economically disadvantaged. Programs are administered by prime sponsors, which are cities and counties of 100,000 or more and consortia. The state government is prime sponsor for the balance of state. Funds are allocated according to each area's prior year's apportionment, number of unemployed, and adults in low-income families. Prime sponsors must submit an acceptable plan to the Secretary of Labor, prepared in consultation with local advisory councils. A state manpower services council reviews local plans and arranges for the cooperation of state agencies.

Title II provides funds to prime sponsors and Indian reservations to hire the unemployed in areas of substantial unemployment for public service jobs. Funds are allotted on the basis of the number of unemployed.

Title III provides for nationally administered programs for Indians, migrant and seasonal farm workers, youth, and other groups that are in particular need of such services. This title also gives the Secretary of Labor responsibility for research, evaluation, experimental and demonstration projects, labor market information, and job banks.

Title IV authorizes the Department of Labor to operate the Job Corps, residential training centers for disadvantaged young men and women.

Title V establishes a National Commission for Manpower Policy to identify goals, evaluate manpower development programs, and make recommendations to the President and to Congress. (The Emergency Jobs Programs Extension Act of 1976 establishes a separate National Commission on Employment and Unemployment Statistics.)

Title VI authorizes public service jobs for the unemployed. Funds are allocated to prime sponsors and Indian tribes, based on the number of unemployed, the unemployed in excess of a 4.5 percent rate, and the unemployed in areas of substantial unemployment. Under 1976 amendments, funds for the expanded Title VI program are in new short-duration projects and most new participants must be long-term, low-income unemployed or welfare recipients.

Title VII contains provisions applicable to all programs such as prohibitions against discrimination and political activity.

Title VIII establishes a Young Adult Conservation Corps to carry out projects on public lands.

CETA's second strategic objective was to discontinue 17 separate and independent programs to give prime sponsors the flexibility to put together a mix of manpower services suitable to their localities. However, in response to new developments, Congress added new categories of service. Categorical programs, which amounted to more than one-half of all CETA resources in 1975, accounted for three-fourths of appropriations in 1978. Indeed, all of the program titles in CETA, except Title I, authorize categorical programs. Proposals now before Congress would continue the trend to address discrete problems with specifically targeted programs. As federal programs expand in response to the needs of particular groups, their purposes are more narrowly defined, the conditions are increased, the federal presence is extended, and the scope of state and local discretion diminished. Under the impact of these developments, CETA has become a "hybrid" program; not entirely decentralized, nor completely decategorized.

There are a number of subsidiary objectives that Congress sought to achieve through the manpower reform: improving the system for allocating resources, eliminating duplication and fragmentation in the delivery of manpower services, assuring that service deliverers of proven ability are given consideration by local sponsors, and providing for wider consultation in planning for manpower services.

PROGRAM OBJECTIVES

CETA has two major program objectives. The original legislation continued the structural objectives of earlier manpower programs—to improve, through remedial training and employment strategies, the employability of persons lacking knowledge, preparation, and connections with the world of work and to expand employment opportunities in areas of chronic and substantial unemployment. Amendments added a countercyclical objective—creation of temporary jobs in the public sector to counter rising unemployment.

Meeting Structural Objectives

The extent to which the structural objectives of CETA are met depends upon who is served, the services they receive, and the outcomes of these services. The original act expressed concern for the poor, youth, minorities, older workers, migrant farm workers, Indians, and others who are at a disadvantage in the labor market. However, the specific eligibility requirements of CETA were much broader. Not only were the disadvantaged eligible, but also the unemployed and underemployed generally. Moreover, rising joblessness in the 1970s expanded the constituency of regular manpower programs to include persons not ordinarily in need of manpower services. In the first 2 years of CETA, the combined effect of these conditions enlarged the pool of program applicants, and Title I enrollees were older, better educated, and less disadvantaged than their predecessors in similar pre-CETA programs.

The assumption that employment and training programs will assist in the development of human capital is still the fundamental premise of the structurally oriented programs of Title I. In the main, the nature of the services provided under Title I is much the same as before CETA. Local sponsors have not used their newly acquired flexibility to undertake radically different programs. Decentralization and decategorization do not necessarily produce abrupt changes from past patterns, especially if the sponsor is unfamiliar with manpower issues and programs. There has been, however, a relative movement away from preparation for economic self-sufficiency toward subsidized jobs. Relative expenditures for the major Title I development programs, classroom and on-the-job training, declined between 1974 and 1976, while the proportion of expenditures for work experience and other income-maintenance programs rose. Some increase in skill-training programs occurred in 1977. The shift towards income maintenance reflected the softening of the economy during these years and sponsors' uncertainty of the usefulness of skill training in a loose labor market. Even where classroom training is prevalent, local sponsors seem to opt for low-cost, short-duration courses.

The National Research Council (NRC) study limited its examination of the outcomes of CETA programs to the extent to which participants obtained unsubsidized employment. Placement outcomes, the ratios of persons who enter jobs to those who terminate from CETA, are lower than before CETA for similar programs, while the annual per person costs of Titles I and VI are in line with the pre-CETA costs. The ratio of people who entered employment from adult-oriented Title I programs was 42 percent in 1976, that is, for every 100 who terminated, 42 were either placed in jobs or obtained jobs on their own. The pre-CETA 1974 estimate for comparable programs was 57 percent. The placement record for the CETA public service jobs programs is also lower than that of the earlier PEP program. Placement rates for both Title I and public service employment rose in 1977, but were still below rates for corresponding pre-CETA programs. The dilemma of manpower policy is its seemingly paradoxical emphasis on job placement, while it urges the enrollment of the least employable.

Meeting Countercyclical Objectives

Central to the countercyclical objective of CETA is the creation of public service jobs in addition to what state and local governments would fund in the absence of federal support: Units of government are required to maintain their regular level of effort and may not substitute federal for state and local funds. However, local officials, especially those struggling with fiscal crises, tend to view federal funds as a source of fiscal relief, and substition has been a thorny issue.

This study estimates that the direct job creation effect of CETA's public service employment (PSE) programs in the public sector averaged about 65 percent between mid-1974 and the end of 1976. That is, out of every 100 positions funded, 65 would not otherwise have existed. (These estimates apply to the period prior to the 1976 amendments to Title VI that attempted to restrict substitution.) Moreover, CETA salaries generate additional jobs in the economy through the indirect multiplier effect. No attempt has been made to estimate the job creation rate of positions allocated to nonprofit organizations, but it is presumed to be greater than the rate achieved in the public sector.

To hard-pressed officials, all dollars, whatever their program labels, are green, and the difficulties of tracking federal dollars through the mazes of local budget processes make substitution difficult to identify, measure, and control. When Congress extended and expanded Title VI in 1976, it also attempted to deal with substitution. The Emergency Jobs Programs Extension Act (EJPEA) required that all Title VI funds above the amount necessary to sustain existing levels of Title VI employment be used to fund positions in short-term "projects" that are not to be part of regular ongoing activities. They were to be specific tasks conducted by nonprofit community organizations or by prime sponsors. The limited duration of projects, their separation from regular government activities, and the encouragement of PSE funding to nonprofit organizations were all intended to constrain substitution. However, in the interests of rapid implementation of the expanded PSE program, the original concept of a project was diluted. It remains to be seen whether the new provisions of EJPEA will reduce job seepage and whether useful public service jobs were created as a result of this amendment.

Balancing Multiple Objectives

As CETA evolved it became a bifurcated program. Titles I, III, and IV were serving predominantly persons with structural handicaps; Titles II and VI, the job creation titles, were enrolling the job-ready unemployed, generally persons higher on the socioeconomic ladder. They were not unlike those in the earlier PEP program, but considerably less disadvantaged than participants in Title I. The existence of two types of programs tended to divide CETA clientele into separate populations and reinforce the distinction between them. The programs were compartmentalized, and this discouraged both the transfer of manpower-training clients to PSE programs jobs under Titles II and VI and the use of Title I resources to train PSE participants. The 1976 amendments to Title VI (EJPEA), which emphasized creating jobs for the long-term, low-income unemployed, introduced a third manpower design: one that embodies both structural and countercyclical objectives. In effect, Title VI, intended as an economic response to cyclical unemployment, was, because of social considerations, enlisted to serve structural purposes as well. Early indications are that the desired changes in clientele are occurring.

The enactment of Title VI and its subsequent expansion brought a large volume of dollars and jobs to prime sponsor jurisdictions. And with these came heightened interest and attention of local elected officials in CETA, especially in the PSE programs. In the face of the urgent and politically attractive job creation programs, the basic employability development programs of Title I, although larger than before, were relegated to the back burner.

The two PSE programs had different objectives. Title II was enacted as a continuing program targeted at selected areas experiencing substantial and persistent unemployment. Title VI, on the other hand, was viewed as a general countercyclical tool, directed to what was believed to be a temporary downturn in the economy. It was authorized initially for 1 year and was applicable to all areas. Despite the original differences between Titles II and VI, they became virtually indistinguishable soon after the programs were implemented. This was due in part to the rise in the national unemployment rate that made almost all localities eligible under Title II.

SUMMING UP

ACCOMPLISHMENTS

On the whole, the study finds that CETA, in terms of organization, delivery of service, and local participation, is a more effective way of handling the nation's employment and training programs than earlier centralized and categorical arrangements. The expansion of the PSE program from a 300,000- to a 700,000-job level in 1977 might not have been possible without the local administrative mechanisms in place.

Resources

The allocation of resources through formulas is a more predictable way of distributing funds than the pre-CETA methods. However, some refinements are necessary to target funds more precisely to people and areas of greatest need and to measure the unemployment and income of areas more accurately.

Planning

The process and substance of local planning for manpower programs has improved, although it is still largely a routine for obtaining funding. A large majority of the local planning councils are passive. But a significant number are quite active, and there is substantially more local participation in decision making than there was in the pre-CETA period.

Administration

The administration of programs by local governments, after a shaky start, is improving. There is closer management and accountability. Local staffs are in a better position to keep track of program operations than the relatively small number of Department of Labor regional office personnel operating from distant locations. These developments have been accompanied by a substantial growth in the number of administrative personnel among prime sponsors.

Delivery Systems

The trend towards the consolidation of systems to deliver manpower services is noteworthy; about half of the local prime sponsors studied were taking steps to streamline intake and placement operations for Title I programs to avoid duplication.

PROBLEMS AND RECOMMENDATIONS

These achievements must be weighed against five major problems that impair the effectiveness of CETA. These problems and proposals to correct them are summarized below. The full recommendations of the

Committee on Evaluation of Employment and Training Programs appear in Chapter 10.

Clientele

There has been a weakening of the commitment to the disadvantaged in Title I programs. The principal reasons for this change include: the broader eligibility criteria under CETA legislation as compared with pre-CETA requirements, the spread of resources into suburban areas with lower proportions of disadvantaged persons, and the inclination of program operators to select applicants most likely to succeed. The proportion of disadvantaged persons in the PSE programs (Titles II and VI) has been markedly lower than in the Title I programs to develop employability. However, the ratio of disadvantaged persons in Title VI has begun to increase as a result of the tighter eligibility requirements in the 1976 amendments to Title VI. *The Committee recommends that eligibility under all titles be restricted to the low-income population (except for some openings in public service employment programs), allocation formulas be revised to reflect the shift in eligibility, public service employment programs be redesigned to include a continuing program limited to the economically disadvantaged, and prime sponsors supervise the client selection process more carefully.*

Quality of Service

The program emphasis of Title I has shifted from activities that enhance human capital to those that basically provide income maintenance. There are also serious questions about the quality of skill-training and work-experience programs. Recent efforts to conduct experimental and demonstration projects to improve the quality of skill-training and youth programs are a step in the right direction, but not enough. *The Committee recommends more thorough and systematic assessment of the content and duration of training programs, experimentation with enriched work experience models, and closer links with the private sector in developing programs that are relevant to the job market. Combinations of public service employment and skill-training activities should be encouraged and more resources devoted to programs to enhance employability under Title I.*

Program Outcomes

There are various ways of evaluating the success of a training and employability program, including increasing proficiency of skills and enhancement of ability to compete independently in the labor market. In the final analysis, however, the primary criterion of success is the extent to which enrollees are able to obtain suitable long-term employment as a result of their CETA experience. The Department of Labor reporting system does not provide information on the duration of employment. However, placement ratios—the percentage of terminees who find jobs either through the sponsor's efforts or on their own—have been lower in the first 3 years of CETA than for comparable pre-CETA programs. The Committee recognizes the special difficulties of placement in a period of high unemployment. There are, however, some steps that Congress and program administrators can take to improve the opportunities for enrollees to obtain unsubsidized employment. *The Committee recommends greater emphasis on job development and placement activities and restoration by Congress of the placement objective in public service employment programs.*

Substitution

One of the major shortcomings of the PSE program is the degree to which its job creation objective is subverted by the substitution of federal for local funds. Recent amendments to Title VI, limiting most newly hired participants to special projects, may tend to constrain substitution. *The Committee recommends renewal of countercyclical revenue sharing to help hard-pressed communities maintain public services, limiting participants' tenure in CETA to 1 year, strengthening the auditing and monitoring capabilities of the Department of Labor, and amending the definition of projects to preclude activities that are incremental to regular ongoing services.*

Institutional Networks

Relations between prime sponsors and other government and nongovernment agencies continue to be unsettled. This is particularly true of the association between the Employment Service and prime sponsors. In its desire to reform the fragmented manpower structure and reduce duplication, Congress fashioned a federal–local system that parallels in several respects the existing federal–state employment service network.

The Committee recommends that studies be conducted of the roles and performance of the Employment Service and CETA systems, of the existing relationships between them, and of the advantages and disadvantages of alternative coordination arrangements.

POLICY ISSUES

Several policy issues are evident in the CETA program and, in one form or another, touch its major problems: the relationship between national policy and local practice, multiple objectives, ambiguous legislation, the balance among program components, and the place of public service employment in the overall design of manpower programs.

One of the most pervasive issues is the degree to which local priorities and practices are consistent with national objectives. The issue is apparent in the structural as well as the countercyclical components of CETA. In both there is divergence between the national emphasis upon enrolling those most in need and the tendency of local program operators to select participants likely to succeed. In the public service employment programs, national attention is riveted on creating jobs to reduce unemployment, while some local officials view the federal funds as an opportunity to support their regular local budgets or as a way to avoid higher taxes. The congressional response to situations in which there are significant local departures from national policy has been to legislate additional provisions that, in turn, limit the degree of local autonomy.

Multiple objectives is another issue that permeates CETA operations and generates organizational and programmatic problems. CETA has become a program for all seasons, but in the pursuit of one set of objectives others are sacrificed, particularly if they appear competitive. For example: emphasis on the job creation program of Title VI results in a deemphasis of the employability development programs of Title I; CETA strives for a high rate of job placement, yet encourages enrolling those most difficult to place; many target groups are singled out for consideration, but, in focusing on some, others are neglected—it is unrealistic to expect prime sponsors to give simultaneous priority to veterans, women, the long-term unemployed, persons on unemployment insurance (UI) rolls, those not eligible for UI, and welfare recipients.

A third issue that significantly affects CETA operations is the ambiguity of the legislation. The political necessity for some ambivalence to ensure the enactment of legislation is understandable. Nevertheless, the ambiguity of some CETA provisions results in confusion and bureaucratic conflicts. For example, the line between prime sponsor and federal authority is not clear. The Secretary of Labor is admonished not to "second guess the good faith judgment of the prime sponsor," but is also directed "to adopt administrative procedures for looking behind the certification of compliance including . . . spot checking. . . . " In effect, the legislative history leaves a large gray area in which the reach of the local authorities contends with the grasp of the federal establishment.

The intent of CETA is also uncertain with respect to the choice of agencies to provide manpower services. Acknowledging the primacy of prime sponsors in a decentralized system, CETA places with them the responsibility for selecting program deliverers. However, prime sponsors are also told to make full use of existing institutions of demonstrated effectiveness. Thus, having come down on both sides of the issue, the legislation leaves it up to the program administrators to sort things out as best they can.

The balancing of CETA objectives and the allocation of resources among CETA programs is another underlying issue. The question arises in several contexts. How should manpower resources be allocated between structural and countercyclical programs? Do the 1976 amendments to Title VI bridge the structural and countercyclical objectives? Within the structural component of CETA, what proportion of funds should be directed to activities that enhance human capital and what proportion for programs that essentially provide income maintenance?

CETA has demonstrated the effectiveness of public service employment as a temporary job creation program, but the tendency to substitute federal for local resources limits its usefulness in the long run. Congress has taken several steps to address this problem: At issue is whether those measures—short-term projects, increased use of nonprofit organizations as employing agencies, and enrollment of low-income persons—will be successful.

With respect to the broader issue of governmental strategies to counter recessions, the question is how much reliance should be placed on creating jobs in the public sector compared with such alternatives as tax incentives in the private sector, extended unemployment insurance, accelerated public works programs, stepped-up government purchases, tax cuts, or monetary policies? What constitutes an appropriate policy mix?

Beyond CETA, Congress is considering the use of public service employment as a major element in welfare reform and full-employment legislation. This raises such issues as the extent to which the public sector should be used to create jobs, the limits of state and local governments' capability to absorb unemployed persons, the degree to which local governments have become dependent on federally funded positions, and the consequences of subsequent withdrawal of these funds.

These are policy issues that need to be resolved in the political process leading to reauthorization of CETA. *The Committee favors the reauthorization of CETA and hopes the findings of the study and recommendations in the pages that follow will provide a basis for discussion and decisions on some of the issues.*[2]

---

[2]On October 27, 1978 (subsequent to the preparation of this report), the President signed into law the Comprehensive Employment and Training Act Amendments of 1978, which reauthorized CETA for 4 years and amended its provisions. The new legislation reflects, in whole or in part, the major recommendations of this report with respect to:

• the establishment of a continuing PSE program for the structurally unemployed and a separate contingency program for the cyclically unemployed;
• closer program links with the private sector of the economy;
• constraining substitution by limiting the tenure of PSE participants and by strengthening the monitoring capabilities of the Department of Labor;
• the enhancement of the employability development programs of CETA;
• the addition of a training component to PSE programs;
• increased emphasis on the placement of CETA participants;
• the use of annual unemployment data to identify areas of substantial unemployment.

2 Resources and Allocations

The $8 billion appropriated for the Comprehensive Employment and Training Act (CETA) in fiscal 1977 and in fiscal 1978 was a new high in manpower funding. It exceeded by far the amount for comparable programs for the entire decade of the 1960s. Together with programs not under CETA, obligations for manpower account for more than 2.5 percent of the federal budget. They are more than one-half of 1 percent of the gross national product compared with about 0.4 percent in the years immediately preceding CETA. The sharp rise in federal funds for manpower over the years attests to the growing significance of employment and training programs in the agenda of national priorities.

CETA replaced earlier manpower operations in which resources were allocated to numerous uncoordinated categorical programs with a system of block grants conveyed directly to state and local units of government—prime sponsors. This system, it was anticipated, would shift program control and management from federal to local officials and permit more flexible use of these resources to reflect local needs more closely. Despite its name, CETA has never been an entirely comprehensive program. Other programs of the Department of Labor (DOL)—the Work Incentive Program (WIN); the Older Americans Act; and the largest of them all, the employment security system—remain separate from CETA. In fiscal 1976, less than 60 percent of federal outlays for manpower-related programs was accounted for by CETA. Another significant change in strategy for distributing manpower resources is the allocation of funds by formula rather than the less formal methods used before CETA.

15

This chapter deals with issues related to the funding of manpower programs and how changes in patterns of resource allocations reflect underlying manpower policies. The major questions discussed are:

1. How do trends in the use of resources for employment and training programs compare with other approaches to unemployment problems? What are the implications for manpower policy?
2. To what extent does CETA represent a comprehensive manpower program? Have there been changes in the emphasis on decategorization and decentralization? To what extent does CETA represent the block grant approach?
3. How has the use of formulas changed the distribution patterns of funds? What problems are associated with the use of formulas and with the use of discretionary funds? What are the measurement problems in the CETA formulas?
4. How has the funding process affected the administration of manpower programs?

TRENDS IN MANPOWER FUNDS

Manpower funding patterns have, over the years, mirrored the policymakers' perceptions of the role of employment and training programs in coping with economic and social problems. The level of funding has reflected the depth of the commitment to those programs and the priority they received in the competition for the federal dollar. The kinds of expenditures have varied with the changing economic and social climate.

In the early 1960s, apprehension over the expected effects of automation led to the Manpower Development and Training Act (MDTA). To implement this act, Congress authorized $70 million to retrain workers whose occupations were expected to become obsolete. The expected large-scale displacement of workers did not occur, but manpower programs were soon enlisted in the war on poverty and were redirected toward the employment and training problems of youth and the disadvantaged. The passage of the Economic Opportunity Act (EOA) of 1964 made greater resources available for manpower programs.

In the early 1960s, emphasis was almost entirely on classroom training. Later in the decade, classroom training funds leveled off, while spending for programs to provide youth with work experience and income more than doubled, as shown in the table below. The increase in level of funding for youth had as much to do with "cooling the street" as providing work experience. On-the-job training also rose significantly as the Department of Labor made greater efforts to enlist the support and cooperation of the private sector.

| | Expenditures for Selected Programs (millions of dollars) | | |
Type of Program	FY 1966	FY 1972	Percent Increase
Classroom training (MDTA institutional and Job Corps)	494	580	17
On-the-job training (JOP, JOBS, PSC)	20	291	1,355
Work experience for youth (NYC in-school, out-of-school, summer)	241	494	105

During the late 1960s, the unemployment rate was relatively low. The concern of manpower programs was to intervene on behalf of those in the labor force who had the most difficulty in getting or holding jobs— the poor, the uneducated, minorities, youth lacking experience, and older workers. Categorical programs were designed for various groups. Each program had its own rules of operations and funding sources. However, the emphasis in each was on the supply side of the employment problem—how to help the individual adjust to the job market. In short, manpower programs during the late 1960s dealt mainly with the employability problems of persons on the margins of the labor market.

The recession of 1970 and 1971 and the phasing down of hostilities in Vietnam signaled a return to the high levels of unemployment of the early 1960s. With the economic slump, attention shifted to the demand side—how could employment be expanded quickly? The passage of the Emergency Employment Act (EEA) in 1971 in response to this economic development added a new dimension to manpower strategy. For the first time since the Great Depression, federal funds were used specifically as a countercyclical measure—to hire the unemployed and underemployed for temporary public service jobs. The EEA authorized expenditures of $2.25 billion over 2 years. Appropriations for employment and training programs—later to be merged into CETA—rose to $2.8 billion in fiscal 1973 and fell back to $2.3 billion in fiscal 1974, as EEA was to be phased out.[1]

The EEA proved to be a useful precedent for the handling of manpower funds under CETA. It demonstrated that formulas based on objective criteria could be used to allot funds and that the channeling of

[1]A total of $250 million was appropriated for the Emergency Employment Act in June 1974 to permit an orderly transfer of EEA activities to CETA.

TABLE 1 Appropriations for Department of Labor Employment and Training Programs, Fiscal 1974-1978 (millions of dollars)

Fiscal Year	All DOL Manpower Programs	Total	Comprehensive Employment and Training Act						Work Incentive Program[a] (WIN)	Older American Programs
			Training and Work Experience (Title I)	Summer Youth (Title III)	Other National (Title III)	Job Corps (Title IV)	Public Service Employment			
							Title II	Title VI		
1974	2,526	2,266	1,010[b]	306[c]	180[c]	150	370	250[d]	250	10
1975	3,894	3,742	1,580	473	243	171	400	875	140	12
1976[e]	6,227	5,741	1,580	528	268	140	1,600[f]	1,625	250	86
1977	8,514	8,053	1,880	595	1,609[g]	266	524	3,179	370	91
1978[h]	8,617	8,062	1,880	693	388	417	1,016	3,668	365	190

SOURCE: Employment and Training Administration, U.S. Department of Labor.

[a] Excludes funds for HEW child care: 1974, $90 million; 1975, $74 million; 1976, $150 million; 1977, $127 million.

[b] Manpower programs comparable to those included under Title I.

[c] Excludes carrying-funds: summer youth, $91 million; migratory farm workers, $33 million.

[d] Emergency Employment Act (PEP).

[e] Transition quarter (July–September 1976) omitted.

[f] Includes supplemental of $1,200 million for Title VI.

[g] Includes $233.3 million for Title VIII, Youth Conservation Corps.

[h] The $1,016 million for Title II and $3,668 million for Title VI forward funded with the fiscal 1977 supplemental.

18

manpower funds directly to state and local governments was not only feasible but could result in effective management of local programs.

FUNDING UNDER CETA

A basic objective of CETA was to combine separate MDTA, EOA, and EEA funding sources into block grants, transferring control and accountability to local officials. Shortly after CETA was passed, the administration requested $2 billion for its implementation in fiscal 1975—10 percent less than 1974 appropriations for comparable training, work experience, and public service employment programs. Congress, however, authorized close to $2.9 billion and later in the year increased the amount to $3.7 billion, when funds for Title VI (the Emergency Jobs and Unemployment Assistance Act) were added. CETA funds increased 2.5 times from the base year of 1974 to 1977. Most of the gain was in public service employment—from $620 million authorized toward the end of fiscal 1974 to $3.7 billion in 1977 (see Table 1).

The initiatives in support of CETA prior to 1977 were taken by the Congress rather than the executive branch and reflected congressional concern over unacceptably high levels of unemployment. The funding of summer jobs for youth illustrates this concern. The initial budget requests for fiscal 1975 and fiscal 1976 did not contain separate requests for summer jobs; the administration intended that prime sponsors finance these programs out of their decategorized Title I allotments. Congress intervened in both years with separate appropriations.

President Carter's economic stimulus package restored the executive initiative. The amount requested and authorized for fiscal 1977 for CETA was raised from $4.1 billion in the Ford budget to $8.1 billion in the Carter budget, and the same amount was appropriated for 1978 (see Figure 1).

CHANGING EMPHASIS IN CETA

Changes in patterns of funding have significantly affected the original decategorized and decentralized emphasis of CETA. The vast additions for the specialized programs for Titles II, III, and VI have significantly increased its categorical nature. Title I, the only decategorized component, accounted for 42 percent of the CETA appropriations in 1975 and 23 percent in 1977. The categorical thrust was sparked by the recession and by the decision to launch a large-scale program directed at the high level of unemployment. The decrease can be attributed to the propensity of Congress and the administration to deal with problems by

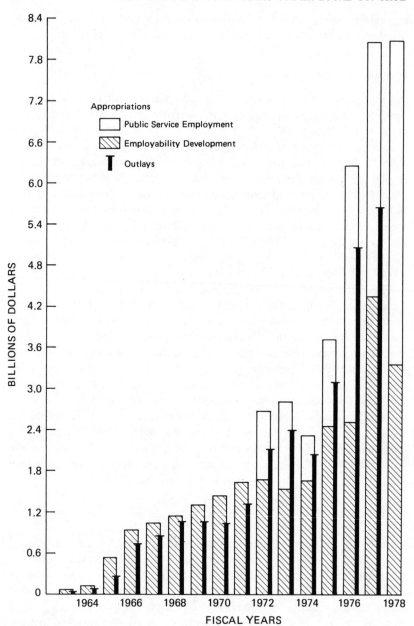

FIGURE 1   Appropriations for CETA rose above $8 billion in fiscal years 1977 and 1978.

TABLE 2 Funds for National Programs, Title III, Fiscal 1974–1978 (millions of dollars)

Title III Program	Funds Obligated 1974[a]	Appropriations			
		FY 1975	FY 1976[b]	FY 1977	FY 1978
Summer employment for youth	459	473	528	595	693
Migrant farm workers	39	63	76	63	95
Indians	12	51	52	51	77
National projects	40	83	94	1,445[c]	171
TOTAL	550	670	750	2,154	1,036

SOURCE: Employment and Training Administration, U.S. Department of Labor.
[a]Amounts for comparable programs.
[b]Excludes transition quarter.
[c]Includes $1 billion for youth, $250 million for Skill Training Improvement Program (STIP), and $120 million for HIRE (veterans).

mandating special programs rather than relying on local authorities to tackle them. The enactment in 1977 of the administration's comprehensive youth program, including a new title for a Young Adult Conservation Corps, has further categorized manpower programs.

The decentralizing thrust of CETA is diminishing to a lesser extent, since some of the categorical programs are managed locally. Though still largely decentralized, the proportion of funds appropriated for programs under local control declined from 93 percent in 1976 to 85 percent in 1977 as more resources were channeled into federally managed programs. The major increase was due to 1977 supplemental funds requested by the Carter Administration for three nationally administered programs: youth, skill improvement, and the hiring of Vietnam veterans (see Table 2). It would appear that the executive branch, under the Carter Administration, and the Congress are now less concerned with the principle of local autonomy than with direct and rapid action on what they perceive to be the major manpower problems.

From their inception, manpower programs were directed to the intractable structural problems that limited the ability of many to participate effectively in the labor market. Their clientele was the disadvantaged, and the strategy called for a combination of programs to develop employability. CETA embodied the same design. However, this was to change, for the same reasons that other aspects of CETA changed—deteriorating economic conditions. The public service employment program (Title VI) was added in the middle of CETA's first fiscal year; but even with this added countercyclical program, three-fourths of all CETA funds were for structural programs—employability development, work experience, training, and subsidized jobs in depressed areas. As the recession intensified, however, more funds were added for Title VI and the balance began to change; only 50 percent of the fiscal 1976 funds was for structural programs.

With the 1977 supplemental appropriation came a renewed emphasis on structural objectives. Two developments moved the program in this direction. More funds were added to the programs directed at structural problems: Titles I, II, III, IV, and summer activities for youth. These programs accounted for 60 percent of the CETA resources that year. Additional funds were also added for Title VI, the counterrecessionary component of CETA. However, in expanding this job creation program, Congress significantly modified its thrust. Limiting the use of the additional resources to the low-income, long-term unemployed gave the program a structural complexion. Title VI now has both countercyclical and structural objectives.[2] If this trend continues, it is possible that CETA may return to its original emphasis on the structural problems of the disadvantaged. The bill proposed by the administration for reauthorization of CETA in 1978 would target CETA almost exclusively to low-income families.

STRATEGIES FOR DEALING WITH UNEMPLOYMENT

Potential clients for manpower programs number in the millions, even in the best of times. The "universe of need" consists of all those who need training or other services—the unemployed with special difficulties, the underemployed, discouraged workers who have given up seeking jobs, and others not in the labor force who could become employed. During recessions, their ranks are swelled by the cyclically unemployed. If the million or so discouraged workers had been counted as unemployed in the fourth quarter of 1976, the total number unemployed would have averaged 8.6 million instead of 7.6 million (see Figure 2). The number of potential CETA clients depends on the measures that are used. Some estimates run as high as 20 million individuals in the course of a year. A conservative estimate for planning purposes in the present economic setting is that there are 12 million people with employment and earnings inadequacies, a large proportion of whom may need some kind of

[2]Emergency Jobs Programs Extension Act of 1976, PL 94-444, October 1, 1976.

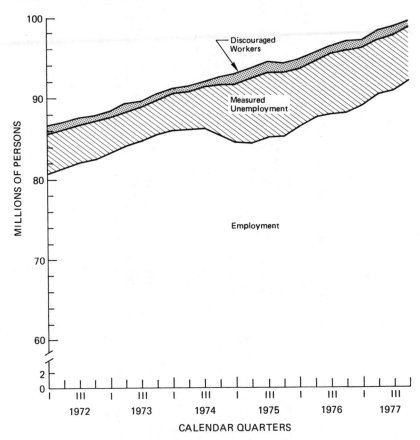

SOURCE: Based on seasonally adjusted data, *Employment and Earnings*, Bureau of Labor Statistics.

FIGURE 2   About 1 million discouraged workers are not counted in measured unemployment.

assistance in getting a decent job at which they can make a living.[3]

The question of what combination of actions would be most effective in helping these 12 million people requires assessing the costs and benefits of various alternatives, such as unemployment insurance (UI), job creation, and manpower training and employability development

[3]Sar A. Levitan and Robert Taggart, "Do Our Statistics Measure the Real Labor Market Hardships?," In Edwin D. Goldfield, ed., *ASA Proceedings*, Social Statistics Section, 1976, Part I, Washington, D.C.: American Statistical Association, August 1976; Julius Shiskin, "Employment and Unemployment: The Doughnut or the Hole?," *Monthly Labor Review* 99(2):3–10, February 1976.

TABLE 3 Trends in Unemployment, Expenditures for Manpower Programs, and Unemployment Insurance Benefits, Fiscal 1972-1977

Fiscal Year	Unemployment Rate (percent)	Annual Average Unemployment (thousands)			Expenditures (millions of dollars)		
					Department of Labor		
		Total	15 Weeks or More	27 Weeks or More	Comprehensive Manpower Assistance[a]	Temporary Public Service[b]	State and Federal Unemployment Insurance Benefits
1972	5.9	4,991	1,234	380	1,592	567	7,088
1973	5.2	4,539	970	432	1,388	1,014	4,796
1974	5.0	4,449	809	327	1,454	605	5,489
1975	7.3	6,704	1,620	655	2,803	372	12,694
1976	8.1	7,743	2,615	1,472	3,158	1,887	18,218
1977	7.3	7,069	2,056	1,114	3,291	2,340	13,058

SOURCE: Computed from data from Bureau of Labor Statistics, U.S. Department of Labor, and Office of Management and Budget.
[a]Excludes WIN, Older Americans; includes CETA Titles I, II, III, and IV.
[b]EEA and CETA Title VI.

programs. Each has advantages and disadvantages in terms of effect on employment, speed of implementation, effect on inflation, focusing on those most in need, and net costs.[4]

Each of these alternatives has expanded in response to the recession, but not at the same rate. Expenditures for unemployment insurance kept pace with the rise in extended joblessness between 1974 and 1976, while increases in spending for employment and training programs lagged (see Table 3). Two temporary programs—Federal Supplemental Benefits (FSB), which increased the duration of benefits, and Special Unemployment Assistance (SUA), which extended coverage—were added.[5] Unemployment insurance has borne the brunt of costs in easing the hardship of cyclical unemployment; in 1976, more than three times as much was spent for UI as for CETA, as shown in the table below. In fiscal 1977, however, the relationship began to change, with higher expenditures for employment and training and sharply lower UI benefit payments as unemployment edged downward.

	Percent Increase	
	FY 1974- FY 1976	FY 1974- FY 1977
Unemployed		
Total	74	59
15 weeks or more	223	154
27 weeks or more	350	241
Outlays		
Comprehensive manpower programs	117	126
Temporary public service	212	287
Unemployment insurance	232	138

[4]U.S. Congress, Congressional Budget Office, *Temporary Measures to Stimulate Employment—An Evaluation of Some Alternatives*, Prepared by Nancy S. Barrett and George Iden, Washington, D.C.: Congressional Budget Office, September 1975; U.S. Congress, Congressional Budget Office, *Employment and Training Programs*, Staff working paper prepared by T. Wendell Butler and Richard Hobbie, Washington, D.C.: Congressional Budget Office, May 1976; National Council on Employment Policy, *Reviving the Recovery by Direct Job Creation*, A policy statement by the National Council on Employment Policy, Washington, D.C., December 14, 1976.

[5]The Federal Supplemental Benefits Program, enacted in December 1974, authorized federal supplemental benefits for persons who had exhausted their unemployment insurance entitlement whenever the insured unemployment rate (either nationally or in specific states) reached 4 percent. The Special Unemployment Assistance Program, enacted in December 1974, was a temporary program covering workers who were not otherwise eligible for unemployment insurance benefits under any other state or federal law. SUA was payable when the total unemployment rate is 6 percent nationally or 6.5 percent at the area level for 3 consecutive months.

DISTRIBUTION OF FUNDS

With more manpower funds available than ever, debate continues on the proper level and mix of funds and how the money is to be divided among geographic areas and client groups.

Almost all CETA funds are distributed on the basis of formulas specified to the local level. The legislation prescribes the manner in which Title I, II, and VI funds are to be allocated, and the Department of Labor has chosen similar formulas for the larger Title III programs (those for Indians and migrant and seasonal farm workers and summer programs for youth). This method of allocation is a departure from earlier methods. Before CETA, formulas were used to distribute MDTA and other program funds to the state level only. However, a great deal of discretion was left to regional offices in allotting funds below state levels and in distributing funds among areas and programs.

The Emergency Employment Act was the first legislation to apply an objective formula based on the extent and severity of unemployment among potentially eligible cities, counties, and states. Experience under the EEA's Public Employment Program (PEP) greatly influenced the way in which allocations are handled under CETA.

One advantage of formulas is that they eliminate grantsmanship and partiality in fund distribution. More important, they assure each qualifying area a share of funds in proportion to need, measured objectively. The effect is to spread funds more broadly than in the past. Among the disadvantages are the lack of flexibility in moving funds about to meet new or emerging situations and the possibility of spreading funds too thin for significant results.

On balance, the use of formulas specified to the local level appears more equitable than earlier methods, but some aspects need consideration: Are the formulas appropriate for the economic and social objectives of each title? Are valid and current statistical data available to measure formula elements?

Selecting the method of allocating limited resources under CETA was one of the most difficult challenges faced by legislators.[6] In addition to designing formulas, they had to decide what size and type of jurisdiction would be eligible to receive funds; how to prevent abrupt declines in existing funding levels; what cutoff rate to use for identifying areas of substantial unemployment under Title II; and how to sustain funds for

---

[6]Robert Guttman, "Intergovernmental Relations Under the New Manpower Act," *Monthly Labor Review* 97(6):10–16, June 1974.

especially disadvantaged groups, such as Indians and migratory farm workers.

PRIME SPONSORS

A central question in drafting CETA was who was to have the primary administrative role. MDTA programs had been administered through the state employment service and state educational agencies, while the EOA programs were usually sponsored by local private nonprofit or public agencies. Except for the temporary Public Employment Program, and in some instances summer programs for youth, state and local units of government had little experience in administering manpower programs.

An early version of the bill to consolidate and simplify administration proposed that state governments be the prime sponsors, with pass-through to local governments. But mayors and other opponents held that state governments would not be responsive to urban needs.[7] Another version favored using labor market areas as the basis to take advantage of training institutions and job opportunities across jurisdictional lines. The economic interdependence of cities and suburbs plus the planning under the Cooperative Area Manpower Planning System (CAMPS) gave added weight to this proposal. On the other hand, successful experience under PEP, the desire to fix accountability, and practical political realities of getting jurisdictions to work together were critical considerations. Congress resolved the issue by designating cities and counties as prime sponsors and by encouraging the formation of consortia where arrangements could be worked out. Each state government would be responsible for the "balance of state"—areas that do not meet the qualifying criteria of size, the smaller, more rural sections.

The decision to establish a minimum population requirement of 100,000 for prime sponsors was based on a number of considerations: limiting sponsors to a manageable number, savings in administrative overhead, and the efficiency of planning for and operating from a geographic base that covers a substantial part of a labor market. To win the support of members of Congress from rural areas, CETA authorized the designation of rural concentrated employment programs (CEPs) with demonstrated capabilities. Under Titles II and VI, certain Indian reservations that do not necessarily meet the population requirement were permitted to be sponsors. As a further compromise, cities or counties with 50,000 population were to be designated "program agents"

[7]Roger H. Davidson, *The Politics of Comprehensive Manpower Legislation*, Policy Studies in Employment and Welfare, no. 15, Baltimore: Johns Hopkins University, 1972.

for Titles II and VI. Prime sponsors pass through funds to program agents, which then manage their own public service employment programs. Thus the act that was intended to streamline administration ended up creating a hodgepodge of many different types of sponsors and a considerable overlap of responsibilities and accountability.[8]

Title II money is earmarked for use only in an "area of substantial unemployment," that is, an area with a 6.5-percent unemployment rate for 3 consecutive months. This may cover a prime sponsor's entire area or simply a pocket of high unemployment of varying size. The rules for delineating such pockets have been very loose, and local sponsors have been known to gerrymander sections or neighborhoods to maximize their funding. A uniform method of identifying Title II areas would ensure that funds were distributed more equitably.[9]

TITLE I, II, AND VI FORMULAS

Allocation formulas can be devised to meet a variety of social, economic, or political objectives, within the limits of data availability. If specific socioeconomic groups are the target, then the key formula elements should be demographic and income criteria. If the major concern is areas of substantial and persistent unemployment, then a combination of unemployment, population, and income criteria would be preferable. If countercyclical objectives are called for, the amount and the severity of unemployment would be the determinants and an automatic unemployment rate trigger phased with the business cycle might be used. Another type of formula would allocate funds by some measure of cost-effectiveness.[10] In each of these, a "hold-harmless" feature, which limits changes in funding levels, could be included to moderate the effect of radical shifts in existing funding levels.

[8]Title I prime sponsors are defined as cities or counties of 100,000 or more population; consortia; balance of states; rural CEPs; areas designated under exceptional circumstances; and U.S. territories (American Samoa, Guam, the Virgin Islands, and the Trust Territories of the Pacific). All Title I prime sponsors are eligible for Title II and VI funds, and in addition, Indian tribes on federal and state reservations are eligible applicants for them.
[9]U.S. General Accounting Office, *Progress and Problems in Allocating Funds Under Titles I and II—Comprehensive Employment and Training Act*, Washington, D.C.: General Accounting Office, January 2, 1976.
[10]Daniel S. Hamermesh and Hugh Pitcher, "Economic Formulas for Manpower Revenue Sharing," *Industrial and Labor Relations Review*, 27(4), July 1974.

Title I

The Title I formula represents a combination of the first two types of formula design described above. The Senate bill based allocation formulas on poverty and unemployment, while the House version based allocations on past funding levels and relative unemployment. The act incorporates all of these with a device for maintaining stability from year to year. Eighty percent of the Title I appropriations is allocated as follows:[11] Half of the funds is allotted on the basis of the sponsor's previous year's funds—37.5 percent according to the area's relative share of total unemployment, and the remaining 12.5 percent according to the proportion of adults in families with earnings below the low-income level defined by the Bureau of Labor Statistics (BLS). To prevent sharp swings in funding from one year to the next, each area must be allotted a minimum of 90 percent and a maximum of 150 percent of its previous year's allotment.

This method has been criticized on the grounds that the emphasis on unemployment rather than income is not appropriate for a program geared to the structurally unemployed. The timing and the frequency of Title I allocations have also been questioned. Lead time has at times been inadequate for planning. More important, the structural nature of the problems addressed in Title I raises a question as to the need for year-to-year funding. It may be more appropriate to determine the proportionate share of each sponsor every 2 or 3 years, with variations in amounts based on the appropriation levels. This would allow for more orderly planning and administration and would alleviate some of the data-gathering problems.

Title II

The Title II formula has only one determining factor—unemployment. Each eligible area receives a share of funds proportionate to its share of the total unemployment in all areas of substantial unemployment in the country.

Issues concerning the Title II formula are the appropriateness of a 6.5-percent unemployment rate criterion for qualifying areas of substantial unemployment, the influence of seasonal unemployment figures, and the lack of a factor in the formula to discriminate among areas on the basis of severity of unemployment. The 6.5-percent rate was chosen when the

---

[11]One percent of the 80 percent allocated by formula was to be reserved for state prime sponsors for support of the state manpower services councils.

national unemployment rate was less than 5 percent; the intent was to concentrate on areas with the most severe problems. With a national unemployment rate that has averaged more than 7.0 percent since CETA was passed, nearly all sponsors qualify for some Title II funds (see Table 4). This suggests that the legislative intent might more effectively be met by using a sliding scale, e.g., setting the local unemployment trigger at a designated percentage above the national average unemployment rate. The same objective might be accomplished by a formula in which the first element would be the number of unemployed in areas of substantial unemployment, and the second would be the number of unemployed in each such area above the trigger level.[12]

In any case, the use of a recent 3-month period for identifying areas of substantial unemployment gives areas with volatile patterns of seasonal unemployment an advantage over those with continuous high unemployment. If the objective of Title II is to provide extra resources to areas with chronic unemployment, it is not achieved with a formula tilted in favor of areas with seasonal or temporary unemployment problems. The General Accounting Office has recommended the use of seasonally adjusted figures, but BLS has not yet resolved the technical problems entailed.[13] The use of annual average figures would channel funds more directly to places with persistent, as well as substantial, unemployment. Discretionary funds could be used for areas that qualify because of a sudden rise in unemployment between allocations.

Title VI

Since Title VI was intended to create as many jobs as possible during an emergency, the allocation formula is also based on unemployment only. The formula has three parts: 50 percent of the total amount is distributed according to each area's unemployment relative to the national total, 25 percent on its share of unemployment in excess of 4.5 percent, and 25 percent on the share of unemployment in its areas of substantial unemployment in relation to unemployment in all such areas. Thus the formula provides an added boost to areas with severe unemployment.

---

[12]Under the Public Works and Economic Development Act of 1965, an area of substantial unemployment may qualify for public works if its unemployment rate is 6 percent or more for 1 year. An area may qualify for other types of assistance if it has unemployment rates of 50 percent above the national average for 3 years, 75 percent above the national average for 2 years, or 100 percent above the national average for 1 year. Under the Emergency Employment Act, a two-part formula was adopted. Fifty percent of Section 6 funds for areas of substantial unemployment were distributed on the basis of total unemployment in qualifying areas, with 50 percent based on unemployment above the 6-percent level.

[13]U.S. General Accounting Office, *Progress and Problems in Allocating Funds.*

TABLE 4   CETA Prime Sponsors Under Title I
and Eligible Applicants Under Title II, Fiscal 1976

Eligible Areas	Number
Title I prime sponsors, total	423
Eligible under Title II	416
Not eligible under Title II	7
Eligible applicants under Title II	416
Entire area qualified	329
Areas of substantial unemployment within area qualified	87
Indian reservations	214
Rural CEPs	4
Total Title II	634

SOURCE: Employment and Training Administration,
U.S. Department of Labor (unpublished data).

Because of the cyclical nature of the unemployment problems addressed by Title VI, the Department of Labor insisted that the latest unemployment data be used in the Title VI formula. In fiscal 1976, BLS used figures for a recent 3-month period, which resulted in a seasonal bias similar to that in Title II. Using a 12-month moving average, instead of a 3-month figure, would overcome this problem.

The administration of public service employment would be more orderly if Title VI were made a permanent part of CETA, triggered automatically whenever national unemployment reaches recession levels. This would avoid the delays in the legislative appropriation cycle that have occurred under CETA.

Title III

Title III authorizes the Department of Labor to continue direct services through national programs for such groups as people with limited English-speaking ability, older workers, offenders, and others with particular disadvantages in the labor market. Indians, migrant and seasonal farm workers, and youth are singled out for special emphasis.

Although not required to do so, the Department of Labor has used formulas to allocate funds for Indians, migratory and seasonal farm workers, and youth summer employment. This produces distributions that conceptually are universal and objective, but problems exist due to lack of satisfactory data.

Data on Indians are obtained from an annual reporting system maintained by the Bureau of Indian Affairs in the Department of the

Interior, but standard measures have little meaning on reservations where underemployment rather than unemployment is the rule. The allotment of funds to states for migrant and seasonal farm workers is derived from annual farm employment data supplied by reporting establishments and compiled by the Department of Agriculture. The sponsoring organization then divides the state's allotment among subareas. Employed workers are reported by place of work rather than by place of residence, which causes an imbalance in fund distribution.

A major problem is the use of the Title I formula for funds for summer employment of youth. That formula gives weight to total unemployment rather than youth unemployment and to adults rather than youth in low-income families, resulting in a skewed distribution, as discussed later in this chapter. Consideration could be given to alternative measures to allot funds more directly to areas with the most severe youth unemployment.

SUBALLOCATION OF FUNDS BY PRIME SPONSORS

Very few of the prime sponsor cities or counties in the survey used formal methods for allocating Title I funds among subareas. Instead, efforts were made to concentrate resources and service in accordance with perceived need, for example, by locating manpower service centers in major cities or in poor neighborhoods within cities.

"Suballocation" takes on more meaning in consortia and the balance of states, in which the sponsor is responsible for an area that includes a federation of separate jurisdictions. Where formulas are used, sponsors developed various combinations of criteria: the Title I formula with more weight to the poverty component (Orange County); unemployed, high school dropouts, and low-income adults (Lansing); labor force, unemployment, poverty, and "output" (balance of North Carolina). The "output" factor in North Carolina was based on how well the substate regions planned to serve the target population. The use of formulas brought complaints in some cases about the validity of unemployment statistics for rural sections and the timeliness of Census poverty data. In the Phoenix–Maricopa consortium, an agreed 60–40 split between the city and the county proved unsatisfactory because the county believed it did not get a fair share of participant slots and services. In Raleigh, the sponsor called in the Department of Labor regional office to suballocate funds among major jurisdictions.

Title II and VI suballotment methods are more straightforward. The Department of Labor determines the amounts for program agents and pockets of substantial unemployment through the standard formulas.

This system proved to be a source of tension in one consortium because some subjurisdictions, in comparing their shares of Title II and VI funds received from DOL with smaller shares of Title I funds under consortium arrangements, found they could do better alone. This was one of the issues that led to the splintering of that consortium. In other cases, in which the sponsor's entire area was itself an area of substantial unemployment, there apparently was little effort to earmark funds for sections with the highest unemployment.

DISTRIBUTIONAL EFFECTS

The relative shares of funds for individual areas under each title have an important bearing on program operations and the direction that manpower is taking under CETA. The amount available for allocation has been increasing each year (see Table 5). When funds from all sources are considered together, each area in the sample had more funds available in 1976 than in the 1974 base year (see Appendix D, Table 5). However, shifts in relative shares among areas do affect clients and programs.

Title I

The major change in Title I allocations has been a relative decline in funds for core cities and an increase in the share going to counties, many of which are suburban areas. The relative share of 56 matched cities declined from 24 percent of the fiscal 1974 allotment to 22 percent in 1976 and to 19 percent in fiscal 1977, while the relative share of 147 matched counties increased from 13 percent in fiscal 1974 to 16 percent in fiscal 1977 (see Table 6). The cities' share would have been less were it not for the 90-percent hold-harmless provision, which limits the extent to which allotments can drop.[14] In fiscal 1975, funds for more than three-fourths of the cities were boosted to keep them close to the fiscal 1974 funding level; more than half the cities, including 7 of the 10 most populous, needed this adjustment in fiscal 1976. The increase of $300 million in Title I appropriations for 1977 eased the problem, but, even with the increase, most cities are still experiencing progressively diminishing Title I funds despite increases in unemployment. Of the 56 matched cities, 36 had less Title I funds in fiscal 1977 than in fiscal 1975, the first year of CETA allocations, while only 9 of 147 matched counties

[14]In fiscal 1974, summer youth funds were included in the base figure. In subsequent years, summer youth funds were separate. When the two allotments (Title I and summer) are combined, the absolute amount for all areas has gone up from 1974. However, in many cases the absolute Title I amounts have been declining since fiscal 1975.

TABLE 5   Appropriations and Amounts Allocated, Titles I, II, and VI and Summer Youth Program Funds, Fiscal 1974-1977 (thousands of dollars)

Title	FY 1974	FY 1975	FY 1976[a]	FY 1977
Title I				
Appropriation	1,407	1,580	1,580	1,880
Allocation				
Formula amount	1,407	1,249	1,249	1,486
Adjusted amount[b]	–	1,354	1,311	1,502
Nonformula allocations				
State vocational education	–	79	79	94
State manpower service	–	63	63	75
Consortium incentives	–	39	38	40
State planning (SMSC)	–	13	13	15
Rural CEPs	–	7	7	9
Territories	–	2	2	3
Balance	–	23	66	142
Title II				
Appropriation	370	400	1,600[c]	1,540[d]
Allocation				
Formula	296	320	1,280	1,232
Discretionary	74	80[e]	320	308
Title VI				
Appropriation	–	875	1,625	6,847[f]
Allocation				
Formula	–	787	1,462	6,176
Discretionary	–	88	163	656
Summer Programs for Youth	(397)[g]	473	528	595

SOURCE: Employment and Training Administration, U.S. Department of Labor.
[a]Excludes transition quarter.
[b]Amount available after adjustment for 90 percent hold harmless factor.
[c]Includes $1,200 million to maintain employment levels under Title VI.
[d]Includes $1,016 million forward-funded for fiscal 1978.
[e]Eighty million dollars distributed with 1976 funds.
[f]Includes $3,668 million forward-funded for fiscal 1978.
[g]Also included in figure for Title I, above.

had decreases. The total amount for the cities declined 7 percent from $311 million in fiscal 1975 to $290 million in 1977. The total for the 147 counties increased 29 percent from $192 million to $246 million over the same period. Gary, with its high unemployment and poverty levels, is an extreme example; it would have received little more than half its fiscal 1975 funds in fiscal 1976 under Title I were it not for the 90-percent floor. Even with the hold-harmless adjustment, Gary's Title I allotment dropped from $5.1 million in 1975 to $4.6 million in 1976 and $4.1

million in 1977, due to the cumulative effect of the formula. Most major cities have had sharp cuts in Title I funds year by year (see Table 7).

The opposite side of the coin, the 150-percent maximum increase in allotment, was designed to limit increases. Only a few areas—nearly all of them counties— are affected by this rule. DuPage County in the Chicago area has gained to an extraordinary degree. The amount of Title I funds in 1976 was more than double the 1974 amount and would have been much higher were it not for the 150-percent maximum. DuPage had the highest median family income in Illinois, according to Census data; only 2.3 percent of its families had incomes below the poverty level. Chicago, on the other hand, has experienced declines each year and would have dropped much lower except for the 90-percent hold-harmless rule.

The redistribution of funds reflects the influence of the three elements in the Title I formula. The change from 1974 to 1975 was due to the introduction of the formula. The year-to-year changes since are due mainly to the influence of unemployment (weighted 37.5 percent) and to a lesser extent to the distribution of adults in low-income families (weighted 12.5 percent).

Congress, in considering various measures of poverty, chose "adults in low-income families" rather than the more familiar Census definition "individuals in families below the poverty threshold." The Census poverty threshold for a nonfarm family of four was $3,745, significantly lower than the BLS estimate of a minimum of $6,940 in 1970 for a family of four at what it calls a lower-level budget in an urban area. At the time of the 1970 census, there were twice as many adults in low-income families as there were in families with incomes below poverty levels (34 versus 17 million).

Critics of the Title I formula have urged that more weight be given to the "adults in low-income families" factor. However, increasing the weight of that factor would probably not increase the relative share going to cities, since the proportion of adults in low-income families in cities is smaller than the proportion in other prime sponsor areas. The likely effect would be to increase the share of funds for the balance of states, as shown by the distribution for fiscal 1976 in the table below.

Type of Sponsor	Unemployed (percent)	Adults in Low-Income Families (percent)
City	18	14
County	21	16
Consortium	33	31
Balance of states	28	39
TOTAL	100	100

TABLE 6 Percentage Distribution of Manpower Funds, Matched Group of Cities and Counties, Fiscal 1974–1977

Type of Sponsor	Number in Matched Group	FY 1974 Manpower Funds[b]	Title I Allocations[a]					
			FY 1975		FY 1976		FY 1977	
			Formula Amount	Adjusted Amount[c]	Formula Amount	Adjusted Amount[c]	Formula Amount	Adjusted Amount[c]
City	56	24.4	21.1	23.0	20.1	21.6	19.1	19.3
County	147	12.6	15.2	14.2	16.0	15.3	16.6	16.4
All others	–	63.0	63.7	62.8	63.9	63.1	64.3	64.3
Total	–	100.0	100.0	100.0	100.0	100.0	100.0	100.0
U.S. total allocation (millions of dollars)	–	1,407	1,249	1,354	1,249	1,311	1,486	1,502

SOURCE: Computed from Employment and Training Administration, U.S. Department of Labor data.
[a]Excludes amounts for consortium incentives, discretionary funds, vocational education and state manpower services grants, funds for rural CEPs, territories, and state planning funds.
[b]Funds for programs corresponding with Title I. Includes summer allotments for youth employment.
[c]Adjusted to provide each prime sponsor at least 90 percent but not more than 150 percent of prior year's funds.

TABLE 7   CETA Title I Allocations, Major Cities,
Fiscal 1975-1977 (thousands of dollars)

Major Cities	FY 1975	FY 1976	FY 1977
New York	63,067	56,760	61,844
Chicago	36,937	33,243	29,919
Los Angeles	22,591	21,115	24,349
Philadelphia	13,932	12,538	13,321
Detroit	15,980	14,427	15,656
Houston	8,830	7,947	8,044
Dallas	4,282	3,854	4,285
Washington, D.C.	15,492	13,942	12,548
Indianapolis	4,568	4,224	4,727
San Francisco	8,002	7,201	7,790
Boston	8,778	7,900	7,695
St. Louis	7,150	6,435	5,791

SOURCE: Employment and Training Administration,
U.S. Department of Labor.

The other alternative, using the standard poverty criterion, would probably have had a similar effect of increasing funds primarily to nonmetropolitan areas. At the time of the 1970 census, 46 percent of families with incomes below the poverty level lived in nonmetropolitan areas, compared with 43 percent of families with less than $7,000 income (see Table 8). The use of the standard poverty criterion would have shifted relatively more funds to the South: 40 percent of adults in low-income families lived in the three southern regions, compared with 44 percent of families below the poverty level.[15]

Summer Programs for Youth

Summer employment programs for youth were originally designed to defuse volatile social situations that tend to peak in the summer. Consequently, they were initially targeted to the large cities in which needs were perceived to be greatest. Later funds were distributed to all states but concentrated in cities. Although CETA does not prescribe a method for allotting summer employment funds, the Department of Labor has adopted the same formula for youth as for all Title I programs. Instead of the 90-percent hold-harmless factor, the amount for each area is adjusted to keep participant slot levels from declining from

[15]Puerto Rico is included in the United States in this calculation.

TABLE 8   Percentage Distribution of Families with Incomes Less Than $7,000, Families in Poverty Status, and Families With Incomes Less Than 125 Percent of Poverty Level, 1969, by Residence

Residence	Families With Incomes Less Than $7,000	Families in Poverty Status	Families With Incomes Less Than 125% of Poverty Level
Metropolitan	57	54	55
Central cities	32	32	32
Other urban	18	15	16
Rural nonfarm	6	6	6
Rural farm	1	1	1
Nonmetropolitan	43	46	45
Urban	15	15	15
Rural nonfarm	21	24	24
Rural farm	7	7	7
Total United States	100	100	100

SOURCE: Computed from Census of Population, 1970 PC(1)-CD, Tables 116 and 117.
NOTE: Details may not add to totals due to rounding.

TABLE 9   Percentage Distribution of Summer Youth Program Funds, by Type of Sponsor, Fiscal 1973 and 1976

Type of Sponsor	Number in Matched Group	FY 1973	FY 1976
City	55	30	26
County	148	10	13
All other	–	60	61
Total United States	–	100	100

SOURCE: Computed from Employment and Training Administration, U.S. Department of Labor data.

year to year. Each area receives more funds in absolute terms than before CETA, but the pattern of allocation has changed so that, as in Title I, the relative share of resources are being shifted from cities to counties (see Table 9).

Title II and Title VI

Fiscal 1976 allotments under Titles II and VI were based on average unemployment figures for a recent 3-month period. Even though the formulas are different, Table 10 shows that the initial distribution by type of sponsor was virtually the same under both titles.

TABLE 10   Percentage Distribution of Public Service
Employment Funds, by Type of Sponsor, Fiscal 1976

Type of Sponsor	Number of Unemployed	Title II Allocation	Title VI Allocation
City	18	19	19
County	20	19	20
Consortium	33	33	32
Balance of state	29	29	29
TOTAL	100	100	100

SOURCE: Computed from Employment and Training Administration, U.S. Department of Labor data.

Discretionary Funds

In addition to funds allocated by formula, a share of the Title I appropriation is reserved by law for use at the discretion of the Secretary of Labor, but this flexibility is illusory. Under Title I, of the 20-percent discretionary amount, 5 percent must be distributed to states for supplemental vocational education, 4 percent is for state manpower services, and up to 5 percent is for consortium incentives. The Secretary must also use part of the discretionary money to guarantee each sponsor at least 90 percent of its prior year's allotment and to fund rural CEPs. In 1976, after these requirements had been met, only about 4 percent remained for discretionary use.

Title II also authorizes the Secretary to use 20 percent of the funds at his discretion, depending on the severity of unemployment in different areas. To meet this stipulation, the Department of Labor distributed most of the fiscal 1975 Title II discretionary funds according to the number of unemployed in excess of 6.5 percent in each area. In fiscal 1976, however, Titles I, II, and VI discretionary funds were combined and apportioned to give each sponsor enough funds to sustain its level of public service employment. This tactic helped to avert layoffs of workers hired with CETA funds but departed from the original intent of using Title II funds to deal with severe unemployment.

Late in fiscal 1976, it became clear that many sponsors would exhaust Title VI funds and lay off their public service employment (PSE) participants. Since authorization for Title VI had expired, Congress passed a supplemental appropriation under Title II, and sponsors were permitted to transfer Title VI participants to Title II. This situation created problems, since Title II residence and eligibility criteria are more restrictive than those for Title VI. In a controversial decision, backed by congressional committees, the Department of Labor used Title II discretionary funds to support public service jobs in some areas that did not have unemployment rates of 6.5 percent or more for 3 months and were technically not eligible for Title II money.[16]

MEASURES OF UNEMPLOYMENT AND POVERTY

For several decades, statistics on joblessness have been available for the nation, for states, for major labor market areas, and for smaller areas. Increasingly, these data are being used to allocate federal funds. This use has generated demand for greater geographic detail and stimulated interest in the methods for estimating unemployment. In 1976, 70 percent of CETA funds was distributed according to the incidence of unemployment. To make these allocations for CETA, labor force, employment, and unemployment data were generated for 416 prime sponsors, 764 program agents, 224 smaller areas of substantial unemployment, and 50 states—a total of 1,450 separate geographic units, not including Indian reservations.[17] However, the system for collecting labor market information was not designed to provide statistics in such detail and at the frequency required. These demands have placed the system under great strain, subjected it to close scrutiny, and engendered considerable controversy.

The two primary sources of labor force data are the Bureau of Labor Statistics and, under a cooperative federal–state program, the state employment security agencies (SESAs). BLS estimates of labor force, employment, and unemployment for the United States and for major states and standard metropolitan statistical areas (SMSAs) are based on a national sample of 55,000 households surveyed each month by the Bureau of the Census through the Current Population Survey (CPS).[18] The SESAs' unemployment estimates for states and for labor market areas are derived from the number of unemployment insurance recipients, using a standard formula to estimate the unemployed labor force not covered by unemployment insurance—primarily new entrants, reen-

[16]This procedure was later confirmed by the Emergency Jobs Programs Extension Act of 1976.

[17]In addition to their use for CETA, local area unemployment estimates are used as a basis for allocating funds under other federal programs. See Bureau of Labor Statistics, *Estimating State and Local Unemployment*, Report no. 500, 1977.

[18]The number of households surveyed was increased from 47,000 in 1974 to 55,000 at present to improve the reliability of state estimates.

trants, agricultural workers, the self-employed, and domestic service workers.

In the past, the BLS and SESA methods differed in concept as well as in technique. An unemployment insurance beneficiary who worked a few hours a week would be counted as unemployed under the SESA method, while the BLS–CPS method would consider that person employed. SESA figures, obtained from establishments, counted a worker twice if he was on two payrolls and listed workers by place of employment rather than residence. This method affected unemployment rates in areas with significant in- or out-commuting. Another problem with SESA labor force data was variation among states in unemployment insurance coverage and duration; the use of standard factors for arriving at components of the unemployed based on national ratios that may not have been equally valid in all areas further complicated the estimating method.

Just prior to the enactment of CETA, responsibility for area as well as national labor force statistics was transferred to BLS in an effort to produce compatible national and local statistics.[19] To make SESA methods conform with the national BLS–CPS series, the employment figures obtained from payroll data were revised to eliminate double counting and to count employed persons by place of residence rather than by place of work.

The second major change was to adjust the monthly SESA unemployment and employment estimates at annual intervals to correspond with the Current Population Survey for all 50 states, 30 of the largest SMSAs, and the central cities of 11 large SMSAs.

While the new sytem of estimating local labor force data has advantages in terms of consistency and better supervision and control, some technical problems remained:

1. The most obvious is that reliable BLS–CPS benchmark data are not available for all SMSAs and for parts of states not in SMSAs. Thus a dual system of labor force estimating is still in effect.

2. The sampling errors in the BLS–CPS annual average and, more particularly, in monthly estimates are magnified in smaller geographic units. This is a serious problem when eligibility for funding is based on a trigger unemployment rate for a 3-month period.

3. The use of 1970 Census ratios for disaggregating labor force data within a labor market area for conversion from place of work to place of

[19]James R. Wetzel, and Martin Ziegler, "Measuring Unemployment in States and Local Areas," *Monthly Labor Review*, 97(6):40–46, June 1974.

residence and for eliminating dual job-holding raised questions because of the time lapse since 1970.[20]

4. The Census undercount, particularly of urban black workers, affects both the CPS sampling frame and the unemployment estimates.

5. Possible errors in field operations and in response rates inevitably affect unemployment estimates. Such errors tend to cancel out when overall U.S. figures are used but can significantly bias local estimates.

6. The most serious problem is the "benchmarking" process at the end of each year, when annual average data became available. This results in significant changes in local employment and unemployment estimates for prior months. Some states and areas have experienced substantial revisions in unemployment data, which may have a significant effect on future allocations.[21]

The Bureau of Labor Statistics is aware of these problems, some of which could be resolved by enlarging the sample. Beginning in January 1978, the BLS introduced several revisions in the estimating methods to correct some of these problems. A new procedure is to be used for linking the UI-based estimates to CPS estimates, to avoid the abrupt benchmarking changes that have occurred in the past. Unemployment insurance data used to estimate local unemployment have been made more uniform from state to state. Unemployment insurance claims data are to be used in disaggregating unemployment within labor market areas instead of the fixed Census ratios that have been used. While these changes will be helpful, Congress should also consider changing the law so that allocations could be based on annual or quarterly instead of on monthly data.

More fundamental are subtle issues surrounding the concept of unemployment. To what extent does "unemployment," as normally defined, measure economic distress? About one million "discouraged" workers are not included in the jobless count, nor are underemployed persons working for substandard wages or part-time workers who want full-time jobs. Those who seek part-time jobs are equivalent, in unemployment statistics, to those who seek full-time employment. The

[20]See Mark Kendall and Harold Wool, "An Evaluation of Procedures for Estimating Unemployment and Unemployment Rates in Cities and Counties," Prepared for the Department of Labor Manpower Administration, Research Center of the National Planning Association, Washington, D.C., 1974.

[21]Hyman B. Kaitz, "Labor Area Estimates of Unemployment Levels and Rates, June 1974" (unpublished); E. Terrence Jones and Donald Phares, "Formula Feedback: The Case of the Comprehensive Employment and Training Act," *Urban Affairs Quarterly* 14(1), September 1978.

figures do not distinguish between a worker in a family where others are also employed and one who is the only employed person in the family. Furthermore, local unemployment statistics (used in allocation formulas) do not distinguish between those who are temporarily unemployed and the long-term, hard-core unemployed.

In further recognition of these problems, a 1976 amendment to CETA established the National Commission on Employment and Unemployment Statistics to identify needs with regard to labor force statistics and to assess the current procedures, concepts, and methods used in data collection, analysis, and presentation.[22] The Commission will also study the information available on the use and effect of education and training programs.

ESTIMATING THE NUMBER OF ADULTS IN LOW-INCOME FAMILIES

Local data for estimating the number of adults in low-income families are available only in the decennial census. The fiscal 1975 Title I allocation used 1970 census data on the number of persons 18 years of age or older in families below the cutoff of $7,000 family income. For subsequent years, it was necessary to update these figures to account for advances in the Consumer Price Index. This was done by changing the income criterion of $7,000 for low-income families to $8,000 for 1976 and $9,000 for 1977 and estimating changes in the number of persons 18 and older in such families based on annual population estimates.[23]

There are, however, some shortcomings in these methods: the use of a uniform low-income standard without farm–nonfarm, regional, or size-of-family differentiations; the lack of local detail in the Current Population Survey, which is used to measure changes from one year to another; the use of outdated census ratios to disaggregate current low-income population figures for small geographic units; and technical problems in the family budget estimates.

The whole question of measuring the poverty or low-income population is made more complex because of the extent of noncash income. Census data (including the CPS) are limited to cash income and do not include the value of farm products used by a farm family or in-kind transfer payments, such as medicare, medicaid, food stamps,

[22]See John E. Bregger, "Establishment of New Employment Statistics Review Commission," *Monthly Labor Review*, 100(3):14–20, March 1977.
[23]For the 1978 Title I allocation, the low-income criterion was $10,000. Estimates of the number of adults by state were obtained from the Bureau of the Census Survey of Income and Education for the year 1975. These estimates were disaggregated to prime sponsor levels by using fixed ratios based on the 1970 census of population.

housing assistance, child instruction, and noncash social services. Yet these in-kind transfers are becoming a very significant component of family income.[24]

More fundamental than the question of measurement is that of where to set the income level and how much weight to give to this component in the Title I formula. These considerations underlie the question of what population group should be counted, keeping in mind the act's objective of enhancing employment prospects for the unemployed and underemployed as well as the economically disadvantaged.

The difficulties in measuring both unemployment and income have been recognized in CETA. The legislation has required the Department of Labor to develop: reliable methods to measure unemployment, underemployment, and labor demand for states, local areas, and poverty areas; data to construct an annual measure of labor-market-related economic hardship; and methods to maintain more comprehensive household budget data, including a level of adequacy, to reflect regional and rural–urban differences in household living.[25]

SUMMARY

The recent upsurge in appropriations for CETA testifies to the growing significance of employment and training programs as a major part of the nation's response to labor market ills. The changes in CETA appropriation and expenditure patterns are significant in demonstrating the changes in policy and emphasis summarized below.

• Most important is the increase in the proportion of CETA funds devoted to countercyclical rather than structural objectives. In the first year under CETA, three-fourths of CETA appropriations were for titles addressed to structural problems. By the second year, the proportion had shrunk to about half, as additional funds went to cyclically oriented programs. Recent appropriations under Title III point to more emphasis on employability development.

• There is a shift away from the concept of decentralization. In fiscal 1976, 93 percent of appropriations was for programs managed by local

[24]According to a Congressional Budget Office analysis, the percentage of families living in poverty in 1976 would decline from 11.4 percent, using a standard measurement of cash income only, to 6.7 percent, including noncash transfers. See U.S. Congress, Congressional Budget Office, *Poverty Status of Families Under Alternative Definitions of Income*, Background paper no. 17, revised, Prepared by John J. Korbel, Washington, D.C.: Congressional Budget Office, 1977.

[25]Section 312, Comprehensive Employment and Training Act of 1973.

officials (Titles I, II, and VI) and 7 percent for national programs (Titles III and IV). But, under the new administration, the proportion used for nationally supervised programs is on the rise.

• In fiscal 1975, 42 percent of appropriations was for Title I—the only title that is essentially decategorized. In 1976, Title I represented only 28 percent of total funds, and, by 1977, only 23 percent, as increases were largely for other titles. This reflects a drift away from the original concept of local decision making, as a result of federal actions to cope with the recession and with other emerging national problems—such as unacceptably high youth unemployment.

• CETA was intended to be a comprehensive manpower program, but other DOL programs (WIN, Older Americans, the employment service) and programs operated by other federal agencies were not folded into CETA. Overlap and lack of coordination persist, and consideration is being given to further consolidation. Congress has been content to continue CETA without change in scope, at least through fiscal 1978.

• There has been a vast increase in outlays for other strategies for dealing with unemployment. The major brunt of the recession has been borne by unemployment insurance: $18 billion spent in fiscal 1976, compared with $5 billion for CETA. Funds were also appropriated for accelerated public works and countercyclical revenue sharing. At the moment, the trend is away from income maintenance toward other cures for the nation's economic ills.

The use of formulas to distribute funds under CETA is a major accomplishment. There is more widespread distribution of funds than before, but this fact has led to changes in the pattern of funding and other problems.

• *Title I.* The relative share of funds going to cities has continued to decline, compared with the pre-CETA distribution under the Title I formula. Despite higher appropriations and a hold-harmless feature in the formula, some of the major cities are losing Title I funds each year, and counties are gaining. The emphasis on unemployment rather than low income in the Title I three-part formula also results in a shift of funds from regions with relatively high-poverty population to those with relatively more unemployment.

• *Title II.* Under Title II, funds are distributed to areas that have had 6.5-percent unemployment rates for 3 consecutive months based on one element only—the volume of unemployment. There are a number of problems with this formula: The 6.5-percent unemployment criterion, when national unemployment is above that level, is too low to identify areas with the most severe unemployment. This tends to diminish the impact on areas with the most severe unemployment. The formula does not have a severity factor to provide progressively more funds for areas with the highest unemployment rates. The use of a 3-month period for qualifying areas introduces a seasonal bias favoring areas with seasonally high unemployment. There are inequities arising from the lack of uniformity in delineating areas of substantial unemployment.

• *Discretionary funds.* Discretionary funds for Titles I, II, and VI have been used to maintain established levels of public service employment rather than to assist areas with unusually severe unemployment or areas with abrupt rises in unemployment.

• *Measurement of unemployment and poverty.* The Bureau of Labor Statistics has made progress in reconciling area and national unemployment estimates and in providing more supervision and control over estimating procedures. However, there are difficulties in obtaining monthly figures for thousands of small areas and for parts of cities. The number of adults in low-income families is even more difficult to determine, since it is derived essentially from 1970 census data. More fundamentally, there is a need for refinement of the concepts of unemployment and poverty and for a means of combining unemployment and poverty data into a useful index that will measure the unemployed who need assistance most.

3 Manpower Planning

Planning is an essential element of the Comprehensive Employment and Training Act. The basic premise of manpower planning is that some of the economic and social developments of recent years can be understood, and to some extent dealt with, through manpower programs. Most of the CETA Title I provisions deal with the components of a comprehensive manpower plan, the character of the local planning process, and the federal responsibility for reviewing plans. Implicit in the legislative requirements are major assumptions about what constitutes effective manpower planning. The first assumption is that state and local sponsors, since they are familiar with varying local conditions and needs, are in a better position to plan than federal program managers. The second assumption is that if the community is broadly represented in the planning process, the programs developed will be closely attuned to local needs.

This chapter examines CETA planning in the light of these assumptions, particularly the changes and trends in the second-year planning. Title I planning is considered separately from planning for public service employment under Titles II and VI, since there are distinct differences in the legislation that result from differences in the nature of the programs and in the pre-CETA planning approaches.

This chapter on planning focuses on three pivotal questions:

1. Who are the key manpower decision makers at the state and local

levels? What are the roles of elected officials? CETA administrators? Planning councils? Program operators?

2. What are the major influences on decision making? Is the end product of the planning effort actually used for making decisions?

3. What is the quality of local planning? How do state and local planners analyze their area's needs, and do they attempt to relate program strategy to these needs?

THE ORIGINS OF MANPOWER PLANNING

For the locality, manpower planning means understanding and evaluating the local labor market: how the supply of labor market skills is developed, how the job opportunities are created, and how the two are matched. It means identifying the problems that restrict economic opportunities for certain groups, selecting priorities or goals among them, and developing for decision makers some alternative choices and recommendations for achieving goals. Planning also implies a continuous process of reviewing what has been accomplished. The performance of a program cycle becomes a source of feedback to the planners, guiding their decisions for the ensuing program. In a broader sense, planning also refers to the continuous process of consultation among agencies and individuals concerned with manpower activities.

Title I requires state and local prime sponsors to draw up formal comprehensive plans for furnishing manpower services that must specify the services to be provided. The act also mandates the establishment of advisory planning councils composed of a broad base of clients, manpower agencies, and business and labor to participate in the planning process. The sponsor's plans must be submitted for approval to the regional offices of the Department of Labor to ensure that they are consistent with the requirements of the act and that the sponsor has demonstrated "maximum efforts" to implement the plan.

This concern with planning is less evident in the sections of the act that authorize public service employment. Under Titles II and VI, sponsors must submit "applications" rather than "plans." However, applications must satisfy a long list of stipulations covering groups to be served and types of jobs to be developed, which implies a considerable and sophisticated planning effort. The Department of Labor in its subsequent regulations made an effort to bring the planning process for public service employment closer to that for Title I by requiring sponsors to submit "plans" for Titles II and VI and to use the planning councils in the process of developing these plans. (Under the Emergency Jobs

Programs Extension Act of 1976, planning councils have a more important role; they must review project applications.)

Planning by local areas for the manpower programs that were forerunners of CETA Title I planning was introduced in 1967. The Cooperative Area Manpower Planning System (CAMPS) established a network of committees at regional, state, and local levels to analyze and make recommendations on local needs and local programs. These committees consisted of representatives of federal agencies administering manpower or related programs. They were to develop plans that related existing categorical programs to each other, minimized duplication, and proposed new programs for the coming year.[1] But the real decision making about what would get funded and for how much was done by federal agencies, and local planning committees were not influential in the allocation of resources. In this context, the CAMPS experience cannot be described as a meaningful planning process; nonetheless, it brought together the agencies concerned with manpower activities and introduced procedures for organizing local demographic and labor market data as a useful framework for program planning.

The CAMPS theme of systematic planning at state and local levels was extended in the early 1970s. CAMPS itself was restructured to include a more broadly based membership and to provide for three levels of planning: a state-level manpower planning council, manpower area planning councils (MAPCs) for large cities, and ancillary manpower planning boards for nonmetropolitan planning districts. Starting with the largest urban areas, the Department of Labor furnished funds to hire state and local staff planners; by 1974, all states, 160 cities, and 161 counties had operational planning grants.

The original CAMPS approach to planning lacked one of the elements that the Congress was later to insist on—the participation of client and community groups. On the other hand, CAMPS originally incorporated a potential for interagency coordination, particularly between HEW and DOL, that CETA may have diminished. The HEW network of vocational rehabilitation, welfare, and vocational education remains largely separate from CETA, despite representation of individual agencies on local councils. Sponsors may pick up program pieces from HEW-funded

---

[1]Categorical programs are federal programs mandated and funded by legislation or otherwise authorized, usually designed for a special purpose, for a designated client group, with defined procedures and objectives.

programs, but "the opportunities for coordination of CETA with other federal programs remain largely undeveloped."[2]

The Title II and VI planning lineage is quite different from that of Title I and can be traced to the temporary countercyclical objectives of the 1971 Emergency Employment Act (EEA). The locus of planning was lodged by the EEA with state and local governments, most frequently in their personnel departments—and, because EEA was thought of as an emergency measure, there was little feeling that it should be integrated with ongoing manpower programs. Participation in the planning process by education and training agencies, or any other agency, was not required or even suggested. Thus, the legacy of EEA set planning for public service employment on a different track, exempting it not only from outside participation but also from integration with other manpower programs. This separation from what was meant to be part of the integral design of CETA has inhibited the best use of resources. And, in many communities, the combined sums available under Titles I, II, and VI constitute very sizable resources in relation to local budgets.

TITLE I DECISION MAKERS

The decentralization of decision making in manpower programs under CETA has created a new set of decision makers and raises the question of how the crucial authority over the allocation of resources is exercised at the local level. Does the decision-making process operate as envisioned by the framers of the legislation—as an open, democratic process in which those most directly affected participate? Or are decisions made, as some skeptics feared, with an eye toward political advantage, or, as others believed, by a self-serving bureaucracy?

The planning process for the first year of CETA was not a fair test. The urgency of drawing up documents in support of grant applications within stringent time limits precluded, in most cases, any meaningful deliberation of alternatives. There were other factors that made it difficult, if not impossible, for sponsors to engage in careful study of existing programs, or to provide time for extended consideration or review of program plans: lack of manpower planning experience, particularly in smaller areas; a rapidly changing economic situation; and the fundamental predisposition of elected officials to move cautiously and to avoid potential sources of embarrassment. About all that fiscal 1975 plans for Title I grants did was to meet immediate administrative requirements.

[2]National Commission for Manpower Policy, *Manpower Program Coordination: A Special Report of the National Commission for Manpower Policy*, Special report no. 2, Washington, D.C.: National Commission for Manpower Policy, 1975.

Even in areas with some staff experience, planning tended to be done primarily by staff of the CETA sponsor and DOL representatives. For the most part, plans were extensions of existing programs, hastily approved by planning councils and elected officials. DOL regional offices focused almost entirely on administrative and procedural grant matters.

In the second year, the dynamics of CETA decision making were much more deliberate. The planning process took shape largely within the framework that the legislation had provided, and certain patterns of decision making have emerged.

LOCAL PLANNING

Role of the Elected Officials

The chief elected official and the CETA staff shape and direct the nature and content of the planning process: The resultant plans reflect their attitudes, philosophies, and competences.

At first, the chief elected officials were generally not disposed to enter actively into Title I decision making, although they were aware of manpower developments in their communities. In larger jurisdictions, responsibilities were delegated to administrative officials; in smaller areas, elected officials were more often involved, either formally or informally, in at least some decisions. By the second year, however, it became clear that CETA administrators were operating under marching orders, ranging from the very broad to the very specific. Of the 24 local prime sponsors in the study sample (excluding the 4 balance of states), only 1 small county reported elected officials to be completely detached from Title I planning. This new interest was awakened by the availability of Title VI funds for public service employment. Once drawn into the CETA decision-making process, elected officials tended to become more sensitive to other manpower issues. In Phoenix, for example, a subcommittee created by the city council to deal with public service employment was soon participating more broadly in CETA activities.

While most elected officials prefer a low profile, at critical periods their presence and influence were quite visible. In St. Paul, for example, the mayor gave full support to the CETA staff in their efforts to introduce a somewhat controversial new program design in 1975. The mayor of Philadelphia was known to lend a hand on at least one occasion to get a project funded. The mayor of Topeka tipped the scales when the Opportunities Industrialization Center (OIC) solicited the support of the city commission against a staff proposal that it be dropped as a CETA contractor, and again when building contractors and unions wanted to continue a hometown plan that the staff had deemed ineffective. In both instances, the staff position was upheld by the mayor and the city commission. The mayor of New York got involved when municipal unions urged the use of Title I funds for PSE in order to rehire laid-off city workers. In fact, Title I funds were used for PSE in fiscal 1976 by 10 local sponsors in the sample. In 7 of the 10, the chief elected official was directly and visibly making the decisions on the allocation of CETA funds for PSE.

The participation of elected officials is likely to be more direct and visible in the smaller counties. The Lorain County planning staff check their plans with the county manager; the Calhoun County CETA administrator "runs commitments by" the elected officials; in Chester County, all three commissioners are on the planning council and chair subcommittees.

The consortium structure appears to dictate even closer attention of elected officials to CETA programs than is the case in cities or counties. Consortia are generally governed by executive boards or committees whose members are the elected officials (or their designees) of the various jurisdictions comprising the consortium. These committees meet regularly and CETA staffs typically keep them informed. Members of the consortium are vigilant to ensure that each gets a fair share of the resources in this potentially competitive situation. In four of the nine consortia in the study sample, the executive committees' participation in the review, recommendation, and decision-making processes have been so extensive as to render the planning councils superfluous. In effect, planning has been an exercise of the staff and the elected officials. In the Kansas City consortium, the planning council reacted by threatening to resign en masse unless its recommendations were seriously considered. In the Austin and the Pinellas–St. Petersburg consortia, on the other hand, there has been practically no participation by elected officials.

The Orange County consortium is a special case, one that more nearly resembles a state model. The county is somewhat unusual in that it contains not just one but five jurisdictions eligible to be prime sponsors. Each is permitted to do its own planning. Consortium planning is decentralized to six units: the four eligible cities plus the balance of the county organized into two planning districts. Each unit has its own planner and develops its own plans, which are cleared with elected officials at the unit level and then forwarded to the consortium. The consortium administration is reluctant to second-guess elected officials of the individual jurisdictions.

The heightened political sensitivity of consortia appears due in some cases to the fragile nature of the agreements between a central city and the surrounding suburb, especially where there are different racial and ethnic compositions. Three consortia in the sample—Cleveland, Phoenix–Maricopa, and Raleigh—have experienced tensions that appear to spring from differences of this nature.

The elected official as a dominant decision maker is certainly a role consistent with the philosophy of decentralization. Congress intended to locate the responsibility for manpower programs with the chief elected officer in a jurisdiction. For better or for worse, the consequence has been to subject manpower programs to the indigenous political process.

Role of the CETA Administrator and Staff

As elected officials are the final arbiters of the planning process, so the CETA staff planners are the initiators of the written word in this process. As such, they decisively influence the planning process and the shape of program plans. In nearly all local planning, CETA staff planners prepare initial drafts of the Title I plan that serve as the basis for subsequent deliberations. The study revealed only a few instances in which assistance from other sources was solicited or received while drafts were being prepared. One was in the North Carolina balance of state: The plan was produced through the interaction of state and substate planning units. Another occurred in Middlesex County. In 1976, the draft for the Middlesex plan was produced in sections, each of which was discussed with a subcommittee of the planning council. A third example was New York City, the only jurisdiction in the study sample in which the council has its own staff; the council staff was consulted by the sponsor staff planners as they drafted the plan.

For the most part, Title I plans are developed and drafted by sponsor staff and then circulated for review and comment. This procedure gives the staff two major opportunities for control. First, they outline the overall program design. Where major ideas for redesign have been proposed, as they were in St. Paul, Topeka, Ramsey County, Union County, and Kansas City, they appear to have originated with the CETA staff. Second, staff members are able to shape the direction and extent of the planning process. In a few situations, council members have complained, criticizing CETA staff for restricting the scope of deliberations by limiting the time for discussion. Others have charged that important background materials are distributed only 1 day before council meetings, or sometimes at the meetings, so that an adequate review of the proposed decisions is not possible.

Field researchers rated CETA administrators and staff as the single "very important" influence in Title I planning in 15 of the 24 local

TABLE 11   Influence of Planning Council Members and CETA Staff in Title I Planning, Sample Local Prime Sponsors, Fiscal 1976

Agency or Group	Number of Sponsors (N = 24)		
	Very Important	Important	Of Little or No Importance
CETA administrator and staff	24	0	0
Employment service	0	5	19
Vocational education or other public education agency	0	8	16
Other public agencies	2	2	20
Elected officials	7	6	11
Community-based organizations	1	10	13
Business or industry	1	3	20
Labor	0	4	20
Client group representatives	1	3	20
Other	0	1	23

TABLE 12   Combinations of Officials and Council Members Rated as Very Important in Title I Planning, Sample Local Prime Sponsors, Fiscal 1976

Combination	Number of Sponsors (N = 24)
CETA administrator and staff only	15
CETA staff plus elected official	5
CETA staff, elected official and other public agency	1
CETA staff, elected official and business	1
CETA staff, CBO and client group	1
CETA staff and other public agency	1

jurisdictions studied (excluding the balance of states). In the other 9 local jurisdictions in the sample, CETA staff shared the "very important" rating, most often with elected officials (see Tables 11 and 12).

Role of the Planning Council

Given the definitive role of the CETA administrator and staff and the ultimate authority of the elected officials, it is easy to understand why many planning councils have had difficulty in exercising an effective role in the planning process. What are the circumstances under which these two powerful decision makers—the elected official and the CETA administrator—will permit the participation of a third—the planning council?

Conceptually, the council role is clear and significant. The framers of CETA viewed the local advisory council as the vehicle through which broad participation in manpower activities could be realized. They carefully specified its membership: representatives of client groups, community-based organizations (CBOs), the employment service, education and training agencies, and business and labor. The intent was to include those who delivered manpower services, those who received them, and others who might be directly affected by their quality and substance. Producers and consumers might be assumed to operate as a check on each other, and the requirement that the plan be made public prior to being submitted to the Department of Labor would facilitate this exchange.

Council functions are defined in the legislation: to submit recommendations regarding program plans and basic goals, policies, and procedures; to monitor and evaluate manpower programs; and to provide for continuing analyses of needs for employment, training, and related services. However, final decisions on such recommendations are reserved for the prime sponsor.

The Congress, having vested decision-making authority in the prime sponsor, did make an effort, however, to provide local groups with an opportunity to participate in the planning process, and it intended this participation to be more than window dressing. What happened is complex and not always what might have been expected.

Prime sponsors published plans in the newspapers, opened planning council meetings to the public, and sponsored public hearings. Perhaps it was naive to have anticipated the kind of participatory response on the part of the general public that is associated with a traditional town meeting. Rarely did anyone attend planning council meetings or otherwise participate unless he or she had a direct interest in the program as a current or potential beneficiary or as a council member. To the extent that general community awareness has been aroused at all, it has been through the scattered efforts of national or regional organizations such as the League of Women Voters, the Urban Coalition, and the Southern Regional Council, which have sponsored citizen-oriented studies of general and special revenue sharing, including CETA.

While CETA did not attract much interest among the general public, it did attract the interest of special publics—groups in particular need of CETA services; service agencies working in areas related to CETA services; and others specifically concerned with employment, training, and education programs. These groups appealed to the council as their principal vehicle for advocacy and recommendations. The council thus became the major channel for communication not only from its own members but also from these external interest groups.

Few CETA councils played any role in preparing the Title I plan in the first year, although some were involved in the planning process later. Time was short, some councils were not yet functioning, and plans assembled hastily by staff and based almost entirely on existing programs were cleared through planning councils without much participation from council members. The interim report of this study identified 8 of the 24 local councils in the sample as having played a role in developing the Title I plan during the first year but only 4 councils as having played a significant role in decision making. In the second year, there was greater opportunity for council activity, and field researchers rated about a third of the councils as having had a substantial effect on decision making, as shown below:

| Type of Prime Sponsor | Effect on Title I Decision Making | |
	Substantial	Little or None
Cities	Long Beach New York	Gary Philadelphia St. Paul Topeka
Counties	Balance of Cook Middlesex Pasco	Calhoun Chester Lorain Ramsey Stanislaus Union
Consortia	Kansas City/Wyandotte Phoenix/Maricopa Orange County Pinellas/St. Petersburg	Capital Area Cleveland Lansing Tri-County Raleigh San Joaquin

The judgments of the field researchers are confirmed and amplified by information about the structure and activities of the councils in the sample: council meetings, subcommittee structure, council composition, the sequence of planning-related events, and CETA staff support. Council activities tend to fall into one of three modes:

1. *Informational*: In five situations the council is convened primarily

to inform members of decisions and developments, rather than to solicit their contribution—the "rubber-stamp" council.

2. *Consultative*: The council is convened to solicit advice from council members. Twelve councils appear to fall into this category, although a few might shade into category 1. It is difficult to determine precisely when pro forma approval or passive response becomes modest but genuine contribution.

3. *Participatory*: Members in these councils participate actively in program planning or in reviewing operations. This is usually done through a subcommittee structure. Seven of the nine councils that were rated as having a substantial or major effect on planning operate through a subcommittee structure.

The policy of the elected officials and the CETA administrator determines the level of council activity. For example, of those councils rated as having little or no impact, members were told explicitly or led to understand that their role was "purely advisory." In these situations, CETA administrators tolerated the council as a federal requirement, but council organization and membership appointments were often delayed, meetings were held infrequently, and background material was delivered late or not at all.

Councils in smaller counties seemed less well established than those in other jurisdictions. This was due in part to their inexperience with manpower programs, manifested in start-up problems, organizational upheavals, and frequent changes in staff directors. Moreover, because elected officials in small counties tend to be directly involved in program decision making, normal election turnover had a disturbing effect on the stability of councils. These kinds of problems plagued council activities in Calhoun, Chester, and Union counties.

Some observers believe that the role of the council is not related to its size and composition; Ripley,[3] for example, concluded that in Ohio the influential councils were characterized not only by a high level of activity and frequent meetings, but also by the relatively low influence of elected officials. The study suggests that the composition of the nine councils judged as having significant effect does not differ significantly from that of the other councils in the study (see Table 13).

Once established, the profiles of local councils tended to be fairly stable. Although individual sponsors enlarged or reduced the size of their councils, the average size and composition did not change significantly

[3]U.S. Department of Labor, Employment and Training Administration, *The Implementation of CETA in Ohio*. R&D monograph 44, Prepared by Randall B. Ripley, 1976, pp. 6–11 (available from NTIS).

TABLE 13   Composition of Sample Local Prime Sponsor Planning Councils and of Councils Having Substantial Effect on Title I Decision Making, Fiscal 1976 (percentage distribution)

Council Membership	Prime Sponsors (N = 24)	Planning Councils Having Substantial Effect (N = 9)
Employment service	5	4
Public education or training agencies	14	14
Other public agencies	13	12
Elected officials	7	6
Business	17	20
Labor	7	6
Community-based organizations	11	11
Client groups	21	24
Other	5	3
All Groups	100	100
Average number of members on council	24	24
Title I service deliverers as percent of total	26	32

between 1975 and 1976. The nine councils identified as having substantial effect are not similar. Their jurisdictions are of all types and sizes; their members range in number from 14 to 39. Two have barred all service deliverers from membership, but, in four of the nine councils, program operators comprise 30 percent or more (72 percent in New York City) of the membership.

As noted earlier, seven of the nine most active councils have program operators as members. In any case, absence from the council appears somewhat illusory, because sponsors that have banned service deliverers from the council itself have permitted or encouraged them to form subgroups or otherwise act in an advisory capacity to the council. This is the case in Kansas City and Orange County.

There is additional evidence that councils active in decision making may be associated with the presence of a number of service deliverers, whether or not they are permitted to be members of the council. Eight of the nine councils that rank high in decision-making impact are associated with delivery systems that use a number of delivery agencies (i.e., "mixed" or "traditional" systems) to provide services (see Chapter 6). For example, in Topeka, which shifted from a system of contracting out services to a sponsor-operated "comprehensive" system, an observer noted that " . . . in fiscal 1976 the council seemed to have some impact on the content of the plan but that was probably due to the interest and activity of the program operators who were also members of the planning council. Since there are no major independent program operators at the present time the role of the planning council has diminished accordingly." It would seem that councils most likely to affect the decision-making process come from among those that have something at stake in the decision.

Not all of the sectors or groups represented on the active council participate equally. The act makes a special point of providing for the participation of client groups in planning—but the study found that client groups (as distinguished from community-based organizations delivering services), business, and labor were the least influential groups on the council (see Table 11). A DOL report on the first year of CETA operations observed that "of all the groups on the council, employer and client group representation was relatively the least adequate."[4] One problem was that client or target groups were sometimes represented by organizations that were also delivering services. Thus, it was not always clear whether it was the interest of the organization or of the clientele that was being represented. On the other hand, individuals who represented clients but had no specific organizational affiliation might find themselves at a disadvantage in terms of informational background and influence.

Active councils frequently play a constructive political role. In New York City, the council helped to protect Title I funds by participating in negotiations among the mayor's office, the CETA administrator, and the Department of Labor over the diversion of such funds to public service employment. In Long Beach and Kansas City, the council was the arena for resolving funding squabbles among community groups.

Inactive councils are generally associated with one of two situations: one in which objective, close monitoring of decision making is not desired for political reasons, the other characterized by a competent, sophisticated staff that resists sharing decision making with a council, perhaps fearing opposition to staff decisions. It is from sponsors with the latter kind of decision-making structure that the most innovative programs and many of the most dramatic changes in programming have come. It remains to be seen whether program efficiency, effectiveness, and innovation are fundamentally consistent with broadly based decision making, particularly when shared by those with a stake in the status quo.

[4]U.S. Department of Labor, Employment and Training Administration, Office of Manpower Program Evaluation, "The Role of Planning Councils and Community Participation in the Planning Process, CETA Staff Evaluation Findings, 1975" (unpublished).

In summary, councils are actively encouraged to participate in decision making when their participation is perceived by elected officials and CETA administrators as useful and not threatening. Otherwise, they are not actively encouraged, and in a few places they may be receiving negative signals. Active and effective councils appear to be characterized by the knowledgeable involvement of council members in the planning and decision-making process, by positive leadership on the part of the CETA administrators, and by the presence on the councils of groups who have something at stake in the decisions.

In 1975, there were four active councils in the sample. Five more were added in 1976. The circumstances that strengthened those five councils during 1976 were various. In Kansas City, the council was reorganized to exclude service deliverers and to replace them with representatives of what was viewed as the traditional power base of the community— business, labor, and the professions. Kansas City is thus an exception to the conclusion that the presence of those who have an interest at stake makes for a stronger council. In New York City, on the other hand, the melding of service deliverers into a constructive body supported by its own staff appears to have been the winning approach. Another council, that of a consortium, may have owed the vigilance and participation of its members to competition, if not distrust, between city and county members. The secret of developing a successful council, from the perspective of the CETA administrator, appears to lie in analyzing the immediate environment and taking advantage of whatever opportunities it offers.

BALANCE OF STATES

The planning process among balance-of-state (BOS) sponsors developed in a distinctive manner. Under CETA, states have responsibilities to act as prime sponsors for all areas too small to be prime sponsors in their own right (i.e., the balance of state), and plans are drawn up in consultation with the balance-of-state manpower planning councils. State governments are also responsible to coordinate plans in the state through the state manpower services council (SMSC). In general, there has been little effective use of the state manpower services council, and there is little evidence of state planning.

The disparate balance-of-state areas are frequently widely scattered, distant from labor market centers, and more or less rural. It is difficult to plan for these areas in terms of conceptuallly integrated economic or social goals. Therefore, it is not surprising that a general pattern of decentralization has evolved, with BOS sponsors redelegating planning responsibility to local levels. All four of the states in the study have decentralized planning responsibility to substate areas or districts. In fiscal 1976, there was no planning process as such at the state level; rather, each local district carried out its own process. The results were aggregated and almost automatically approved by state CETA staff and the balance-of-state planning councils. Other studies of CETA implementation in Ohio, Michigan, and Washington also point to the same pattern of decentralization of responsibility for planning.[5]

This decentralization of planning responsibility to substate areas has the advantage of using planning regions, such as councils of government, that already exist to plan, review, or carry out other types of programs. This should make possible greater coordination with other programs. (In North Carolina, for example, substate planning regions are also responsible for programs concerning child development, aging services, family planning, and nutrition.)

Planning by substate areas follows the logic of decentralization, which suggests that those closest to the problems should be in the best position to solve them. The major disadvantage is that recourse to a multitude of planning units may also lead to undesirable duplication of effort and planning for geographic areas that do not have the economic viability for program success.

One study of the state role in CETA develops a typology of planning and administration in which decentralized planning, along with a somewhat centralized responsibility for administration, is described as a typical BOS arrangement deriving logically from the CETA concept.[6] Under this model, substate areas are free to generate local plans, but monitoring, evaluating, and contracting authority (and sometimes choice of contractor) resides with the state. Centralized administration is generally justified as a means of achieving some economies of scale, avoiding political patronage at the local level, and maintaining enough control to meet BOS responsibilities under the law.

Another study argues that the reverse—centralized planning and decentralized administration—might be a better approach.[7] Centralized planning would be preferable to achieve economic efficiency within and

[5]Peter Kobrak, "CETA Implementation in Michigan," Unpublished paper prepared for the CETA Evaluation Seminar sponsored by the National Manpower Policy Task Force, Washington, D.C., June 13, 1975, Western Michigan State University, Kalamazoo; U.S. Department of Labor, Employment and Training Administration, *The Role of the State in the CETA Process: A Case Study of Washington State*, Final report PB-245 602/8ST, Prepared by V. Lane Rawlins, Washington State University, May 1975 (available from NTIS); U.S. Department of Labor, *The Implementation of CETA in Ohio*.
[6]U.S. Department of Labor, *The Implementation of CETA in Ohio*, p. 41.
[7]U.S. Department of Labor, *The Role of the State in the CETA Process*, pp. 4 and 29.

among the balance-of-state areas, as well as to overcome the scarcity of experienced, competent planners and the tendency of small, new planning units to "reinvent the wheel." Decentralized authority for the selection of program contractors and the supervision of operations, including monitoring and evaluation, would bring program success or failure closer to community awareness and would make continual program observation more feasible.

Although all four of the states in the sample have decentralized planning and a more or less centralized administrative structure, there are some interesting differences. In Maine, Title I funds are allocated and plans are developed at the local level by 8 area committees representing 12 counties. The local areas also select their own service deliverers, but contracting is done at the state level. Half of the membership of the balance-of-state planning council is comprised of the chairpersons of these 8 local planning councils; therefore, it would be unlikely for any significant revision of local plans to be made at the state level. This was made clear at a council meeting that considered fiscal 1977 plans. The council heard formal protests on four of the eight plans from agencies that were being dropped as deliverers. In three cases, the local council chairmen rose to defend their positions and were quickly supported by the state council; one local council's plan was returned for further discussion and resolution of its deficiencies.

In Arizona, too, Title I funds are allocated and plans developed at the local level—in this case, by four councils of government (COGs) and seven Indian groups. Through state-level review, again perfunctory, each plan is considered separately; there is no effort to develop an integrated BOS plan. In the view of some observers, fragmentation of the planning effort is a particular problem because plans are developed by the Indian groups independently of the COGs within whose areas they are physically located.

Texas has 14 substate planning regions, corresponding to councils of government, each with its own planning council and Title I plan. Again, review at the state level is routine. The dynamic that appears to underlie the BOS planning process was pinpointed by one observer, who noted that "since most of the plan is basically developed at the local area, a hands off policy seems to prevail, with members [of the state planning council] reluctant to challenge the wisdom of other representatives regarding what's best for their own area and problems."

For the most part, the state CETA staff in Texas viewed themselves as advocates for the local governments. In at least one instance, however, local planners felt that their autonomy was infringed by a decision of the governor's office to use 20 percent of Title I funds for a BOS-wide migrant worker program in fiscal 1977. Local councils were upset because the state was, in effect, planning to serve this group on their behalf and with their funds. In some communities, this situation resulted in three separate and uncoordinated migrant programs: a local effort, under its own Title I program; the special BOS Title I program; and an additional migrant program funded by the Department of Labor under Title III through another agency.

Despite the decentralization of planning responsibility, state governors did participate in Title I activities when there were political problems or an overriding state concern. In Texas, as noted, the governor's office decided on the 20-percent set aside for migrant programs. In North Carolina, the governor intervened in early 1975, when unemployment was very high, to reallocate all available Title I funds into work experience activities, so as to create more jobs. In Arizona, the governor was urged during fiscal 1976 to address a dispute on the allocation of Title I funds: It was claimed that Indian tribes were receiving 40 percent of the funds while constituting only 18 percent of the population.

In only one of the states studied—North Carolina—has there been an effort to develop a cooperative planning process between the state and local levels of government. The intent was to develop a mutually agreed-upon plan with broadly based community support through a series of communications between the regions and the state.

State planning staff instituted such a process, designed not only to maintain local autonomy but also to achieve "real planning" and "real control over program operations." Funds were provided to hire planners for each of the 16 substate planning regions (known as "lead regional organizations" or LROs) and local planning councils were established for each. Meetings between state planning staff and regional planners began in January 1975. A two-stage approach was adopted: an initial round of draft plans focusing on goals and priorities and a second round concerned with program design, management, and operations. First-round drafts prepared by LROs were reviewed at the state level by staff and council. State planners also provided considerable technical assistance to the LROs in the preparation of second-round drafts during many formal and informal meetings. Because of this close and continuing association, the state CETA planning staff was able to act as advocate for the local planners at the state level. Although there were differences among state-level staff with respect to whether local autonomy should be guaranteed, the principle of respecting local decisions prevailed.

Because of its difficult and ambitious objectives, the North Carolina planning process encountered numerous obstacles and fell far short of what might be considered exemplary in terms of state–local sharing of planning responsibility. The fundamental issue of how to achieve congruence between state manpower policy and local autonomy was not resolved. Contracting procedures, under which the LROs issued requests for proposals and made recommendations on selection to the state which had the final say and did the contracting), turned out to be confused and lengthy. A novel proposal to set aside 10 percent of Title I funds for LROs with outstanding plans was never fully implemented. Bureaucratic delays, inefficiencies, and dissension plagued the planning process, particularly during the second round of planning. Nonetheless, the North Carolina effort to create an integrated state-level planning process was unusual. Although it had mixed success, it did represent an important break with the past and the initiation of a more rational planning procedure.

INFLUENCES ON TITLE I DECISION MAKING

CETA critics predicted that the principals on the manpower scene would make choices not through objective consideration of alternatives but in terms of their own interests. Stereotypes persist that link such interests to the decisions that are made. Thus, the involvement of elected officials is associated with "political" decisions in the pejorative sense; participation in decision making by service deliverers is supposed to perpetuate the status quo and stifle objective program assessment; the domination of decision making by CETA staff may be perceived as leading to bureaucratic aggrandizement. The study tried to find out the extent to which these kinds of considerations influence decision making.

POLITICAL FACTORS

There is limited evidence of political intervention in the CETA planning process, in the Tammany Hall sense of trading political favors, nepotism, and patronage. Field reports suggest that, in one city, CETA staff were chosen more for political loyalty than for professional talent. In two other areas political power was said to be the biggest factor in determining who got the major contracts, but a recent change in administration altered the situations in one of these areas.

Another type of political intervention is illustrated by the decision of the mayor of New York City to use Title I funds to relieve fiscal pressure: Four of the local sponsors studied reported an "excessive" fiscal crunch (see Chapter 7); all of them allocated Title I funds to public service employment.

Political considerations seem to have dominated the Title I planning process in Cleveland and Raleigh. In Cleveland, consideration of financial stringencies apparently resulted in the allocation of a very large proportion of Title I funds to public sector employment; in Raleigh in fiscal 1975, political pressures determined the selection of a major service deliverer.

On the whole, however, the most important political concern of chief elected officials is to avoid embarrassment or "problems." This concern, which lies behind the insistence of elected officials that program decisions be cleared with them, induces a cautious approach and tends to constrain risk-creating innovations or controversial proposals.

SERVICE DELIVERERS

Politicking by service deliverers, particularly community organizations with specific racial or ethnic constituencies, is also reflected in the planning process. Program operators were viewed by some as concerned solely with securing or retaining their territories. Thus, in the Lansing consortium, it was observed that "the political reality seems to be that each minority group . . . gets at least one program designed specifically for them, and the size of the program depends more on the aggressiveness and competency of the program operators [than on the level of need]."

These conflict-of-interest concerns prompted the Department of Labor to issue a regulation in fiscal 1977 barring planning council members from voting on their own contracts. Three of the councils studied exclude all program operators from membership; two more exclude private-sector program operators (i.e., private, nonprofit community organizations) but permit public-sector program operators, such as the employment service and vocational education agencies, to be members.

The new regulations do not necessarily solve the conflict-of-interest situation; as one local observer noted: "this doesn't prevent log rolling, since you vote on the other group's program and he [sic] votes on yours." Backscratching may be extended to include the CETA administrator as well as the program operators, with the latter deferring to the former as disburser of funds. Then, as another observer noted, "CETA becomes a self-serving, closed system." Moreover, even in situations in which operators do not have council membership, they are permitted to serve on commitees or to organize as an advisory group.[8]

But there is some evidence that conflicts of interest may be diminished by other developments. As will be seen in Chapters 5 and 6, the importance of the established program operators within the CETA delivery system has decreased. Community action agencies and the employment service have had significant reductions in Title I funding; vocational education agencies have lost some of their influence. Community-based organizations, such as Opportunities Industrialization Center, Jobs for Progress, and the Urban League, no longer exercise control over a total program sequence from client entry to exit, but they compete for contracts on individual program pieces. Thus, while their funding is higher, their span of control is more limited. As sponsor staffs have gained more experience, the ability of service deliverers to influence planning decisions also appears to have declined.

Thus, in some cases, the grip of the service deliverers has been loosened. Elsewhere, under skillful leadership, they have become a force for constructive program improvement. Seven of the nine councils that were identified as important participants in decision making pay close attention to relative program performance. These councils concern themselves with placement rates, costs, and other aspects of individual contractor performance that are considered in planning for the next year. In Long Beach, council subcommittees set the rules and make recommendations on program proposals. In Orange County, program operators participate on subcommittees that work with sponsor staff to set specific performance goals and objectives for contractors. Program operators in Lansing are kept apprised of one another's progress by detailed comparative analyses. In New York City, one observer commented that the council as a whole was a major force in program planning and implementation. It has its own staff that conducts extensive analyses of contractor performance, and program operators have come to see that their competitive advantage lies in program success.

In Union, Calhoun, and Cook counties and in Philadelphia, staff planners are reported to rely on program operators for informal contributions to the planning process. Service deliverers are also reported to be influential in some of the consortia, notably Cleveland, Phoenix, Raleigh, and San Joaquin, although it is difficult in some of these cases to sort out helpful suggestion from self-serving influence.

[8]Originally, the Department of Labor proposed that council members be prohibited from even discussing matters affecting their own organizations, but in the final version of the regulations the prohibition extended only to voting on matters affecting their own organizations.

In summary, the representatives of service deliverers on the council are certainly interested in protecting and advancing their organizational interests. Some sponsors have sought to curtail the role of the program operators, while others have tried to channel it constructively. The challenge is to derive maximum benefit from the available expertise of service deliverers while minimizing conflicts of interest.

THE STAFF ROLE IN PLANNING

The decentralization of manpower programs shifted the responsibility for local programs from individual project managers to the elected official and the CETA administrator. In many instances, the CETA administrator has also opted to operate some of the manpower program components directly.

It is alleged that planning decisions on the allocation of resources among various service deliverers are influenced by the desire of some administrators to operate programs themselves rather than to use existing manpower resources. Such allegations, especially if made by service deliverers threatened with loss of a contract, are difficult to prove or disprove.

In Pinellas–St. Petersburg, for example, the CETA staff proposed a new comprehensive delivery system that would have enhanced staff participation and reduced that of some deliverers. Council members rejected the proposal, claiming that they were not furnished with enough information on objectives, costs, and how the new system would improve arrangements. In another consortium, a council member complained: "I and others question some of the staff recommendations, but they make a person feel like a fool and there are very few of us knowledgeable enough to even ask these questions. . . . " In Topeka, the staff presented to the council a proposal that the sponsor operate the intake center directly rather than contract with the employment service. According to one observer, no written documentation was provided to support the staff position that they could operate the center as efficiently as the employment service: "there were no data on the cost of the two proposals nor any impact study as to how the programs would be affected by a change in locations." In another city, an observer noted: "It appears that experienced competent suppliers such as the Urban League had their field of service restricted so that inexperienced individuals employed directly by [the CETA] staff could attempt to develop . . . a broad program . . . [N]othing I was told or read led me to conclude that the net result of [staff's] playing a larger role was a real gain in efficiency of operation or an enlargement of opportunities presented to the clients."

There is thus some concern that increasing responsibility for program operations is beginning to infringe on the objectivity of the administrator's planning function.

THE QUALITY OF TITLE I PLANNING

Central to the CETA concept is the premise that states and localities can plan more suitably for local needs than can the federal government. Nationally mandated manpower policies are not equally appropriate in every community; they may require adjustment to local conditions. More precise understanding may be easier to reach at the community level of an individual labor market. Such an understanding can generate a fresh look at local problems and possible solutions.

There had been some progress in the art of manpower planning before CETA. The CAMPS system, especially the funding of some 1,200 planning positions in state, city, and county governments, at the very least developed a core of manpower planners. CAMPS also provided a technical approach to planning, requiring analysis of the supply and demand dynamics of the labor market that was carried into the CETA system.

In 1974, the Department of Labor issued a technical assistance guide on planning for CETA sponsors.[9] The guide described the steps to be followed in identifying needs and establishing the priorities among them as a basis for decisions on program goals, groups to be served, and services to be offered.

First, demographic data for the sponsor area were to be analyzed to identify those groups in the population in special need of manpower services, i.e., youth, older workers, dropouts, and minorities. Next, the local labor market was to be examined to identify occupations with good career potential; then, information on existing local programs and other resources and their effectiveness was to be assembled and reviewed. This analysis was to be used to select priorities in target groups and services to be offered.

One characteristic of a planning model that calls for a detailed analysis of the labor market is that it permits, and indeed encourages, a fundamental rethinking of community and clientele needs and responsive program strategies. It may of course be used to make incremental changes in existing programs. It differs from other planning approaches

[9]U.S. Department of Labor, Employment and Training Administration, *Manpower Program Planning Guide*, April 1974.

that accept whatever is already in place and focus mainly on fine tuning of the existing design.[10]

However desirable the zero-base approach, it proved to be impossible in the first year of CETA for reasons beyond the control of most sponsors. A DOL study notes that "in the initial planning year, strategic planning was powerfully influenced by five key structural factors: the legacy of past programming, the new funding allocation formula under CETA, the time constraints, the rapidly changing economic situation, and the relative size of sponsor program efforts."[11] The net effect was to predispose sponsors to maintain what was in place, unless there was a particular reason for doing otherwise. The majority of sponsors did not plan at all in fiscal 1975, if by planning is meant "foresighted relating of action to needs or goals." Rather, they continued with what existed and concentrated on gathering up the reins of administrative control.

The second year was expected to be a better reflection of state and local planning capabilities; there was more time, greater familiarity with the programs, and a better understanding of the problems. Assessments of fiscal 1976 planning, however, have tended to be somewhat disappointing. The major problems were analytical weaknesses in identifying needs for manpower services and in conceptualizing approaches to meet those needs. Planning was still largely perfunctory. For the most part there was no serious, in-depth analysis or strategic planning. Observers close to the scene made these various comments regarding Title I planning:

The decision making process . . . was essentially the same as it was in the 1975 fiscal year, which in turn was essentially the same as it was prior to the passage of CETA.

Planning has tended to be . . . a ritual appendage to funding.

Where the plan does not show improvement is in defining needs in the city and in providing any rationale for allocating resources.

In depth and serious manpower planning does not occur.

. . . Document is primarily descriptive.

. . . Plan wasn't internally consistent—did not serve the groups that the analysis of need showed needed the most serving.

[10]For example, a planning and evaluation guide prepared by the staff of one large urban sponsor notes that "if a manpower program is operating, and if an annual . . . plan is prepared in a form acceptable to the Federal government, planning is going on." Part One, p. 35, In U.S. Department of Labor, Employment and Training Administration, *Planning and Evaluation Under CETA—A Guide for Large Prime Sponsors*, Prepared by Samuel B. Karp and Ralph S. Walker for the Mayor's Office of Manpower, Chicago, January 1976 (available from NTIS).

[11]U.S. Department of Labor, Employment and Training Administration, Office of Manpower Program Evaluation, "Prime Sponsor Planning for Fiscal 1975, CETA Staff Evaluation Findings, 1975" (unpublished), p. 12.

In some respects, the 1976 planning was an improvement over the year before and presaged further improvement for fiscal 1977. From a substantive point of view, the single most consistent accomplishment was the increased use of data on program performance (stemming from the management information system) as an aid to planning. The New York City, Topeka, Middlesex County, Lansing, and Kansas City sponsors made specific use of program data for planning in fiscal 1976. The Title I plan for each of the 16 regions in North Carolina showed an unusual level of detail that incorporated separate cost projections for each major Title I program activity (i.e., administration, allowances, and training). Less experienced sponsors or those that got a late start were not able to accomplish as much in fiscal 1976, but they expected to do more effective planning for fiscal 1977. Thus Pasco, Chester, and Union counties made significant improvements in their fiscal 1977 planning process, not only by greater council involvement, but also by more intensive staff planning.

The effort made by the Department of Labor to assist sponsors in installing adequate program management tools appeared to have paid off, since sponsors were clearly improving their capability of judging contractor performance. In many cases, however, the result of this improved capability was to demonstrate to sponsors the further difficulty and complexity of developing adequate evaluation techniques for comparative analyses of programs. Observers in a number of areas commented on the need for DOL guidance in developing standardized approaches that would be adjustable to varying sponsor needs.

The quality of planning improved. But if total reform and a rethinking of program strategies were expected, Title I planning for fiscal 1976 fell short. The annual planning and grant cycle itself puts a premium on short-range planning. As noted earlier, there were structural and environmental factors that tended to limit comprehensive and objective planning: the attitude and philosophy of the elected official, the leadership exercised by the CETA administrator, economic and fiscal pressures that diverted Title I funds, and attention to countercyclical problems.

TITLE I PROGRAM GOALS AND OBJECTIVES

There is a persistent confusion about program goals and objectives. What exactly are Title I manpower programs intended to accomplish? The language of the act is vague and general: Training and services are to be designed to lead to "maximum employment opportunities and enhance self-sufficiency." This phrase does not help the planner discriminate among alternative strategies to make better use of scarce resources. It does not suggest a balance between long-term and short-term objectives, between crisis intervention in times of unemployment and longer-term efforts to improve job-related skills. It does not suggest a balance between those who need much help and those who need only a little. It contains no guides for the appropriate role of employers in the program or of schools and other existing training institutions.

The planners in the North Carolina balance of state attempted to focus on identifying goals. The first round of draft planning within the BOS was devoted entirely to the development by each lead regional organization of a policy statement that would serve as "the basis on which the region has and will make decisions concerning the development, utilization and maintenance of the . . . labor force." But when the staff analyzed these first drafts, they found that the regions were having considerable problems in formulating policy statements for reasons that included inexperience, the influence of existing categorical programs and operations, lack of time, insufficient data, and lack of skill in the use of available data.

The initial technical assistance provided by the Department of Labor was confusing. The 1974 Manpower Program Planning Guide advised sponsors to establish a program "purpose," and also to define for themselves program "goals."

"Purpose" is defined as a "statement(s) describing the focus or thrust of a program." The example given in the guide attempts to narrow the broad statement of purpose in the act by focusing on a specific group: "The purpose of this program is to improve the overall employment prospect of the economically disadvantaged residents of the area." Most sponsors, however, tended to quote or paraphrase the more general statement of purpose in the CETA legislation in their fiscal 1975 plans.

The 1974 Manpower Program Planning Guide defined "goals" in one place as "statements of desired aims or outcomes." Although not as general as statements of purpose, goals are broad statements and do not represent a specific quantifiable level.[12] The example was poor: "A goal of this program is to move 16–19-year-old minority youth into laborer and operative positions." Such statements do not define a long-term program goal or explain why one activity is selected rather than another.

Nevertheless, for some sponsors, the fiscal 1976 plans represented an improvement over the year before in terms of meaningful goals. At least one Department of Labor regional office required its sponsors to present

---

[12]U.S. Department of Labor, *Manpower Program Planning Guide*, pp. 1–2.

a specific statement of longer-term needs as a rationale for its activities. Sponsor plans in this region included such goal statements as increasing income levels of specific target groups, decreasing the percentage of specific target groups with incomes below the poverty level, and increasing the percentage of minorities employed in various occupations and industries. Two sponsors in the study sample from this region (Cleveland and Lansing) have such statements in their plans. Some plans of sponsors in other regions also referred to longer-term goals such as the intention to move workers from secondary to primary labor markets (Philadelphia) or to bring about a more equitable distribution of jobs and incomes with respect to minorities and females (St. Paul). In all, half of the 14 plans examined contained some statement of specific long-term goals, although none proposed any mechanism to measure achievement, and none furnished any evidence of the extent to which such goals actively guided program decision making.

LINKS TO THE PRIVATE SECTOR

Inadequate attention to the private sector was cited as a significant impediment to effective planning for a number of sponsors studied.

A representative of the chamber of commerce in the central city of a consortium deplored the failure of CETA to cultivate relations with business more actively. In another consortium, a representative of the Urban League viewed the low level of business involvement, despite representation on the planning council, as a significant problem. An observer in still another consortium noted: "There seems to be some reticence among manpower staff to deal with private sector employers. No major employers in the consortium have sat on the council. . . . It appears that little systematic outreach has been conducted to make contact with them."

In one urban area, an observer noted: "job development personnel get a list of terminations when the course is completed, instead of being forewarned of job needs. . . . Overlaying the entire process [of job development] is the failure . . . to interest the business community where the jobs are to be sought."

Union County, making an effort to overcome this lack, held a luncheon for 50 local employers to acquaint them with CETA staff and programs. Also, CETA staff in Union planned to provide direct placement referrals to employers as a way of building a relationship and paving the way for graduates of their training programs.

THE REGIONAL OFFICE FOCUS

The Department of Labor was preoccupied in fiscal 1975 and 1976 with administrative rather than substantive matters of planning. DOL argued that getting the act implemented was the first priority; more attention to program content and quality would follow.

Because of the urgency of implementing CETA, DOL regional office attention for the most part was limited to procedural and technical aspects of grant applications. San Francisco was an exception; sponsors in that region were asked for information on the results of CETA classroom training in the previous year—i.e., enrollments, completions, and placements by occupation. Sponsors in this region were also asked to include a table of skill shortage occupations that would show not only projected demand but also projected supply of labor for each occupation from sources other than CETA. This information was furnished by one sponsor.

It would appear that a knowledge of other manpower-related activities, especially those funded under Title III of CETA, would be essential if unnecessary duplication were to be avoided. In New York City, for example, the field researcher noted: "There are manpower programs in the Department of Employment, . . . in the Housing and Development Agency, in the Department for the Aging, in the Health and Hospital Corp . . . but nowhere are they (all) listed, nowhere can you even get an overview of all these programs and the relationships between them." A recommendation by the 1974 planning guide to develop inventories of other training efforts had relatively low priority with sponsors. However, the San Francisco regional office, by requesting this information, introduced a key element to link the program to the general framework of labor demand. This was a significant step in tightening the analysis, even though the responses were limited and fragmentary.

The Department of Labor practice of comparing sponsors' plans with performance reports may have contributed to some distorted thinking concerning the proper role of planning. The DOL regional offices suggested that plans be modified if quarterly performance reports by prime sponsors show substantial variance from the plan. This procedure implies that the regional office places a greater premium on accurate guesses as to what will happen than on a challenging blueprint for what should happen. Through successive modifications, planning comes to reflect rather than guide program operations.

Some sponsors also felt hindered by regulations and regional office interpretations that limited the options for programs. Programs to upgrade the skills of individuals currently at work—even if the upgrading would mean job openings for others when those in the program were upgraded—were not approved by DOL.[13] Regulations on paying (or waiving) allowances also restrict discretion—not a minor matter when allowances may consume half or more of Title I funds.

The Department of Labor has presided over a difficult transition in the nature and scope of planning. The pre-CETA view, as Mangum notes, "saw manpower planning as an effort to accept federal resources and develop a program to meet federal guidelines, and to make programs work in some local environment."[14] CETA requires a broader and more complex understanding and analysis of how federal programs and resources should be brought to bear upon a labor market.

Inadequate Data

For small areas, lack of data is a major problem in planning. Economic analysis has traditionally employed the integrated labor market (e.g., standard metropolitan statistical areas [SMSAs] as the major unit of analysis, a practice that continued under CAMPS). Under CETA, however, the labor market area was replaced with the political jurisdiction as the planning unit. Sixteen of the 24 local prime sponsors in the sample were serving only part of a labor market area. A Department of Labor study found that, despite the widespread formation of consortia, a significant number of sponsors were planning for smaller geographic areas than were planned for under CAMPS. Moreover, the plans, particularly those for Title II, required information on unemployment and other economic indicators for even smaller units, such as neighborhoods and census tracts.

For information on labor market supply, many sponsors used the package of 1970 census data made available by the Department of Labor, while noting that it was out of date and consequently had shortcomings.

Because the needs for manpower services are much larger than can be met, considerable refinement of detail is necessary in the data to support informed choices in allocating resources. The detail available, however, is frequently not adequate. As a result, it is difficult for planners to set objective priorities or preferences. For example, sponsors were asked to

[13]The Department of Labor argued that CETA Title I funds should be used to assist directly those in greatest need and that the individuals already employed who would benefit initially from upgrading did not, in many cases, fall into this category.
[14]Garth Mangum and David Snedeker, *Manpower Planning for Local Labor Markets*, Salt Lake City: Olympus Publishing Co., 1974, p. 29.

list in their plans the "significant segments" of the population in need of service and the degree to which each group would be served; in the 16 jurisdictions examined, the average number of significant segments listed was 7. Long Beach proposed to serve more than a dozen target groups directly in proportion to their incidence among the poor and/or unemployed. This tendency to allocate resources over a long list of significant segments was noticeable in fiscal 1975, and it became entrenched in fiscal 1976.

To analyze labor market demand in order to determine where the employment opportunities lay and what kinds of training were needed, sponsors were expected to have available a list of occupations for which training might be offered, based on the local skill shortages and anticipated economic growth. This information has been difficult to obtain for areas smaller than smsas, and in fiscal 1976 the Department of Labor began a major effort to improve data collection for small areas. Congress also recognized the problem and, in extending Title VI in fall 1976, established the National Commission on Employment and Unemployment Statistics to review and suggest improvements in current employment data and recommend the collection of additional information on occupations, education and training, job vacancies and turnover, and related demand indicators.

PUBLIC SERVICE EMPLOYMENT

It was not anticipated that planning for public service employment would be a large part of CETA planning. The original public service employment component of the act (Title II) consisted of a modest program for areas of substantial unemployment, emphasizing the transition of program participants to unsubsidized employment. Much of the Title II language is similar to that of the 1971 Emergency Employment Act, which also spoke of unmet public service needs, significant segments, and transition prospects. In the urgency of Title II planning, the first impulse of many sponsors was to pick up their lists of EEA slots from the shelf.

When Title VI was passed, planning was compressed into a 6-week period. Given the tremendous pressure to get the new public service employment money spent rapidly, there was neither the time nor the inclination for extensive analysis of needs and opportunities. Virtually all sponsor planning for public service employment consisted of a single series of decisions: the allocation of slots among potential employing agencies. For the most part, the distribution of their slots was left to each agency.

TABLE 14   Relationship between Public Service Employment Decision Makers and Degree of Fiscal Pressure, Sample Local Prime Sponsors

Degree of Fiscal Pressure in Major Jurisdictions[a]	Sponsors by Principal Decision Makers			
	All Sponsors	Elected Official	Elected Official and CETA Administrator	CETA Administrator
Extreme	4	3	1	0
Moderate	14	7	3	4
Little or none	6	0	3	3
TOTAL	24	10	7	7

[a]Fiscal pressure refers to the financial position of the major unit of government, based on revenues, expenditures, and other relevant information.

DECISION MAKERS

Elected officials were reported to be the decision makers for at least two-thirds of the local jurisdictions studied. Plans for the disposition of Title II and VI funds were made directly by elected officials, by their immediate offices, or by planning or budgeting offices reporting to them, rather than by the CETA office. The extent to which elected officials were willing to share their authority, even with the CETA administrator, appears to be related to the fiscal position of the jurisdiction. The greater the financial need, the more likely elected officials were to be sole decision makers; where fiscal straits were less acute, elected officials tended to share more of the decision making with CETA staff. Table 14 indicates that 18 of the 24 local jurisdictions studied were reported to be under some fiscal pressure, ranging from moderate to extreme. In 10 of these, the chief elected officials were the sole decision makers. On the other hand, in 3 of the 6 jurisdictions in which there was little or no fiscal pressure, CETA administrators and staff made the principal decisions; in the other 3, staff and elected officials worked together. There were no jurisdictions under extreme pressure in which CETA administrators were permitted to make the key decisions, nor were there any with little or no financial difficulty in which elected officials acted as sole decision makers.

CETA planning councils had virtually no role with regard to public service employment. In only 2 of the 24 local jurisdictions studied was there any record of the council's making even a modest contribution to the Title II or VI plan. Thus it appears that chief elected officials or their representatives and the CETA staff controlled public service employment at the local level.

The role of the planning councils in public service employment planning was expected to become more significant in fiscal 1976 as the Emergency Jobs Programs Extension Act was implemented. That act required, for the first time, that the planning council have an opportunity to comment on project applications and make recommendations to the prime sponsor. This gave planning councils a direct responsiblity for administration and therefore a clearer mandate for participating in planning.

At the state level, Title II and VI decision making generally was decentralized to substate units. In the sample, the three states that had decentralized Title I decision making followed the same policy for public service employment. In part this decision reflects the importance that local governments attach to control over jobs. In Maine, for example, although 12 counties in the balance of state had agreed to merge into 8 planning units for Title I purposes, they were not willing to do the same for Titles II and VI; instead, they received permission to establish 12 separate planning councils for Title II and VI planning. Typically, under BOS sponsors, local planning units sent their plans to the state staff, which then submitted them to the BOS council for approval. In one state, the BOS council made some suggestions, but it does not appear that they resulted in any significant changes.

On the other hand, in North Carolina, where the state directed and coordinated Title I planning, some PSE decisions were also made at the state level. For example, the decision to allocate half the Title VI jobs to state agencies and half to local units of government was made by the governor.

THE PLANNING PROCESS

The fiscal 1975 planning process for Titles II and VI reflected three modes of decision making. If the chief elected official was the sole decision maker, the essentials of the plan were likely to be prepared by the official's budget and personnel office and handed to the CETA staff, who affixed the necessary "boiler plate" data from the Title I plan, reviewed it with the CETA planning council, and forwarded it to the Department of Labor. In New York City, the Bureau of the Budget worked out the allocation of job slots; in Philadelphia, it was the city manager's office.

When planning was done jointly by the chief elected official and the CETA administrator, the division of work varied. Generally, however,

CETA staff drew up the plans. In some instances the staff acted as scribe; in other cases their participation was more significant. Gary exemplified the former situation. In St. Paul, the CETA staff consulted with the mayor and with government agencies. In Austin, the CETA staff worked with the city personnel department to identify the agencies most likely to be able to absorb PSE participants. In Ramsey, staff prepared a draft allocation of slots, which was subsequently reviewed and revised by the county commissioners.

In cases in which the CETA administrator and staff exercised the leading role, the usual procedure was to solicit requests for slots from government agencies and, in some cases, from nonprofit organizations. The staff reviewed the requests and allocated the positions. In Middlesex County, Title II slots were allocated on the basis of a weighting system. The 16 municipalities eligible for Title II funds were grouped into five categories according to severity of unemployment. Weights were assigned to each category, and funds distributed on this basis. Title VI funds, on the other hand, were distributed on the basis of such considerations as feasibility and the speed of implementation.

The general practice among consortia was to distribute PSE slots among consortium members on the basis of a fixed formula. Topeka was the only consortium in the sample in which this was not done; the distribution was made by CETA staff primarily on the basis of commitments of employing agencies to absorb PSE workers into regular unsubsidized jobs.

Title VI planning began in early 1975, and fiscal 1976 planning was scheduled to begin 2 or 3 months later. The proximity of the two periods, together with initial difficulties in implementing PSE, obviated any real efforts to take a fresh look at plans for fiscal 1976. Consequently, for the fiscal 1976 planning cycle, nearly all sponsors merely modified their grants to continue whatever package of jobs was listed in the original grant. If new jobs were to be added or substituted for previously planned jobs, the existing, established decision-making process was used.

In summary, the disposition of a major part of public service employment funds was decided on by state and local governments within about a month early in 1975. Decisions were made by chief elected officials and CETA staff, with little additional participation. The major planning consideration in most sponsor jurisdictions was the fiscal situation: If it was severe, the principal goal seems to have been to relieve it. Otherwise, perceptions of how long the program might last, how rigorously placement goals might be enforced, and the administrative concerns of staffing and organizing to provide or improve public services were among the considerations.

The hastiness of the initial PSE planning and the absence of a new formal round of planning for fiscal 1976 precluded any coordination or integral relationships between the plans for Title I and those for Titles II and VI. In a sense, the opportunity was there, because the same staff units usually prepared the plans for all three titles. (Of the 24 local prime sponsors studied, 19 used the same staff for all three plans.) Large chunks of the Title I grant materials—such as those describing the universe of need and local economic conditions—were inserted into PSE grant documents.

However, had there been time enough, there were yet other factors that militated against any real integration in planning. The basic purposes of Title I and of Titles II and VI were different and prompted different decision-making processes. Pre-CETA planning approaches had been different, as discussed earlier. To the extent that PSE funds appeared to be a temporary phenomenon, there might seem to be little merit in putting a lot of effort into detailed coordination of the two, even if it were possible.

The complex aspects of the recession, however, particularly the combination of inflation and unemployment, suggest that PSE may become a permanent activity among other fiscal options. In this event, it might be wise to consider the possibilities of overall planning strategies that would draw upon all of the CETA resources in an integrated fashion. On the average, funds available to a given jurisdiction from all three titles of CETA probably amount to about 5 percent of local government budgets (other than education) in a given year—not an insignificant resource itself. Teamed with funds from other federal or local sources, it could be sufficient to effect major social or economic goals.

SUMMARY

The *raison d'etre* of decentralization is to promote more effective allocation and use of resources. State and local governments are expected to be able to plan better than the federal government to meet local needs. The study has addressed this assumption through three central questions: Who are the key decision makers under CETA? What factors influence the decisions? What is the quality of state and local planning under CETA?

First, the locus of decision making has shifted. CETA administrators and elected officials are the primary decision makers; the extent to which others participate reflects the attitudes and philosophy of these two groups. This discovery has different policy implications at different levels of program management. At the local level, planners may or may not be participating more fully in decision making. Before CETA, program planning was conducted by program operators such as the local employment service, but program decisions were made by federal officials. Now planners have much better access to the decision makers, but the scope of their operations is still limited by whatever mandate is laid down by the chief elected official. From a national perspective, the desired transfer of responsibility and authority has been fully accomplished: State and local elected officials, through their CETA organizations, now control and shape the decision-making process.

On the whole, the move has been slow toward a participatory style of decision making. About a third of the sponsors in the sample brought their advisory planning councils fully into fiscal 1976 planning. A number of factors continue to restrain sponsor enthusiasm for the councils. One is the difficulty of organizing service deliverers as a constructive force for program improvement. Another is that sponsors tend to be less interested in councils if the program is subject to undue political influence, or if it is very nonpolitical. In the former instance the sponsor staff may prefer to avoid close or objective scrutiny of program performance; in the latter, the sponsor's staff may wish to avoid interference in program change.

The influences governing Title I decision making tend generally to be constructive. Those who anticipated large-scale political patronage, lack of interest, or other negative stereotypes will be disappointed. Although self-interest in various guises can and does enter into decision making, local prime sponsors have on the whole demonstrated a capability of responding to careful, objective analysis of services and needs, as well as a serious search for program improvement.

Fiscal 1976 planning for Title I was better than that of the previous year, but confusion as to goals and objectives, DOL regional office preoccupation with administrative and procedural matters, and inadequate data hampered the development of truly comprehensive planning. Sponsors were still in transition between the mechanical grinding out of numbers that constituted much of pre-CETA planning and a thoroughgoing overhaul of program strategy. Department of Labor assistance to sponsors in installing management information systems began to pay off in terms of increased sponsor attention to program performance and the use of program data to support changes and shifts in the plan. This growing awareness also highlighted the difficulties and complexities of developing adequate measures for comparative analysis or evaluation of program activities. A number of observations by field researchers focused on the need to upgrade planning skills in this area and to promulgate national evaluation approaches flexible enough for varying program designs.

Respondents in some jurisdictions also expressed concern that staff planning was weakened by staff operation of programs. The separation of planning and evaluation functions from operating responsibilities needs serious consideration.

Sponsors have paid very little attention to longer-term manpower policy and program goals. They need assistance in identifying and choosing among disparate objectives—countercyclical assistance, income maintenance, and alleviation of structural unemployment—that fall within the CETA framework.

Inadequate attention to the private sector by many sponsors was cited as a significant impediment to effective planning. Longer-term planning strategies benefit from integration with the private sector's plans for expansion and new investment; short-term planning should rely on firm employer support.

There has been considerable delegation of planning responsibilities to smaller planning areas within prime sponsor jurisdictions. This is most obvious in BOS Title I planning, in which planning authority is typically delegated to substate planning bodies such as councils of government. Some consortia have also decentralized planning responsibility to individual jurisdictions. Such delegation of planning to units that are only portions of labor markets raises questions about the economic viability of the plans, as well as about duplication of effort.

The expanding role of the elected official in the decision-making process became evident in 1976 Title I planning. The direct participation of elected officials in manpower programs is new under CETA and, for the most part, beneficial: It gives the program the support and visibility it needs to be effective. It does, however, carry some drawbacks. Here and there the negative effects of trading in political favors have been noted. A more frequent and somewhat unexpected effect is that the participation of elected officials tends to work for caution and conservatism. Their participation has also been associated in fiscally hard-pressed jurisdictions with the diversion of Title I funds to public service employment programs designed to provide fiscal relief.

Elected officials and the CETA administrators together generally shape and control the role of the planning council. About one-third of the local councils are rated as having significant effect on Title I planning. Active councils open up decision making and focus attention on program performance. They are, in effect, the primary vehicle for establishing accountability, since there is virtually no other citizen input. Field researchers saw a continuing need for the training of council members to help them improve their understanding and capability for participation.

Representation on the council, as specified in the act, was designed to include both program producers (e.g., program operators) and program consumers (e.g., clients and employers). Conflicts of interest among program operators serving on the council have continued to be a problem for many sponsors, who feel that council membership should be broadened or revised to exclude or reduce the influence of program operators. On the other hand, their presence seems almost necessary for an active council.

There is some evidence that councils are more effective when elected officials do not serve as council members. A minority view, however, holds that direct contact between the official and the council lends needed support to council activities. The role of the elected official appears to be a particular problem in consortia, where executive committees composed exclusively of elected officials have in some cases nearly usurped the planning council role. Even among active councils, observers have noted a continuing problem in securing adequate participation by program consumers—i.e., clients and employers.

Title II and VI decision making was controlled much more tightly than that for Title I by elected officials. The greater the degree of fiscal pressure experienced by the jurisdiction, the more likely elected officials were to act alone. Officials under less financial pressure delegated more of the PSE decision making to CETA staff. Planning councils played little or no role in decision making. Strained treasuries aside, it is difficult to get elected officials to view public service employment as anything but an extension of their normal authority over employment in their agencies and departments.

Planning for Titles II and VI was hasty and perfunctory. For the most part, it did not go beyond assignment of slots to employing agencies. Only three local sponsors gave any serious attention to transition. Some field observers believe that in view of the difficulties of bending PSE to serve structural as well as countercyclical purposes, the countercyclical component should be dropped from CETA and perhaps be converted into general revenue-sharing funds. Others believe that, given more time for planning, PSE could serve both goals. Or, taken together, funds from the three titles might be sufficient to generate a major change in a local condition.

4 Administration

The transfer of responsibility for and control of manpower programs from federal to state and local officials marks a major change in the administration of employment and training programs. This decentralization, embodied in CETA, resulted from the confluence of two developments: the recognition of the need to reform the rapidly expanding but uncoordinated manpower system and the commitment of the Nixon Administration to the concept of "New Federalism."

In the mid-1960s, responsibility for manpower training and employment programs stemming from the Manpower Development and Training Act (MDTA) and the Economic Opportunity Act (EOA) was divided among the Department of Labor, the Office of Economic Opportunity (OEO), and the Department of Health, Education, and Welfare. The OEO programs were eventually placed under the newly created Manpower Administration of DOL (now named the Employment and Training Administration).[1] At the state and local level, two major administrative channels had emerged: MDTA classroom training funds went through state employment service and vocational education agencies to their local counterparts, and on-the-job training funds were handled by the state employment service or other organizations. Programs stemming from the EOA went from the Manpower Administra-

---

[1]Stanley H. Ruttenberg, assisted by Jocelyn Gutchess, *Manpower Challenge of the 1970s*, Baltimore: Johns Hopkins Press, 1970, pp. 74–97.

tion to local sponsors such as community action agencies, community-based organizations, or governmental units.

Some of the major cities became sponsors for youth summer employment programs or concentrated employment programs, but, for the most part, the hundreds of local governments had little opportunity to manage federal manpower programs until the Emergency Employment Act of 1971. Even under that act, their experience was limited to hiring the unemployed for public service jobs.

A 1967 amendment to the EOA assigned responsibility for a comprehensive work and training program to local organizations, mostly community action agencies. The 1968 amendments to MDTA gave state governments the authority to approve all manpower projects funded by the federal government, provided they conformed to an approved state plan. But these amendments were not fully implemented, and the Department of Labor continued to operate manpower programs through its national and regional offices.

The question of how to organize and coordinate a decentralized manpower development system had been debated for some time.[2] Beginning in 1969, several legislative attempts were made to define more clearly the administrative roles of federal, state, and local governments and to replace the compartmentalized system of categorical programs with a more flexible design.[3] One proposal would have given state governments a preeminent role; another envisioned decategorization of local programs under strong federal control. The Manpower Training Act of 1969, proposed by the administration, called for local prime sponsors to be designated by governors. Several variations were considered in the Senate and the House, but there were disagreements over such key matters as defining local prime sponsors, the role of state governments, the fate of various established categorical programs, and the type and scope of a public service jobs program. The bill that finally cleared the Congress in December 1970 was vetoed on the grounds that it would create "dead-end" jobs in the public sector and because it appeared to preserve categorical programs.

This legislative activity was not in vain, however; it consolidated support among congressional committees and within the administration for legislation embodying the principles of local determination and management of programs. Although no agreement was reached on the

[2]Robert Guttman, "Intergovernmental Relations Under the New Manpower Act," *Monthly Labor Review* 97(6):10–16, June 1974.
[3]Roger H. Davidson, *The Politics of Comprehensive Manpower Legislation*, Policy Studies in Employment and Welfare, no. 15, Baltimore: Johns Hopkins Press, 1972, pp. 10–20.

mechanics, there was broad consensus on the need for rationalizing the system, and the groundwork was laid for the eventual passage of CETA in December 1973.

CETA structured a direct federal–local relationship and placed local units of government in the central role in administering manpower programs, albeit with strong federal oversight. States were given responsibility for areas not under the jurisdictions of the established local prime sponsors—the balance of states.

This chapter examines the manner in which local government has managed a new and complex area of public administration, the problems encountered at various levels of government, and the adjustments made to resolve such difficulties. It attempts to furnish some insight into the major administrative questions about the CETA block grant approach, i.e., whether the handling of manpower programs has been simplified or made more complex and whether clients are served in a more effective and efficient fashion.

THE ADMINISTRATIVE NETWORK

One purpose of CETA was to move decision making and management of manpower programs closer to grass roots, to make it more responsive to local needs and more responsible to local officials. In the process, CETA has changed existing interorganizational relationships and modified the roles of federal, state, and local officials. Ambiguities in the act, as well as in the administrative regulations, have tended to weaken the thrust of decentralization, but the situation is dynamic and a final accomodation among the roles and responsibilities of the various levels of government does not seem imminent.

FEDERAL–LOCAL RELATIONS

The federal–local relationship is the crux of decentralization, but the compromises made during the legislative activity that produced CETA left the relationship less than clear. Title III, which provides for direct federal supervision of programs for Indians, migrant and seasonal farm workers, youth, and other special groups, and Title IV, which authorizes continued federal direction of the Job Corps, are federally controlled.

Titles II and VI, although managed at the local level, are categorical programs. Funds are intended mainly for public service employment, although they may also be used for employability development. Consideration must be given to certain clients, and, in the case of Title II, only residents of specific areas can qualify.

Only Title I programs are both decentralized and decategorized, and they afford local officials the most authority and flexibility. But even for Title I, Congress provided for significant federal presence at critical points. Most important is the authority of the Department of Labor to approve prime sponsor plans prior to funding. The Secretary of Labor may withhold funds from any sponsor that fails to comply with the act.

The CETA legislative history reflects ambivalence regarding federal versus local control. Sponsors must give assurances that statutory provisions are being met. However, a House committee report admonishes the Secretary of Labor not to rely on prime sponsor certification alone, but to exercise judgment to ensure that the requirements of the act are fulfilled. This implies a strong federal role. On the other hand, the same report "does not expect the Secretary of Labor to second guess the good faith judgment of the prime sponsor."[4] Apparently, the intent was to permit some degree of freedom within the broad limits imposed by the statute. These limits, however, are not clearly delineated.

Since the enactment of CETA, there has been a gradual erosion of the freedom and flexibility of the local authorities as a consequence of the congressional approach in dealing with new problems.[5] Congress tends to deal with emerging problems by enacting categorical legislation. This tendency, in turn, has the effect of limiting prime sponsor options in using manpower resources. The enactment of Title VI of CETA (the Emergency Jobs and Unemployment Act of 1974) as a countercyclical device is a case in point. Although the program is administered locally, the prime sponsor is restricted in program eligibility, types of employment, and wage rates. The 1976 extension of Title VI imposed additional stipulations to ensure that locally administered programs are not at variance with national policies and priorities. In this instance, Congress detailed specific eligibility requirements and limited the employment of new hires to "projects."

Appropriation decisions providing additional funds for newly perceived needs have tended to tilt manpower programs toward increased federal control and recategorization. The systematic funding for the youth program for summer jobs and the supplemental appropriation for President Carter's economic stimulus package greatly increased the size

---

[4]U.S. Congress, House, Committee on Education and Labor, *Comprehensive Manpower Act of 1973*, Report No. 93-659, 93rd Congress, 1st Session, 1973, p. 8.
[5]See Robert McPherson, "CETA—The Basic Assumptions and Future Prospects", In National Commission for Manpower Policy, *Directions for a National Manpower Policy: A Collection of Policy Papers Prepared for Three Regional Conferences*, Special report no. 14, Washington, D.C.: National Commission for Manpower Policy, December 1976, pp. 195–214.

of categorical programs for youth and recent veterans. The effect of these new, special programs has been to constrain local authority and program flexibility. The proportion of CETA resources reserved for programs subject to unfettered local control (Title I) is shrinking.

Some congressional initiatives have had the effect of curtailing the federal role as well. A clause in the Emergency Jobs Program Extension Act of 1976 prohibited the Department of Labor from establishing limits on the extent to which Title VI slots can be filled with regular public service workers who have been laid off and rehired.

As CETA develops, the issues in federal–local relationships come into sharper focus. Obviously, under its responsibilities to ensure that the act is administered properly, the federal government is concerned with such matters as organization and the processes of administration. What is less clear is the extent to which federal officials should participate in decisions on such matters as the type of programs to be offered locally, the delivery system for these programs, the selection of agencies to deliver the services, and the clientele to be served.

Put even more broadly, should the Department of Labor be responsible within the CETA framework for setting national goals and priorities to respond to emerging needs and new situations? If so, should these be binding on prime sponsors or merely guides for consideration and emphasis?

The National Role

In the 6 months from the passage of CETA to its implementation, the Manpower Administration designated sponsors, allocated funds, and established planning and management systems. Arranging for the continuance and orderly transfer of existing programs was a major achievement.

In an effort to define the limits of the federal role, the Department of Labor outlined several major functions for itself, in addition to designating prime sponsors and allocating funds. Its key responsibility is to review plans for conformity with the legislation. Other major responsibilities are to implement and interpret national policy through regulations and guidelines, provide technical assistance, assess prime sponsor performance, and establish a mechanism for hearings and appeals. Some prime sponsors believe that, in carrying out these functions, the federal establishment has exceeded its congressionally mandated role, especially for Title I programs. DOL, on the other hand, is convinced that its activities are necessary for the proper discharge of its

88   CETA: MANPOWER PROGRAMS UNDER LOCAL CONTROL

oversight responsibilities. The statutory language is broad enough to accommodate both positions.

The unfamiliarity of many local governments with manpower programs, requests for clarification and specific guidance, and the belief that there is a need for uniformity have occasioned a steady stream of written instructions from DOL. With continual changes in legislation, policies, directives, and regulations, the stream has become a torrent, and some prime sponsors complain that excessively burdensome regulations restrict their flexibility to design and conduct local programs.[6]

The issuance of performance guidelines to be used by DOL regional offices in reviewing prime sponsor Title I grant applications created a major furor.[7] The purpose of the standards was "to provide a common framework against which regional offices and prime sponsors could compare their fiscal 1977 program plans and performance goals." The main performance indicators used were placement, "non-positive" termination, unassigned participant rates, and cost ratios. Although indicators were expressed as "ranges" rather than as absolute standards, sponsors felt that their use tended to constrain the kinds of programs and services they could offer and placed a premium on low-cost strategies. Moreover, as they argued, the emphasis on placement tends to discourage youth or adult work-experience programs, which are not oriented primarily toward obtaining regular employment. These guidelines have since been revised by a federal–local task force and are now more acceptable.

Equally controversial was DOL's decision to pressure prime sponsors into arrangements with local employment service offices for placing job-ready clients. The Department of Labor's purpose was to make maximum use of existing institutions and avoid duplication of effort and costs, but its action was viewed by prime sponsors as an effort to place the employment service in an advantageous position and to undermine the prerogatives of local officials in selecting program deliverers. This issue has not yet been completely resolved.

Symptomatic of the continuing ambivalence in the federal role is a

[6]See, for example, "Statement of John V. N. Klein, County Executive, Suffolk County, N.Y. on Behalf of the National Association of Counties," In U.S. Congress, House, Committee on Education and Labor, *Oversight Hearings on the Comprehensive Employment and Training Act*, Part 3, Hearings before the Subcommittee on Manpower, Compensation, and Health and Safety, 94th Congress, 2nd Session, 1976, p. 700.
[7]U.S. Department of Labor, Employment and Training Administration, "Comprehensive Employment and Training Act," Field memorandum no. 224-76, 41 F.R. 35245–35254, 1976.

statement of national program emphasis in the federal regulations of June 1976.[8] That statement called for improvement of performance, elimination of duplication, and high priority in linking operations to the private sector. While no one could disagree with these objectives, issuing a statement of national program emphasis in this manner gives it force that could be construed as imposing national goals on local sponsors.

The Regional Office

The federal establishment is linked to the local prime sponsors through a network of regional offices of the Employment and Training Administration. These offices transmit national policy, review and act on prime sponsors' plans, interpret regulations, provide assistance, assess programs, and handle complaints.

CETA altered the regional offices' responsibilities and required a new approach appropriate to dealing with prime sponsors. Contact is maintained through a federal representative assigned to each prime sponsor. The amount of time spent in each area varies considerably, depending on each regional office's style of operations and the amount of assistance requested. Some representatives attend local planning meetings; others are seldom seen even by local staff.

At the outset, there was considerable uncertainty as to where to draw the line between the autonomy of the prime sponsor and the responsibility of the DOL regional office. The survey found widely different regional office practices during the first year, ranging from hesitantly offered advice to strenuous arm twisting. A vigorous regional office role became more common about the middle of the first fiscal year, as DOL attempted to step up lagging implementation of Title II.

Although the difficult start-up problems were largely resolved by the second year, the federal role continued to grow. Fifteen of the 28 sponsors in the sample reported increased regional office contact; 2 reported less. Monitoring and assessment activities and frequent grant modifications, partly due to funding changes, were the occasion for most contacts. Assessment emphasized meeting goals in the prime sponsor plans, which, at the beginning, often led to revisions that brought goals closer in line with experience.

In the area of administration, the regional office focused on the rate at which prime sponsors were allocating funds, the manner in which they allocated administrative costs, the system for managing finances, and

[8]U.S. Department of Labor, Office of the Secretary, "General Provisions for Programs under the Comprehensive Employment and Training Act" (94.1[c]), 41 F.R. 26339, 1976.

reporting. Less frequently, regional staff were involved in program areas such as placement policies, public service employment, maintenance of effort, and rehiring policies.

Relations between DOL regional offices and local staff continued to be uneven in the second year. In a number of jurisdictions, federal representatives were described as helpful and relationships positive. Two of these jurisdictions had new CETA administrators who relied on regional office advice. A few sponsors were very dissatisfied, and relationships with their regional offices were described as "ragged" or "adversary." Difficulties caused by the high turnover of regional office staff and their lack of response to inquiries were common.

Other problems related more to the system as a whole. Prime sponsors were unhappy about too-frequent requests to modify plans, lack of uniformity in interpreting rules, interference by the regional office in such matters as setting allowances or choosing subgrantees, and the irregular and unpredictable funding process.

Local officials in several jurisdictions criticized regional office representatives for lack of familiarity with substantive program areas and for paying too much attention to the details of administrative statistics, forms, and mechanics rather than to the content and quality of the program. A slightly different perspective comes from a study in one state that queried regional office representatives on their perception of national office performance. The major criticisms were unclear communications, inconsistent policy positions, lack of technical support, and lack of training to enable them to do their jobs effectively.[9]

In summary, relationships between the DOL regional offices and local prime sponsors were becoming more stable by the end of the second year, but many problems remained due to the complexity of programs and the turnover of regional office and local staff. The federal presence is definitely felt in most jurisdictions and relationships vary, reflecting fundamental tensions between the federal and the local role. As CETA moved into its third year, the federal role appeared to be getting stronger.[10]

STATE–LOCAL RELATIONSHIPS

In the long legislative process leading to the enactment of CETA manpower reform, state governments lost the struggle for the dominant

[9]U.S. Department of Labor, Employment and Training Administration, *The Implementation of CETA in Ohio*, R&D monograph 44, Prepared by Randall B. Ripley, 1977, p. 48 (available from NTIS).

[10]CETA was extended for 1 year, from June 1977 to June 1978, without substantive change.

position in the new manpower system. Most state governments had had little experience in manpower program administration.

In the years preceding the enactment of CETA, MDTA programs were administered through state employment security and vocational education agencies, usually with little supervision from the governor's office. However, some governors were beginning to participate in manpower and economic development planning, partly as a result of CAMPS planning grants from the Manpower Administration. A number of states had human resources development departments, of which manpower was a component. Most states had offices that included manpower-related planning, and several participated in the experimental Comprehensive Manpower Program.[11]

Although supported initially by DOL, which sought a strong state role, the states did not rally sufficient support to win a key position in CETA. Vigorous opposition had come from mayors, community action agencies, and representatives of the poor and minorities—all of whom believed that state governments would turn the programs over to the state employment service agencies, which, they alleged, would not be sensitive to the problems of cities.[12] A federal–local model for implementing CETA was finally agreed on. However, there were certain compromises that gave states responsibility as prime sponsor for balance-of-state areas and statewide planning and coordination. While the responsibilities of state governments are not clearly defined, the amount of funds flowing through the governor's office is substantial. Balance-of-state sponsors receive about 30 percent of Title I, II, and VI funds. In addition, the states receive about 10 percent of the Title I funds for vocational education, state manpower services, and planning activities.

New responsibilities under CETA plus the considerable amount of funds flowing through the governors' offices have increased the importance of state manpower activities. About one-third of the state manpower services councils (SMSCs) are chaired either by governors or members of their immediate staffs. In a number of cases, the SMSCs, as well as the balance-of-state managers, are part of the governors' offices, according to surveys made by the National Governors Conference.[13]

[11]Statement of Martin L. Peterson, National Governors' Conference Human Resources Committee, in U.S. Congress, House, Committee on Education and Labor, *Comprehensive Manpower Act of 1973*, Hearings before the Select Subcommittee on Labor, October 1973, p. 105.

[12]Roger H. Davidson, *The Politics of Comprehensive Manpower Legislation*, pp. 25–30.

[13]Robert P. Goss, *State Manpower Services Councils: Promises—Problems—Progress*, Washington, D.C.: National Governors' Conference, Center for Policy Research and Analysis, September 1975.

Even in North Carolina, where the SMSC and the administration of BOS manpower programs are not in the executive office, the governor was reported to have reviewed plans for the balance of state and participated in decisions.

In most states, CETA and the employment service system are organizationally separate, according to the National Governors' Conference. The CETA organization usually handles both the SMSC and balance-of-state functions, but with separate staffs. The various patterns are illustrated by the four states studied. In none of these states does the employment service administer the CETA program; in three of the four, the SMSC and balance-of-state functions are lodged in the same administrative unit.

State	SMSC	BOS/MPC
Maine	Office of Manpower, Planning and Coordination, Office of Governor	Same
North Carolina	Department of Administration	Same
Texas	Division of Planning, Office of Governor	Department of Community Affairs
Arizona	Department of Economic Security	Same

State Manpower Services Councils

Prior to CETA there was a state manpower planning council in each state, which had little real reponsibility except to coordinate and transmit local plans. There are now two state bodies with CETA responsibilities. The SMSC is responsible for reviewing local prime sponsor plans and making recommendations for more effective coordination. The SMSC also monitors the operation of local programs and prepares an annual report to the governor. The role of the SMSC is mainly advisory to the governor; this is consistent with CETA's objective to keep responsibility with local elected officials. The balance-of-state manpower planning council coordinates planning for the balance-of-state area.

One-third of the members of the SMSC are appointed from among local prime sponsors in the state. The rest are from the employment service, vocational education and other manpower-related state agencies, business and labor, and client groups. This composition was designed to bring about closer relationships among agencies and groups concerned with manpower. Indeed, providing informal communication has turned out to be the most important accomplishment of the SMSC.

SMSCs have not proved to be effective in carrying out their formal assignments so far. In the first year, the survey found that SMSCs were just getting under way and there was little activity. SMSC review of local plans was generally perfunctory; state councils had virtually no effect on local programs. The second year brought little change; a number of local sponsors reported that there had been no meaningful review of plans from state sponsors; others said it was perfunctory. Only one sponsor of those surveyed reported receiving substantive assistance from the SMSC; the SMSC had advised that sponsor on establishing on-the-job training and construction crafts projects. More typical was the experience of another jurisdiction, in which the extent of review was a form letter acknowledging receipt of the sponsor's plan. In a large state with a number of local prime sponsors, the SMSC devoted one meeting to a perfunctory review of plans. The presence of prime sponsors on the SMSC apparently has a log-rolling effect and inhibits any critical comments on local plans.

The act requires that SMSCs monitor the operation of prime sponsors, with particular attention to the availibility, responsiveness, and adequacy of state services. Theoretically, one advantage of such review is to promote the coordination of plans and operations of contiguous areas. Although there was somewhat more monitoring of local programs by SMSCs during the second year, their impact remained negligible in most cases. Eight of the 28 areas surveyed reported that some monitoring took place in fiscal 1976, ranging from site visits to a panel-type review. One prime sponsor reported that the SMSC made a study of its problems and wrote a report that had some influence on the subsequent reorganization. In that state, the SMSC made statewide investigations of specific program components such as work experience, classroom training, and client assessment procedures. Systematic monitoring took place in two states: Maine contracted with an outside firm for assessment, while Texas used a detailed and structured monitoring guide.

Except for Arizona, where the SMSC arranged a workshop on DOL–HEW relationships, and Texas, where various representatives of state agencies on the council made presentations, most of the prime sponsors interviewed were not aware of SMSC coordination activities. The Texas SMSC staff worked with various state agencies to fund projects jointly. On the whole, coordination through the plan review and monitoring functions was not significant, although informal contacts facilitated by the councils may have contributed to better relationships.

Aller and Kropp, who have studied SMSC functions in five states, conclude that SMSCs have not yet established a systematic planning, monitoring, or coordination role. They note, however, that some SMSCs have been assigned additional responsibilities by governors, such as making special studies, arranging conferences, and making recommendations for use of the Title I 4-percent manpower services fund.[14]

The major reason for the ineffectiveness of the SMSC is that CETA did not assign to it any real authority. SMSCs are required to help coordinate state agencies with CETA, but these agencies and sponsors may resist interference. A study made by the National Commission on Manpower Policy in 1975 found that locating the SMSC within the governor's office gave the best results. This was confirmed by a 1977 study of nine states made for the Department of Labor by the Manpower Development Corporation. That study also concluded that SMSCs are seldom perceived as primary instruments for the development of statewide policies.[15] The SMSC is responsible for an annual report to the governors but is not required to be consulted in preparing the state's comprehensive manpower plan, which is more important. Another reason for ineffectiveness is the possibility of overlap or conflict with the BOS manpower planning council in those areas in which the two staffs are not integrated.

State Grants

Four percent of the Title I appropriation is allocated to states to provide supplemental manpower services by state agencies, assist rural areas, furnish economic and labor market information, and fund model programs. In 1976, $63 million was available for these activities. The assumption was that this fund would give states the needed flexibility to extend manpower programs and services to areas and groups not adequately covered and to ensure the cooperation and support of state agencies with local sponsors.

Most local prime sponsors in the sample reported that they were not consulted on how the 4-percent fund was to be used during the first year. Some indicated that data systems were being established from this fund, while others reported that their states planned to use the funds for special projects and for technical assistance. In fiscal 1976, too, it appeared that most of the 4-percent money in the states represented in

---

[14]National Commission for Manpower Policy, "State Manpower Services Councils: A Field Study Assessment," Unpublished paper prepared by Curtis C. Aller and Richard R. Kropp, Center for Applied Manpower Research, Berkeley, California, 1977.

[15]See National Commission for Manpower Policy, *Manpower Program Coordination*, A special report of the National Commission for Manpower Policy, Washington, D.C.: National Commission for Manpower Policy, October 1975; U.S. Department of Labor, Employment and Training Administration, Office of Research and Development, *The Utilization and Effectiveness of CETA Title I Special Grants to Governors*, Final report PB-268 230/OST, prepared by MDC, Inc., Chapel Hill, April 1977 (available from NTIS).

the sample was used for special projects, funded directly, or sponsored with other state agencies. Four of the 24 local sponsors in the sample participated in state-sponsored projects. State projects, in some instances, conflicted with local programs. In Philadelphia, for example, where the manpower office arranged for a welding program for its own clients, the state also sponsored a welding course. In other cases, the governor used the 4-percent fund for projects outside the normal scope of CETA training.

Some states are also using the 4-percent money for training local prime sponsor staff and for expanding labor market information. In California, $6 million was allotted to the state employment service for developing detailed labor market information for local planning throughout the state.

The availability of the manpower services fund attracted many applications, and, in trying to accommodate as many requests as possible, states have tended to splinter the 4-percent money among myriad small projects. Approval is often influenced politically. Other studies confirm that the 4-percent fund is not being used generally to fulfill an overall plan by supplementing local efforts. Aller and Kropp reported that even where the SMSC controls the allocation of funds, ad hoc projects that do not contribute to long-range goals are funded. According to a National Manpower Commission study, local prime sponsors would prefer to see a greater proportion of state grant funds used for labor market information, program evaluation, and research and development and less on miscellaneous projects.[16]

To encourage local sponsors to use the public vocational education system as part of their manpower programs, Congress reserved 5 percent of Title I funds for state boards of vocational education. These funds, amounting to $79 million in 1976, are distributed by agreement between state boards and the local sponsors.

During the first year of CETA, there were delays and problems in negotiating agreements between local sponsors and state boards and disagreements on the appropriate use of the funds for allowances. Nevertheless, the vocational education money has been a substantial resource in local classroom training. In most cases, grants are used to supplement regular institutional training, but some sponsors have used these funds for special projects that might not otherwise have been supported.

[16]National Commission for Manpower Policy, *Manpower Program Coordination.*

Consortia

Since CETA policy is to encourage planning and administration on a broader geographic basis than individual political jurisdictions, DOL allocates the 5-percent consortium incentive fund to consortia that cover a significant proportion of a labor market area. During CETA's first year, 135 consortia were established; by 1977 there were 144, including several that were statewide. This figure represents about a third of all prime sponsors.

Incentive payments were only a minor consideration in the decision of jurisdictions to form consortia. In some cases, the central cities had more experience in handling manpower programs, and it was natural for surrounding counties to rely on this expertise rather than to set up new administrative units. The decisive factors were mutual trust, based on prior experience in joint planning or other activities, and the ability to work out arrangements for the division of responsibility and resources. In a few cases, suburbs preferred the anonymity of a consortium to handling the manpower problems in their own jurisdiction.

There are many difficulties in organizing and administering a consortium. Carefully designed agreements on the allotment of resources and on the management of programs across jurisdictional lines did not prove to be workable in all cases. Although most consortia have endured for 2 years, some show signs of strain. Of the nine in the sample, one was dissolved (Phoenix–Maricopa), and three lost some of their component jurisdictions (Raleigh–Wake, Cleveland, and the Capital Area). One of the cities in the sample became a consortium. The reasons for the breakup of consortia help to illuminate the interjurisdictional problems.

Raleigh is a classic example of city–county conflict over program with political, social, and racial overtones. Originally the consortium was composed of the city of Raleigh and the balance of Wake County (each of which was eligible to become an independent prime sponsor), plus Johnston, Lee, and Chatham counties. The balance of Wake County split off at the end of the first year. The mayor of Raleigh and the chairman of the Wake County board of commissioners initially agreed on an integrated delivery system, which they thought would best use the capabilities of three agencies: Wake Opportunities, a predominantly black community action agency in Raleigh; Wake Technical Institute, located in a predominantly white section of the county; and the state employment service. The system collapsed because of numerous disagreements as to the proportionate share of city and county clients to be served, type of courses to be offered at Wake Technical Institute, and kinds of manpower services to be offered.[17] Behind the disagreements, however, were political rivalry between city and county and differences in the social and economic characteristics of their residents. The disagreement on service deliverers was only a proximate cause. The secession of Wake County left Raleigh with Johnston, Lee, and Chatham counties. The truncated consortium is structurally stable because each of the components arranges for its own delivery system.

The Phoenix–Maricopa split resulted from disagreements on the allocation of resources and the selection of program operators, as well as from a complex and unwieldy administrative setup. The initial consortium agreement gave the county 40 percent of resources and the city 60 percent, but such a fine balance could not be maintained. The administrative unit for the consortium was lodged in the city of Phoenix, which had prior experience in operating a concentrated employment program, but all significant decisions had to be approved by both the city and county legislative bodies.

The city of Cleveland formed a consortium with surrounding Cuyahoga, Lake, and Geauga counties and the city of Parma. Because of the heavy concentration of manpower problems in Cleveland and the availability of experienced manpower staff there, administration was entrusted to the city. More than 90 percent of the Title I funds were allotted to Cleveland, with the concurrence of elected officials of the remaining jurisdictions. However, under Title II and Title VI formulas, the counties received a much larger share of funds. Growing expertise in Lake County and the realization that it could receive a larger share of funds on its own led to its withdrawal as of fiscal 1977.

In these cases, the causes for dissolution of the consortium or withdrawal of units were conflicting priorities, dissatisfaction with the division of resources, unequal service by program operators, the growing expertise of subunits, lack of perception of common interests between city and suburb, and circumstances unrelated to manpower, such as political rivalries among jurisdictions.

Another type of situation is exemplified by the splintering off of Llano County from the Capital Area consortium (Austin, Texas) to join the balance of state. Llano, a small rural county on the fringe of the nine-county consortium, had been served by a community action agency that arranged for manpower programs throughout the area outside Austin.

[17]Robert M. Fearn, "Raleigh Consortium, North Carolina," In William Mirengoff, ed., *Transition to Decentralized Manpower Programs: Eight Area Studies*, Committee on Evaluation of Employment and Training Programs, Washington, D.C.: National Academy of Sciences, 1976, pp. 85–104.

There was no incentive for Llano County to remain in the consortium, since the same services were available from the balance of state without requiring the county to be committed to a consortium.

Of nine consortia in the sample, six have a strong central administration, a board of elected officials that establishes ground rules, and a clear agreement for division of resources. Three are confederations of separate units, operating their own programs or "buying into" the central city program. Theoretically, the decentralized form should have fewer stresses than the centralized type, but this is not always the case. Consortia designed to operate with a unified delivery system may be just as stable. The pertinent elements are the relative size and power of units, whether the component jurisdictions have manpower expertise, and the extent of conflicts of interest among the jurisdictions.

Whether the breakup of SMSAs into individual prime sponsors is more efficient from an administrative standpoint and, even more to the point, whether clients have better opportunities for training and employment are essential questions from the standpoint of national policy. The evidence accumulated in the study does not prove the case for or against consortia. In terms of program outcome, service to the disadvantaged and minorities, and administrative cost ratios, consortia average between cities and counties. The facts that many consortia do not themselves correspond with SMSAs and that some are "paper" consortia, with each unit substantially on its own, further obscure any conclusion. The breakup of a minority of consortia along city–county lines (with counties withdrawing) lends support to the premise that a consortium may be more beneficial to the inner city with its concentrated poverty and unemployment, since the consortium affords a wider job market. However, the experience of the Raleigh consortium suggests that there may also be disadvantages to the inner city in terms of service delivery, distances to training sites, and internal conflicts as to kinds of programs and services offered.

Balance of States

In the first year of CETA, three of the states in the sample were attempting to cope with the problem of providing manpower services over large areas by delegating part of the planning and administrative responsibilities to substate units. Texas delegated responsibility to councils of government and community action agencies, while Arizona used COGs and Indian groups as subgrantees. Administration in North Carolina was handled at the state level, while planning was done by lead regional organizations. Maine was the only one of the four states that centralized administration at the state level.

For the most part, the trend toward decentralization continued in the second year. Texas pursued the decentralization concept, and some counties gained experience and formed independent consortia. The balance of Texas has been whittled from 161 counties in 1975 to 150 in 1976 and 134 in 1977. In Arizona, the decentralization concept was strained, as the state insisted on a stronger role for the employment service in recruitment and placement; councils of government viewed this as interference in local affairs. There were also problems of coordination with Indian groups in Arizona. In Maine, two of the larger counties splintered off in 1976 and two others left in 1977 to join them.[18] Maine has now established eight regional planning councils representing the remaining counties. In North Carolina, where there was little change, administration is still largely handled at the state level.

Moving the locus of administration from the state to substate units has two important implications. One is that the balance-of-state area may be unwieldy to manage. Communication, the distance from the state office to the local programs, the difficulty in applying consistent policies to dissimilar areas, and political pressures from various subareas on the governor's office are cited as problems. More important is that decentralization tends to change the character of COGs and other intermediate units originally established for planning purposes; they now have operational functions as well.

In North Carolina, for example, defining the role of the lead regional organizations has been a matter of concern.[19] In fiscal 1976, administration was still centralized, but in a few cases, LROs, which previously had only planning duties, began to contract with program deliverers. The balance of state in Texas has had decentralized CETA operations from the beginning due to its vast, noncontiguous territory and the heterogeneity of its economic, social, and ethnic composition. The state as prime sponsor for the balance of state generally contracts with councils of governments to deliver services within their areas. The COGs, in turn, either subcontract or operate programs themselves. In several instances, Texas administers regional or local programs through community action agencies, community-based organizations, or directly with counties. But in any case, the central office exercises only limited control over local programs.

[18]Cumberland and Penobscot counties became a consortium in fiscal 1976, and Hancock and Oxford became another consortium in 1977.

[19]See Alvin L. Cruze, "North Carolina Balance of State," In William Mirengoff, ed., *Transition to Decentralized Manpower Programs*, pp. 153–178.

PRIME SPONSOR ORGANIZATIONS

Despite the first year's growing pains, CETA prime sponsors succeeded in establishing the framework for local administration of manpower programs, a new and difficult area of public administration. However, before the framework was firmly in place, the prime sponsors were faced with implementing a new large-scale program of public service employment. Many had serious administrative problems, and the DOL regional offices, not fully familiar with their CETA roles, were not always able to give helpful advice and technical assistance.

In the second year, many prime sponsors were still plagued with difficulties as they sought to administer their greatly expanded manpower programs, but considerable progress was made in building prime sponsors' capability of managing manpower programs. With their organizations beginning to coalesce, prime sponsors have turned to more substantive concerns and exercised greater supervision over local programs.

LOCAL ADMINISTRATION

As a result of CETA, manpower activities are now an integral part of local government. CETA funds available for local governments in fiscal 1976—over $5 billion—amounted to about 2.3 percent of state and local government expenditures. In at least one area, because of the way the allocation formulas operated, expenditures for manpower amounted to 10 percent of total expenditures, including education (see Table 15). Public service employees hired under Titles II and VI made up a substantial proportion of total public service employment in the community. In most of the cities, counties, and consortia in the sample, manpower administration is an important and visible part of the local government structure and is commanding increasing attention from local officials.

The organizational structures established in the first year under CETA generally remained in effect in fiscal 1976, although there were changes in procedures, functions, and personnel. In 10 cases, the CETA manpower office was originally organized as a separate department or, in the cases of New York City and Cleveland, merged with an existing manpower agency. In 7 other cases, it was attached to the office of the mayor or the county executive; and in the remaining 5, CETA became a unit reporting to a division or other office of the local government. Thus, in most areas, manpower occupies an important position in the organizational structure.

TABLE 15 CETA Title I, II, and VI Expenditures As a Proportion of Total Local Government Expenditures, Sample Local Prime Sponsors (amounts in millions of dollars)

Jurisdiction	Local Government Expenditures FY 1974-1975[a]	CETA Expenditures FY 1976[b]	CETA Expenditures As Percent of Total
City			
Gary[c]	88.5	9.3	10.5
Long Beach[c]	210.2	8.4	4.0
New York	11,571.5	214.3	1.8
Philadelphia	1,422.9	44.9	3.2
County			
St. Paul/Ramsey[d]	474.3	8.2	1.7
Chester	138.7	2.0	1.4
Balance of Cook	2,031.7	15.5	0.8
Pasco	53.6	1.4	2.6
Middlesex	440.9	11.3	2.6
Balance of Union	293.8	5.4	1.8
Consortium			
Kansas City/Wyandotte	104.3	6.9	6.7
Cleveland	1,374.0	38.2	2.8
Phoenix/Maricopa	826.7	24.1	2.9
Orange County	1,189.9	25.8	2.2
Pinellas/St. Petersburg	305.0	7.7	2.5

SOURCE: Local Government Finances in Selected Metropolitan Areas and Large Counties: 1974-1975, GF75 No. 6, Bureau of the Census; Employment and Training Administration, U.S. Department of Labor.
[a]Expenditures of all government units within the jurisdiction.
[b]Titles I, II, and VI for four quarters.
[c]1972-1973 expenditures for school districts substituted for unavailable 1974-1975 data.
[d]St. Paul and Ramsey County are combined because census data on government expenditures were not completed for each jurisdiction separately.

Two major changes did occur in organizational placement in 1976. In Topeka, which formed a consortium with Shawnee County, the manpower office was taken out of the mayor's office and made a separate department of labor with added responsibilities. In St. Paul, the CETA manpower unit was transferred from the mayor's office to the department of community services.

Major reorganizations occurred in two other sample areas because of the intervention of the DOL regional offices. In Philadelphia, the regional office recommended a functional reorganization with a separate unit for public service employment following allegations of political influence. The change was made to separate the administration of the public service jobs program from other intake and referral activities. All intake of PSE participants is now handled through the state employment service, and applicants are referred either to the prime sponsor (for city jobs) or to the employing agency. The administration of Calhoun County was also reorganized at the insistence of the regional office. There was a shift from sponsor-provided manpower services to the use of contractors to provide such services because of the lack of experience of the prime sponsor staff in actual operations.

Several other areas reported internal reorganizations to improve administrative effectiveness and to bring administration close to the community. Manpower programs in Cook County were administered through three local offices for closer contact with program deliverers. In the balance of Texas, the manpower services division has had three reorganizations. The division was first organized along functional lines, with each unit dealing with both the balance of state and activities of the state manpower services fund. Subsequent reorganizations separated the responsibilities of the balance-of-state and the state manpower services council activities.

Integration of Titles II and VI with Title I

Prime sponsors originally placed the responsibility for Titles I and II in a single organizational entity. When Title VI with its expanded public service program was added, all sponsors in the survey assigned the Title VI program to the same agency that handled the other manpower programs, although often as a separate unit.

However, even under a single organizational umbrella, responsibilities are divided between employability development activities (Title I) and public service employment programs (Titles II and VI). In one pattern that emerged, two subunits, each with its own staff, were established to handle the two kinds of programs. New York City has a deputy commissioner of the department of employment for Title I and another deputy commissioner for the public service employment titles. Another pattern divides staff along functional lines: Each function, irrespective of title, is handled either by the same individuals or by small units with interchangeable staff. Reasons advanced for jointly administering Title II and VI employment programs with Title I were that the original CETA administrative unit was already in place and staffed by personnel familiar with the programs and that better coordination and better integration of services to clients were possible, as well as better staff utilization, lower overhead, and economies of scale.

When one looks beyond the organizational charts at the dynamics of the program, the organizational integration of public service employment frequently becomes more nominal than real. Moreover, the extent of administrative coordination varies considerably. In one major city, decisions on public service employment are made by an executive in the mayor's office and merely transmitted through the CETA office.

The separation of public service employment administration from Title I is more evident where there are program agents. In fiscal 1976, there were 764 program agents—that is, cities or counties of 50,000 population eligible to operate their own programs with allotments specified by the Department of Labor—for an average of about 2 program agents for each prime sponsor. Eighteen of the 28 prime sponsors in the sample had program agents. Prime sponsors pass funds to program agents, who are responsible for carrying out their programs in accordance with the area plan, so much of the public service program is decentralized to program agents, who have considerable independence. Program agents administer programs through various municipal or county departments. The city of Phoenix, which was part of the Phoenix–Maricopa consortium, administered Titles II and VI through a municipal agency responsible for economic development, while Maricopa County used its personnel department.

The pass-through to program agents in one sense tends to make the administration of programs for public service employment less complex than that for Title I. Although sponsors are accountable for the entire program within their jurisdictions, some decisions for occupations and employing agencies are delegated to program agents.

On the whole, the imposition of public service employment programs interfered with the orderly administration of Title I. In the midst of trying to organize methods of handling comprehensive manpower employability programs, sponsors were pressed, under very tight deadlines, to take on large-scale public service employment programs. Without the Title VI diversion, such Title I activities as arranging for services, supervising contracts, establishing reporting and accounting controls, and developing management information systems should have gone more smoothly.

In the second year, conflicts between the administration of Title VI and Title I were less evident as CETA staffs were increased, procedures were formalized, and the recruiting of new enrollees diminished. Nevertheless, Title II and VI activities required a disproportionate amount of attention in some jurisdictions because of frequent modifications of plans, a large number of employing agencies, and changing guidelines regarding the phasing out of programs.

STAFFING

Staffing continued to be a major concern during the second year of CETA. For the most part, sponsors reported larger staffs in fiscal 1976 (the average was about 40). This was mainly attributed to new responsibilities for Title VI but also reflected the tendency on the part of some sponsors to take a more direct role in program operations. In several areas, staffs were reduced as functions were better defined.

The total staff size in the sample areas varied from 5 in Stanislaus County to 200 in New York City. In counties, consortia, and the balance of states, administrative staff were divided between the central office and outlying areas. The Raleigh central staff consisted of 11 people, but 22 others were engaged in similar administrative functions for the city of Raleigh and for Johnston, Lee, and Chatham counties.

In selecting staff originally for the central administrative unit, some local sponsors hired former manpower planners; others drew on personnel with varying backgrounds. A study of 25 sponsors in New York State showed that three of every four persons in managerial or staff positions held at least an associate degree from a 2-year college. Two-thirds of CETA personnel had experience in the public sector, and the majority had held positions that were identical or similar to that of their CETA job.[20]

CETA participants are used frequently to augment administrative staff; in one county, half of the 72 prime sponsor staff were CETA enrollees. On occasion, prime sponsors borrowed staff from program operators to help with administration.

Thus a new administrative layer emerged between program operators and regional offices of the Employment and Training Administration (ETA). Although the total size of all the prime sponsor staffs has not been determined, according to an estimate made by the ETA, in 1976 about 20,000 man-year equivalents were employed on state and local administrative staffs (both prime sponsors and program operators) compared with about 11,400 in 1974.[21] The increase in staff is related

[20]Benjamin Chinitz and Richard A. Rehberg, *Local Planning and Special Revenue Sharing,* Center for Social Analysis, State University of New York, Binghamton, New York, 1975.
[21]That estimate was derived by applying average salary figures to administrative expenditures. The concept of allowable administrative costs may vary from pre-CETA programs.

partly to the increase in the size of programs and partly to the buildup of several levels of local administration. Reduction in staff of the state employment service and ETA staff during this period has not offset this buildup. Staffing problems did not end with the buildup of administrative and operating personnel. Personnel turnover was equally troublesome. Six of the 28 prime sponsors in the sample had changed CETA administrators since the program began; Maine, for example, reported three balance-of-state administrators in 2 years. Other areas lost deputy directors, planning directors, fiscal officers, and operations supervisors. One county had a 100-percent turnover of staff in the 2-year period under study. CETA administrators are still struggling to define staff functions, provide appropriate training, and integrate personnel with varying backgrounds and political sponsorship into functioning organizations. In consortia and counties, staff from several jurisdictions must be blended to accommodate the interests of those jurisdictions.

ADMINISTRATIVE HEADACHES

The administrative problems of sponsors were not limited to staffing. The Employment and Training Administration, in its annual performance review, evaluated prime sponsors on six aspects of administration: grant management, financial reporting, management information systems, adherence to regional office directives, program performance compared with approved plan, and advisory councils. Prime sponsors were rated "satisfactory," "marginal," or "unsatisfactory" on each element and then assigned an overall rating. In fiscal 1976, 39 percent of the prime sponsors were rated marginal or unsatisfactory on Title I program performance; 35 percent received these ratings for Title II. Management information systems and grant management were the aspects most frequently rated unsatisfactory.

The administrative problems most frequently mentioned by respondents in the survey were difficulties with the management information system, lack of planning capability, excessive administrative costs, and organizational problems. The latter include training, duplication of functions, poor staff coordination, and lack of skill in program areas. In the second year, sponsors criticized less frequently tight DOL deadlines, excessive paperwork, and problems with statistical reports. However, prime sponsors still considered inconsistent policy, changing interpretations in regulations and guidelines, and inadequate evaluation systems to be major concerns.

OFF-AGAIN, ON-AGAIN FUNDING

Perhaps the most frustrating task faced by prime sponsors was attempting to administer an orderly program of public service jobs despite highly erratic funding. Public service employment originally was intended to be a modest program for selected areas of substantial unemployment. Before the program started, however, Congress appropriated $370 million for fiscal 1974, all of which was carried forward into fiscal 1975, making $770 million available for Title II that year.[22] By the middle of fiscal 1975, Congress appropriated an additional $875 million for countercyclical public service programs under Title VI. Thus, in a period of less than a year, prime sponsors found themselves with four times the amount of money they expected, being pressed by the Department of Labor to accelerate hiring.

The funding picture was even more confusing in fiscal 1976. The Department of Labor expected to have $400 million for Title II and $1,625 million for Title VI—a total of $2,025 million, which was $380 million more than the total available fiscal 1975. Moreover, there were substantial carry-overs of unspent funds. Sponsors were expected to continue the June 1975 level of public service employment throughout the year, but, because of stepped-up hiring, some sponsors exhausted their Title II funds early in the year. To avoid layoffs, they were permitted to transfer Title II participants to their Title VI account. By the middle of the fiscal year, however, it became apparent that many other sponsors would exhaust their Title VI funds as well. Since the authorization for funds under that title was to expire in December 1975, the administration chose not to seek an extension of the enabling law, but instead requested a supplemental appropriation under the continuing Title II to phase out the Title VI program. The supplemental $1,200 million, received in March 1976, came none too soon. But sponsors who had run out of Title VI funds were now obliged to transfer enrollees back to Title II.

This erratic funding was an administrative nightmare. Sponsors were urged by the Department of Labor to hire above their support levels and then were faced with the possibility of mass layoffs as funds were used up. This entailed hiring freezes, plans to phase out those on board, and rescinding layoff notices when new funds became available. All of this was accompanied by grant modifications and voluminous paperwork.

Thirteen of the 28 sample sponsors reported that irregular funding and

[22]In addition, $250 million in Emergency Employment Act funds appropriated in June 1974 was administered through program agents, some of which were also prime sponsors.

overhiring in response to DOL pressures created major administrative tangles. The Middlesex County experience illustrates the muddle in which many prime sponsors found themselves. In 1975, the county had what amounted to two years of Title II funds. Because it attempted to find unsubsidized jobs for half of its PSE participants, very little of its Title II money had been spent by the time Title VI funds were added. A period of heavy enrollment followed, and careful plans for geographic and occupational distribution had to be scrapped. To fill slots quickly, the agency recruited to levels that could not be supported indefinitely. By late 1975, faced with a shortage of funds, Middlesex County sought to transfer enrollees to Title I but was not permitted to do so by the DOL regional office. Calhoun County, too, was pressured to accelerate hiring under Title II to the point that all Title II funds were exhausted by November 1975 and participants were transferred for accounting purposes to Title VI. When supplemental Title II funds became available, a large portion of the PSE participants was shifted back to Title II.

With the supplemental appropriation under Title II, New York City's CETA enrollees were rescued temporarily. Both New York and Cleveland had used Title I funds to help maintain public service employment. In Cleveland, 50 percent of Title I funds had been diverted from employability development.

Administrative headaches have also been caused by delays in announcing planning estimates. In December 1975, the ETA set up a timetable for fiscal 1977 Title I and Title II grants that called for preliminary plans to be prepared by sponsors in June 1976 and for final plans to be forwarded on September 2. Because of delays in appropriations and in unemployment calculations, however, tentative allocations for Title II were not announced until September 15, more than three months late. Final allocations had not been made by mid-November, more than a month after the beginning of the new grant year.[23] Title VI allocations for fiscal 1977 were also held up due to congressional delay in enacting the extension of Title VI and failure to authorize a definite sum for fiscal 1977.[24]

Meanwhile, the Department of Labor lost credibility, and the "Perils

[23]Title II allocations for fiscal 1977 originally were to be based on unemployment estimates for 3 consecutive months in the period January 1975 through May 1976. In August 1976, the Department of Labor decided to drop the first 5 months of that period, a decision that resulted in the loss of eligibility for some areas and delays in calculating unemployment.
[24]U.S.Congress, Senate, *Continuing Appropriations, 1977,* Senate report no. 94-1378, September 1976. The act authorized sufficient funds to maintain 260,000 public service jobs under Title VI.

of Pauline" atmosphere made orderly administration nearly impossible. It affected the selection of types of participants, blurred the distinction between the objectives of Titles II and VI, and adversely affected the management of Title I programs. To some extent, the cause was the usual delay in the appropriations cycle; this was exacerbated by the administration's attempts to hold the lid on expenditures for public service jobs and summer programs for youth, with the expectation that the recession would end and the unemployed would be able to find work in an expanding economy. But the unsteady funding generated uncertainty and impeded long-range planning.

LOOKING AT RESULTS

During the first year of CETA, prime sponsors were concerned largely with the nuts and bolts of administration. In the second year, they were to turn more of their attention to substantive matters. Under Department of Labor prodding, there was considerable evaluation activity, although its extent and scope varied from area to area. For the most part, prime sponsors conceive of evaluation in the narrow sense of performance assessment, that is, monitoring the performance of individual operators with regard to their contracts or comparing results of overall performance with plans. Rarely is evaluation viewed in the broader context—as a device for comparing different service strategies, assessing the effects of programs on various target groups, or studying the effects of the program as a whole in terms of the objectives and goals of manpower programs. In short, current evaluation is mainly an extended form of monitoring individual program operations.

Monitoring ranges from informal, unstructured activity to the use of highly structured systems. One-fourth of the sponsors in the study have installed or are in the process of installing formal procedures. The outstanding example is the Lansing consortium, which developed a highly structured overall performance rating system. Each Title I contractor's performance is graded on a number of objective, quantified elements, which are combined to measure unit cost per placement and "effectiveness rate." The effectiveness rate is derived from a weighted formula whose principal elements are the placement rate, a target group index, and the number of enrollees. Other weighted elements in the effectiveness formula are the follow-up rate, the retention rate, and the post-program wage index. This system addresses a whole spectrum of outcomes as well as costs. A similar formula, with fewer elements, is used to rate Title II and Title VI contractors; under this formula, the expenditure rate and the job-fill rate are given the greatest weight.[25] This quantified approach is supplemented by on-site visits by the evaluation staff. The results of the formal rating system are given serious consideration by the consortium board and the planning council. These extremely complex formulas can be used only with a very detailed management information system, which is nonexistent in most areas. Other sponsors with structured monitoring systems are Topeka, Calhoun County, Phoenix–Maricopa, San Joaquin, New York City (where reviews are performed by the planning staff), and the balance of Texas. Generally, less formal approaches, involving some combination of contract compliance review, activity reports, and on-site visits, were employed. In some cases, monitoring is either assigned to a separate unit or handled by staff in addition to their other duties. In Kansas City, management information system reports on placements, the characteristics of clients, client outcomes, and costs for each contractor are examined to flag a situation that may require attention. A team of monitors visits each subcontractor monthly, and operators receive reports so that they can compare their performance with others. Philadelphia assigns a full-time monitor to each Title I subgrantee, who goes beyond checking statistical results to evaluate processes and propose changes. In Stanislaus County, one full-time monitor assists the planning council's evaluation committee. Cook County supplements its monitoring by having counseling and education specialists to evaluate program content in each subarea.

There are sharp differences regarding the merits of the structured, quantitative approach to monitoring. Prime sponsors and DOL regional office staff, on one hand, favor it because they believe it will help hold down costs, lead to better performance and accountability, and help identify areas that need corrective action.

Critics point out that the structured approach requires good management information, which is often missing; that it places too much emphasis on placement; and that it fosters "creaming," that is, selecting applicants with the best chance for success. Some program operators fear that clients may be shortchanged because a quantitative approach discourages high-quality services, encourages shorter programs, creates an excessive amount of paperwork that often cannot be analyzed properly, and tends to impose uniform standards on a number of programs with unique characteristics. A common criticism is that an

---

[25] The Lansing consortium uses a different formula called the Systematic Ranking Technique Methodology (SRTM) to compare proposals submitted for funding.

exclusively quantitative approach substitutes a mechanical "numbers game" for a more discriminating type of program examination. A balanced evaluation should include consideration of such factors as the qualifications of enrollees and labor market conditions. But there is some question as to whether the competency for comprehensive evaluation exists. In one case, an observer found that neither the sponsor nor the DOL regional office employed persons properly qualified to make a meaningful assessment.

Monitoring in balance-of-state areas is hampered by the extensive territory to be covered and dependence on COGs or other substate units. In Maine, Arizona, and North Carolina, field staffs conduct routine on-site visits to check performance with contracts. Texas has a more formal system, using a field-assessment guide and a monitoring-evaluation guide for planned annual on-site visits to each program operator. However, there are shortcomings—lack of data, criteria that may not apply to all cases, and staff shortages.

Opinions among respondents vary as to whether assessment and monitoring by regional offices and state agencies have been stepped up since CETA. The prevailing view is that the monitoring of individual programs is much more extensive, more frequent, and more substantive and constructive than it was prior to CETA. It is generaly agreed that the DOL regional office staff was stretched too thin to conduct the kind of reviews that the prime sponsor can do now. For example, a regional office field representative who supervised 36 contracts in one county before CETA could make only cursory visits and spot checks. Now, in one of the smaller counties, each new CETA staff member is assigned to work directly for a while with each subcontractor to become familiar with all the activities.

COMPETING FOR CONTRACTS

In giving the prime sponsor control over manpower programs, CETA reversed the earlier pattern of designating deliverers of manpower services and placed responsibility for selecting program operators with the prime sponsor. The expectation was that, through competitive bidding, operators best able to meet performance standards at the lowest costs would be chosen. However, the expected competition did not materialize. In most cases, established operators are the only ones with the facilities and the staff necessary to perform the services required. Moreover, the decisions of sponsors are often subject to the political influence of community-based organizations.

Only 6 of the 28 areas in the sample reported using competitive bidding. Lansing and Kansas City have used bidding successfully, but even in these areas there were hints of political interference. In Philadelphia and Topeka, the system is nominally in use, but only for activities remaining after major operators have been dealt in.

North Carolina tried unsuccessfully to use requests for proposals for its balance-of-state programs, but the system bogged down as lead regional organizations attempted to handle them. The balance of Texas, required by law to use competitive bids, soon encountered difficulties. Program operators tried to control their success rate and thus to win contracts by not accepting new clients and terminating those currently enrolled toward the end of the year. The emphasis was on looking good rather than doing good. Established agencies often brought political pressure to have their grants renewed.

WATCHING COSTS

Total expenditures for manpower activities corresponding with Title I, II, and VI programs rose from $2 billion in fiscal 1974 to $4 billion in fiscal 1976. Administrative costs have increased commensurately. Because of changes in the number of participants, the content of services, and the definitions of administrative costs, comparisons of CETA with pre-CETA administrative costs are difficult. In fiscal 1976 and 1977, charges to administration for state and local prime sponsors under Titles I, II, and VI combined averaged less than 10 percent of total expenditures (see Table 16). The major expenditures for all three titles are for allowances, wages, and fringe benefits. According to one estimate, administrative costs for pre-CETA categorical programs averaged 11 percent in fiscal 1974, compared with 16.4 percent under Title I for CETA in 1976. Title II and VI ratios (4.6 and 3.4 percent, respectively) are slightly higher than the PEP program ratio. But under PEP, local sponsors had a 10-percent matching requirement that does not apply under CETA, so the figures are not entirely comparable.

The biggest element in administrative costs is wages, and it is obvious that the number of people employed in manpower program administration is greater under CETA than previously. Except for small planning units, most cities and counties had no manpower staffs before CETA; administrative staffs have now been established, not only at the prime sponsor level, but also in subareas. Second, there has been a great expansion in the number of program operators, and part of their staff and overhead costs are allotted to administration, although there is widespread use of CETA participants in management and clerical positions whose salaries are charged to program budgets.

TABLE 16 Percentage Distribution of CETA Title I, II, and VI Expenditures by Cost Category, Fiscal 1976 and 1977

Cost Category	Title I		Title II		Title VI	
	FY 1976	FY 1977	FY 1976	FY 1977	FY 1976	FY 1977
Administration	16.4	16.2	4.6	6.1	3.4	5.9
Allowances	16.6	18.9	0.2	0.3	0.5	0.1
Wages	38.4	31.1	82.2	79.6	83.4	81.1
Fringe benefits	3.4	2.7	12.4	13.1	12.2	12.1
Training	13.5	16.4	0.2	0.3	0.2	0.2
Services to clients	11.7	14.8	0.4	0.7	0.3	0.7
TOTAL	100.0	100.0	100.0	100.0	100.0	100.0
Amount (thousands of dollars)	1,528,600	1,538,987	556,103	880,121	1,934,302	1,562,458

SOURCE: Computed from Employment and Training Administration, U.S. Department of Labor data.
NOTE: Details may not add to totals due to rounding.

Charges to administration include not only direct costs to the prime sponsor, but also certain expenditures by program operators that are considered to be for administration. The complex definitions in the regulations and accounting procedures have been a source of conflict between prime sponsors and the regional offices of ETA. Two of the problems are the allocation of costs between the program and the administrative budget and the allocation of certain Title II and Title VI costs to the Title I administrative account.

The latter was a more serious problem. Because the cost of acquisition or rental of supplies, equipment, material, and real property was not allowable under Titles II and VI, some sponsors apparently were charging certain costs, particularly rent and supplies, to Title I. The recent Title VI amendment to CETA has raised the administrative cost limit from 10 to 15 percent for Titles II and VI and lifted the restriction on the use of public service employment funds for supplies, equipment, etc.[26]

Prime sponsors in the sample were not troubled by the limit of 20 percent on administrative costs for Title I and the limit of 10 percent for Titles II and VI. Only one sponsor indicated that the restriction on supplies and equipment or the limit on expenditures of funds has hindered the development of special projects that could have been funded under CETA.

Administrative cost ratios tend to be higher for cities than for other types of sponsors. This tendency may reflect the higher salaries and more complex administrative and program structures of urban centers. Administrative costs for Title I programs are lowest among balance-of-state sponsors, which tend to offer more work experience than training projects (see Table 17).

In comparing the efficiency of the CETA program with corresponding programs before CETA, one must consider management aspects as well as cost ratios. Field research associates in nine of the sample areas concluded that manpower programs are operating with better control under CETA than before. They found better coordination, less duplication of effort, and more monitoring of local program operators. Field researchers in three other areas found the present system to be less well managed, mainly because new layers of administration had been introduced with no visible improvement in program or outcome. In the other areas, the field researchers concluded that there were insufficient data to make reliable comparisons. While they noted that site visits were

---

[26]Emergency Jobs Programs Extension Act of 1976, Section 2.

TABLE 17   Percentage Distribution of CETA Title I Expenditures by Cost Category and Type of Sponsor, Fiscal 1976 (cumulative to third quarter)

Cost Category	Type of Sponsor			
	City	County	Consortium	State
Administration	21.2	16.1	17.6	14.2
Allowances	15.6	16.5	17.6	17.1
Wages	30.7	37.1	34.3	44.0
Fringe benefits	2.2	3.1	3.1	3.9
Training	15.4	14.9	13.7	11.8
Services to clients	14.9	12.3	13.7	9.1
TOTAL	100.0	100.0	100.0	100.1

SOURCE: Computed from Employment and Training Administration, U.S. Department of Labor unpublished data.

more frequent and program analysis was more extensive, standards were still lacking and monitoring tended to be cursory.

SUMMARY

CETA's major objective of institutionalizing employment and training programs in local government has been achieved. Considerable progress has been made in building the capabilities of local units of government to manage manpower programs, but difficult administrative problems remain. Part of the turmoil and chaos of the first 2 years is attributable as much to changes in legislation, irregular funding, and unusual growth patterns as to the unfamiliarity of local governments with the administration of manpower assistance programs.

• On the whole, program administration was better in the second year than in the first, despite excessive turnover of key staff. Lack of experience in conducting programs and inadequate management information systems seriously hampered program management.
• The uncertainty of funding has made orderly planning and management of public service employment programs very difficult.
• The administration of Titles II and VI is under the same organizational roof as that of Title I, although often handled by separate units. Basic decisions, however, are often made outside the CETA establishment.

• Competitive bidding is used rarely as a means of selecting program operators.

• Structured program monitoring and evaluation systems have been developed in some places, but most sponsors use less formal procedures and rely on desk audits and on-site visits for program evaluation. Monitoring tends to be mechanical, with insufficient attention paid to the broad objectives of the act.

• Administrative costs for Titles I, II, and VI as a whole are lower than the statutory limits but higher than those for comparable pre-CETA programs.

• In 9 of the 28 areas surveyed, administration is believed to be better than before CETA, particularly with respect to accountability and cost consciousness. In 3 areas, local administration was considered by field analysts to be less well managed than before, despite more staff. For the remaining cases, a judgment could not be made because of lack of hard data.

• CETA and its subsequent modifications have not delineated sharply the relationship between the federal establishment and prime sponsors. In some ways, the scope of local autonomy was narrowed in the first 2 years, but restrictions on federal intervention were also added. The consequence has been continuing tension in relationships between federal authorities and prime sponsors. Such tension can be constructive, however, and it may prevent extreme swings of policy or action that could be damaging.

• Increased federal presence was noted in the second year, and the extent and the nature of the Department of Labor's oversight have continued to be an issue.

• Some sponsors assert that DOL regional office staff do not provide adequate substantive assistance.

• Plan review, monitoring, and coordination activities by state governments have little effect on local programs. State manpower services grants are fragmented into numerous special projects. The supplemental vocational education fund is making a significant contribution in supporting local classroom training, but there are still differences as to how best to use state funds.

• Consortia have generally remained stable and their number has increased. However, tension between central cities and suburbs has led to the withdrawal of some governmental units. Disagreements on the allocation of resources, conflicting priorities, lack of common interest, political rivalries, and growing manpower expertise in subunits are common reasons. Some balance-of-state administrators are moving toward decentralization, but they have encountered difficulties because of lack of substate administrative structure.

• CETA has introduced new administrative layers between program operators and the DOL regional offices, a fact that, on the whole, has promoted greater local responsibility and concern for manpower at the cost of increased complexity in administrative channels.

5 Program Choices

CETA was expected to promote two types of change in manpower programs. It was anticipated that the distribution of funds among major programs (e.g., classroom training and on-the-job training) would shift as sponsors began to adapt existing approaches to the needs of their clients and the demands of their labor markets. It was also hoped that the elimination of categorical restraints would release a flood of local new ideas that would redesign the program.

Examination of the changes in the pattern of Title I funding over the first 2 years suggests a departure from the pre-CETA program configuration. There was a shift from employability improvement and training approaches to such programs as work experience and public service employment that relate more to income maintenance. How did this come about and why? Review of the allocation of Title I funds by sponsors for fiscal 1975 and 1976 offers some clues.

SPENDING PATTERNS

In the first year, there was a predisposition to use programs that were in place because of lack of time, reluctance to "rock the boat," and lack of the experience necessary to develop better alternatives. Any inclination to continue the status quo, however, was soon modified by a set of circumstances that tended to alter the program mix. The nature and the direction of these early changes were to persist throughout the first 2 years (see Table 18).

117

TABLE 18 CETA Title I Expenditures by Program Activity, Fiscal 1974-1977 (amounts in millions of dollars)

Program Activity	FY 1974		FY 1975		FY 1976[a]		FY 1977	
	Amount	Percent	Amount	Percent	Amount	Percent	Amount	Percent
Classroom training[b]	361	42	276	32	524	33	620	39
On-the-job training	154	18	70	8	144	9	173	11
Work experience	319	37	375	43	606	38	566	35
Public service employment	NA	—	56	6	171	11	93	6
Services and other	33	4	99	11	145	9	157	10
TOTAL	868	100	876	100	1,590	100	1,608	100

SOURCE: Computed from Employment and Training Administration, U.S. Department of Labor data.
NOTE: Details may not add to totals due to rounding.
NA = Not applicable.
[a]Four quarters.
[b]Includes expenditures under 5 percent vocational education grant to governors in fiscal years 1975 and 1976.

TABLE 19 Percentage Distribution of CETA Title I Enrollees by Type of
Sponsor and Activity, Fiscal 1976 (cumulative to third quarter)

Program Activity[a]	All Sponsors	City	County	Consortia	Balance of States
Classroom training	32	31	37	36	28
On-the-job training	9	7	9	8	12
Work experience	48	49	43	44	54
Public service employment	4	2	4	5	5
Services and other[b]	7	12	7	8	2
TOTAL	100	100	100	100	100

SOURCE: Computed from Employment and Training Administration, U.S. Department
of Labor, unpublished data.
NOTE: Details may not add to totals due to rounding.
[a]Some enrollees counted in more than one activity.
[b]Enrollees in activities such as removal of artificial barriers to employment, job restructuring, and implementation of affirmative action plans. Does not include enrollees receiving only manpower or supportive services.

One reason for the changes was the spread of manpower funds to
small geographic units. Even sponsors with large areas, such as consortia
and the balance of states, tended to decentralize planning. Smaller
jurisdictions tended to favor work experience over other activities
because it requires the least preparation, expertise, or special facilities.
The increase in work experience in fiscal 1975 was also due in part to
prodding by the Department of Labor to reserve part of the Title I
allotment for summer employment of youth.

Classroom training in rural areas frequently runs into difficulties
because of lack of transportation, buildings, and equipment. Moreover,
job opportunities for graduates of vocational courses in these areas are
likely to be limited. Enrollments by type of sponsor show a heavier
concentration of classroom training among cities than among other types
of sponsors, particularly states and the balance of states that have a
higher proportion of rural areas and small communities (see Table 19).

The decline from 1974 in relative expenditures for classroom training
and on-the-job training (OJT) may have actually been less than is shown
in Table 18, and the increase in work experience may have been
somewhat greater, since the differences are partly due to record-keeping
changes. Under CETA, "services" is identified as a separate expenditure
category. Prior to CETA, most expenditures for manpower and support
services had not been shown as separate items but had been included as
part of the program activity they accompanied.

The decline in expenditures for on-the-job training in 1975 is generally

TABLE 20 Percentage Distribution of CETA Title I Expenditures by Program Activity and Degree of Unemployment in Sample Prime Sponsor Areas, Fiscal 1975 and 1976

| | Level of Unemployment[a] | | | | | |
| | High, N = 8 | | Moderate, N = 12 | | Low, N = 8 | |
Program Activity	FY 1975	FY 1976	FY 1975	FY 1976	FY 1975	FY 1976
Classroom training	25	27	39	38	32	35
On-the-job training	11	13	6	8	4	8
Work experience	44	46	35	32	46	38
Public service employment	0	4	7	9	3	8
Services and other	19	9	14	14	14	12

SOURCE: Computed from Employment and Training Administration, U.S. Department of Labor data.
NOTE: Numbers are averages of percents.
[a]Twenty-eight sponsors classified on the basis of annual average unemployment rate in calendar 1975. High is defined as 10 percent and over; moderate is 7.6–9.9 percent; low is 7.5 percent and below. National average unemployment rate for 1975 was 8.5 percent.

attributed to the recession, but other factors may also have contributed. Table 20 shows that among the sponsors studied, ojt expenditures were relatively highest in both fiscal 1975 and fiscal 1976 in areas with the highest unemployment rates—contrary to expectations. A regression analysis of on-the-job training with unemployment rates confirms the finding that factors other than unemployment account for variations in ojt expenditures.[1] The New York City experience offers some insight on this point. Over the years, New York built up a network of effective subcontractors who arranged for ojt opportunities; even with one of the highest unemployment rates in the country (10.6 percent in 1975), its outlays for ojt dipped only slightly in fiscal 1975 and rose in fiscal 1976. This experience suggests that the effects of a sluggish economy can be overcome if effort is made to develop ojt opportunities. A dol in-house evaluation found that while many sponsors cited layoffs and limited job openings as a reason for reducing ojt funding, "the majority of sponsors had planned some alterations in their approach to ojt, principally involving changes in the delivery agent responsible for developing training arrangements with employers."[2]

Difficulties attendant in changes in program deliverers (see Chapter 6) were also partly responsible for the decline in classroom training: At least four sponsors in the study sample (Topeka, Raleigh, Lansing, and Cook County) encountered difficulties with deliverers of classroom training that delayed the start of programs and caused fiscal 1975 expenditures to decline.

As fiscal 1975 progressed, it became evident that Title I as well as Title II expenditures would fall far short of projections because of delays in getting programs operating. Halfway through the year, only 12 percent of the fiscal year's Title I money and 10 percent of the Title II funds had been spent by sponsors. The slow pace of expenditures concerned the Department of Labor as a reflection of its ability to mount new programs quickly: It might reduce the expected stimulus to economic recovery and raise questions as to whether the funds were really needed. The department resorted to a series of expediencies that affected the program mix.

[1] A cross-sectional regression of the percentage of Title I expenditures for on-the-job-training by 423 prime sponsors in fiscal 1976, with annual average unemployment rates for the prime sponsor areas in calendar year 1975 as the independent variable, produced a correlation coefficient (r^2) of 0.001. An analysis of changes in unemployment rates related to percentage of ojt expenditures (28 areas) showed no signficant relationship.

[2] U.S. Department of Labor, Employment and Training Administration, Office of Manpower Program Evaluation, "Prime Sponsor Planning for Fiscal 1975, CETA Staff Evaluation Findings," Employment and Training Administration, 1975, pp. 1–62 (unpublished).

TABLE 21 Percentage Distribution of CETA Title I Expenditures, by Program Activity and Population of Area, Sample Local Prime Sponsors, Fiscal 1975 and 1976

Program Activity	Size of Sponsor[a]					
	Large, N = 5		Medium, N = 9		Small, N = 10	
	FY 1975	FY 1976	FY 1975	FY 1976	FY 1975	FY 1976
Classroom training	37	34	35	39	34	31
On-the-job training	10	9	7	10	6	10
Work experience	35	33	37	32	40	41
Public service employment	10	19	0	3	2	4
Services and other	8	6	20	16	18	18

SOURCE: Computed from Employment and Training Administration, U.S. Department of Labor data.

NOTE: Numbers are averages of percents for each group.

[a]Size categories based on 1970 census data. Large = population of 1 million or more; medium = 300,000 to 1 million; small = less than 300,000. Includes six cities, nine counties, and nine consortia, no states.

122

At DOL urging, sponsors managed to spend in fiscal 1975 about as much as had been spent in fiscal 1974 (see Table 18). There may, however, be a question as to whether the resulting combination of programs was responsive to local needs or to the funding exigencies of the moment. Outlays for classroom training and for OJT were down both in absolute and relative terms, while work experience and public service employment took up the slack. The largest jurisdictions spent relatively much more on PSE than smaller jurisdictions (see Table 21).

The decision on the part of some sponsors to use Title I funds for PSE had litle to do with manpower considerations. Rather, they represented an effort by hard-pressed urban areas to use PSE resources to alleviate their fiscal problems. Four of the five large sponsors in the sample used some Title I funds for PSE in fiscal 1975; all five did in fiscal 1976. Thus, funds were spent differently than planned in the initial year because of pressures to obligate funds quickly and to respond to the fiscal hard times of the cities.

By the end of fiscal 1975, sponsors had managed to obligate about $1.1 billion of the $1.4 billion of allocated Title I funds and to spend about 80 percent of what they had obligated. Combined with the fiscal 1976 allocation of $1.4 billion, the unspent balance of about $500 million made available to sponsors about $2 billion in fiscal 1976, more than double their fiscal 1975 expenditures. However, many sponsors were reluctant to double their expenditures in fiscal 1976 because they believed that an operating level based on a temporary increase in funds could not be sustained the following year.

Expenditures in fiscal 1976 followed the pattern of those in 1975. Thus, in 2 years, the direction of the Title I program had shifted from emphasis on classroom training and OJT to emphasis on work experience and public service employment. Traditionally, classroom training and OJT had been expected to produce significant proportions of successful program outcomes—placements of participants in training-related jobs. This was not the case with work experience, for which placement expectations were commonly much lower, since most enrollees are school youth and others not seeking regular employment.

The large change in the relative funding of the various existing programs resulted, after 2 years, in a major change in manpower activities, from employability enhancement to programs that have, in some cases, become income maintenance. The crucial question then became how to protect the former objective during a period of high unemployment.

The Department of Labor, in its revised regulations of June 25, 1976, expressed its concern with "redirecting the program's preoccupation with work experience and public service employment during the recent period of high unemployment, back to an emphasis on employability, training, and transition to meaningful employment at the soonest possible point."[3] Data for fiscal 1977 show a higher proportion of expenditures in classroom and on-the-job training.

PROGRAM APPROACHES

Nearly all CETA sponsors inherited some sort of manpower program, along with staff, equipment, and established delivery agencies. Typically, rural counties had only a public employment program and a youth program; large cities had full-range programs, competing agencies, organizations, and community groups. In either case, it was hard for sponsors to divest themselves of their inheritance, had they wished to do so. Efforts to eliminate programs would run into problems of finding other qualified resources as well as political and bureaucratic pressures to maintain the status quo. The principal charge made by elected officials to their CETA planners, at least in the first year, was "Don't make waves."

The advent of recession in 1974 changed priorities, disrupted time schedules, and generated enormous pressures on the Department of Labor and the prime sponsors. In the midst of assuming new administrative responsibilities and pressured by DOL to spend a series of new funding allocations hastily, most sponsors simply did not have time in either the first or the second year to develop new program designs, and the department itself gave higher priority to other matters.

This state of affairs intensified the risks ordinarily inherent in program innovation. Relatively little is known about what combinations of manpower activities lead to increased earnings or about the extent to which the caliber rather than the type of program may be influential. There is no proven formula for training and supportive services that will produce a predictable outcome; the categorical programs were, among other things, a series of experiments to find the right combination. But they embodied so many variations in scope, duration, quality, target group, and locale that no clear relationships emerged. The transfer of responsibility for manpower programs to state and local authorities was not accompanied by prescriptions for exactly what a client would need to improve his or her employability.

Yet somehow, local sponsors were to find the key to the mystery that had eluded others for so long—namely, how to enhance the employabili-

---

[3] *Federal Regulations*, Title 29:94.1 (c)(3).

ty of the disadvantaged so that they could support themselves. Before CETA, federal manpower programs had offered three substantive approaches, singly or in combination:[4]

1. education and/or training (classroom and on-the-job training);
2. subsidized employment in the public or private nonprofit sector (work experience and public service employment); and
3. support services (counseling, job referral, child care, etc.).

These approaches to manpower shared a common assumption that the problem lay in a deficiency in the level of skill or capability of an individual. Their solution was to improve the ability of the individual to cope with the job market by building skill levels and other work-related capabilities. Oriented to the supply side of the labor market, these approaches assumed that, for any given level of demand, these intractable deficiencies would persist in operating against the disadvantaged. However, recent research reinforces the position of those who call for a complementary strategy on the demand side of the labor market. The dual labor market theories and other studies of the rigidities and barriers inherent in the demand side of the labor market have underscored the need for intervention in the labor market processes.[5]

But no one has a crystal ball to determine which approaches will be effective and where. The initiatives of the 1960s, with the objective of improving competitive status in the labor market, were lost in a welter of ad hoc, add-on programs.

Unclear about what should be accomplished, uncertain as to how it should be done, and burdened by time and organizational pressures, few CETA sponsors made extensive changes in program design. Only one of the sponsors studied, St. Paul, developed a different program design based on a conceptualization of the causes and remedies for unemployment: "it is . . . apparent that this maldistribution of employment and its rewards is multi-causal and has its roots in social and economic customs and practices. . . . Any help offered . . . should deal with the whole individual and his relationships with his environment, not only his obvious economic difficulties."[6] The St. Paul approach, which relies heavily on counseling, assessment, and employer contacts as part of an

[4]See Charles R. Perry, Bernard E. Anderson, Richard L. Rowan, and Herbert R. Northrup, *The Impact of Government Manpower Programs: In General, and On Minorities and Women*, Philadelphia: Industrial Research Unit, Wharton School, University of Pennsylvania, 1975.
[5]See Glen G. Cain, "The Challenge of Segmented Labor Market Theories to Orthodox Theory: A Survey," In *Journal of Economic Literature* 14(4):1215–1255, December 1976.
[6]St. Paul Title I Plan, Fiscal Year 1976, pp. 16, 25.

individual approach to each client, was instituted in the first year of CETA. These innovations were possible because St. Paul had a sophisticated staff with a great deal of experience in developing new program techniques. Such competence and confidence might be necessary in assuming the risks of innovation.

Other studies and reports have also noted the absence of any fundamental sponsor effort or DOL assistance for the rethinking of program content through fiscal 1976 planning. A study of CETA in the state of Washington concluded that "there were few major changes in Washington in actual manpower operations. . . . The same people planned within essentially the same framework to meet the same problems."[7] A study of CETA planning and program implementation in North Carolina and South Carolina concluded that

Whether planning is "responsive to local needs" is problematical. It would be safe to say that those who have done the planning up to now . . . have tried to satisfy needs as they perceive them. . . . [But] the simple truth is that nobody knows what the real local needs are. There are myriads of statistics, but nobody has given the prime sponsor a method or methods of converting these statistics into a means of determining need, and, hence, the preferred program mix. Until something is advanced, local needs more often than not are going to turn out to be whatever manpower programs . . . have been in the past.[8]

About half of the sponsors studied reported that they established some type of new program under Title I in fiscal 1976. These in the main were small-scale innovations. Half consisted of offering more or less standard programs to new groups (or at least groups new to that sponsor): ex-offenders, the handicapped, out-of-work union members, and senior citizens. Long Beach reported some novel features of its summer program for youth, such as training youngsters to use movie cameras and to produce films, a project that resulted in an award-winning film. Calhoun County experimented with two alternatives for ex-offender programs, and the Lansing consortium conducted a controlled experiment with a new assessment and counseling program. Cook County and Cleveland used work experience funds to subsidize theater groups. St. Paul, along with its major program overhaul, remodeled its Neighborhood Youth Corps program into a year-round work-study program for

[7]Rawlins, V. Lane, U.S. Department of Labor, Employment and Training Administration, *The Role of the State in the CETA Process: A Case Study of Washington State*, PB-245 602/8ST, Prepared by V. Lane Rawlins, Washington State University, May 1975.

[8]U.S. Department of Labor, Employment and Training Administration, "An Analytical Study of CETA Planning and Program Implementation in North Carolina and South Carolina," Unpublished study prepared by Edward F. Dement, North Carolina Manpower Development Corporation, Chapel Hill, N.C., August 1975 (available from MDC).

youth tied directly to the school curriculum, which carries a student over a 3-year period. Pinellas–St. Petersburg revived "cottage trades" to provide contract work at home to the elderly, the handicapped, mothers of small children, and others unable to leave home. Orange County introduced a pilot project involving the local community action agency, the community college, and the county welfare department. Mothers on welfare were provided with a combination of education and training to qualify them for a license to furnish day care in their homes. The county welfare department then paid them to care for children of other mothers on welfare who could then seek jobs.

Other new projects reported by the Department of Labor include the use of mobile rather than stationary service centers, voucher systems permitting participants to seek out and arrange for their own training or subsidized employment, and variations and improvements of traditional work experience and work-study concepts.

VOCATIONAL EDUCATION

Perhaps the greatest substantive program changes have been made in classroom training. Prior to CETA, classroom training was funded under the Manpower Development and Training Act. Under this act, major decision making took place in the state and local offices of the employment service and the education agencies. Through its local offices, the employment service proposed the occupations for training, secured the participants, and attempted to place them upon completion of training. The vocational education agencies selected the facility that did the training. Three general kinds of programs were funded: single-occupation training courses, multi-occupational projects, and individual referrals. The most common programs were class-size courses in a particular skill or occupation. These presented problems in keeping classrooms full and minimizing costs because of their set entry and exit dates. Multi-occupational projects, usually conducted in skill centers, had the advantage of open entry–exit, occcupational clustering, and a range of supportive services. However, they were costly and required a lot of coordination. The third type of project, individual referral, assigned an individual to a particular school and, in contrast to the other two, did not imply that the existence of the institution or the class depended on maintaining a given number or flow of individual participants. However, each referral often required as much time-consuming paperwork as a class-size project. Partly for this reason, but also because some believed that standard training institutions were inappropriate for the educationally disadvantaged, individual referral was not widely used.

Before CETA, no transactions of any significance occurred between the local employment service and the local training agency: Any decision made at the local level had to travel up the hierarchy to the state level of the initiating agency, across to the state level of the other agency, and then down again to the local level. The split responsibilities at the local level resulted in delays, less-than-full use of projects that were funded, and some difficulty in establishing accountability for program results.[9]

Under CETA, prime sponsors assumed the decision-making responsibilities previously exercised by the state employment service and the vocational education agency. Many sponsors moved decisively away from the class-size projects and skill centers to much wider use of individual referral. Almost half (10 of 24) of the sample sponsors reported more individual referrals in fiscal 1976. Its advantages to them were a wider range of training facilities and occupational choices,[10] greater flexibility to tailor programs to individual needs, and avoidance of costly commitments to single institutions. Some training could be obtained from public schools at no instruction cost, incidentally achieving a CETA goal of closer coordination with existing agencies.

However, vocational education agency officials have pointed to flaws in a policy of large-scale individual referral: It usually does not address the long-term manpower needs of an area. Because each individual makes a choice from courses that already exist, there is not much motivation for sponsors to add new courses that would be useful. Individual referral may also lead to a policy of selecting the most qualified applicants, because persons without enough education to keep abreast of a standard course may not be referred to such programs. Some vocational educators feel that an academically able CETA enrollee, capable of completing a standard course in a vocational institution, probably should not be consuming CETA resources. If sponsors give up the more costly special training centers for the educationally disadvantaged, there is a question as to whether they are substituting equally effective training.

Interviews with vocational educators and manpower planners revealed very different views of vocational training. Some of the conflict arises from differences in perception of what constitutes effective training and some comes from a clash of bureaucratic interests. The differences are

[9]North American Rockwell Information Systems Co., *A Systems Analysis of the MDTA Institutional Training Program*, Arlington, Va., 1971.
[10]One consortium (Pinellas–St. Petersburg), previously limited to class-size groups in 5 occupations, expanded its offerings to 35.

highlighted in a study of vocational education and manpower planning in Texas,[11] which observes that manpower programs are commonly directed at narrow, short-term objectives—the minimum amount of training necessary to get a person a job.[12] In contrast, vocational educators prefer a somewhat more generalized, more enriched training curriculum, which over the long run is presumably more effective in improving employment prospects. A report[13] on a 1976 conference of state vocational educators illustrating bureaucratic inertia describes the reluctance of vocational educators to "move away from traditional, time-honored activities and to establish new operational priorities." (Sponsor relationships with institutions delivering classroom training are discussed in Chapter 6.)

There is evidence that some prime sponsors were adjusting classroom training content to conform to a low-cost strategy. For example, several sponsors—New York City, Topeka, and Calhoun, Cook, and Pasco counties—reported a shift in occupational skill training from industrial and manufacturing skills to less costly training in service skills. For the most part, sponsors reported that they had made these changes in response to the recession, because job opportunities in the service fields were better. But two in the sample (Calhoun County and Cleveland) reported that shifts to the service fields were made to reduce costs by shifting to a less expensive training area and shortening the training to provide just enough preparation to get the immediate job. The Chester County fiscal 1976 Title I plan, for example, stated that classroom training would be limited to 11 weeks. If an individual could not master the material within this period, he or she might continue to attend "as necessary for proficiency" but would have to attend in the evening, without allowances.

A few sponsors planned to move in the other direction: St. Paul reported a broadening of skill training by adding courses in basic math, science, and communications. Ramsey County planned most of its classroom training to continue for an academic year or longer. However, the DOL grant-review guidelines for fiscal 1977 seem to favor a relatively low-cost Title I program strategy and could have the effect of diminishing the educational content of classroom training. Key indica-

---

[11]Lyndon B. Johnson School of Public Affairs, "Manpower and Vocational Education Planning Processes: Four Regional Case Studies," University of Texas at Austin, 1975.
[12]See North American Rockwell Information Systems Co., *A Systems Analysis of the MDTA Institutional Training Program*, pp. 2–126.
[13]A mimeographed summary of the proceedings of this meeting was circulated by the National Governors' Conference (now the National Governors' Association), Washington, D.C.

tors continue to be placement, cost ratios, rate of expenditures related to the characteristics of participants, the mix of services, and general economic conditions.[14] Recognizing the pressures toward concentration on low-skill, short-term training, the Department of Labor undertook in 1977 to encourage a number of experimental, advanced-skill, long-term training projects through the Skill Training Improvement Program (STIP). These emphasized the involvement of private industry in identifying needs for skilled occupation and in the oversight of programs.

Sponsors were responsive to the legislative emphasis on meeting the needs of persons of limited English-speaking ability. Four of the sample sponsors reported adding English as a second language (ESL) to curricula in 1976, bringing to 12 (of 19 local sponsors for which data are available) the number that offered this program. Other programs included orientation, which was offered by 13 sponsors, and adult basic education or preparation for a general equivalency diploma (GED—equivalent to a high school degree), which was offered by 16 sponsors. All 19 sponsors offered some type of skill training.

WORK EXPERIENCE

Before CETA, work experience was in many cases the main activity for youth or a last resort for adults, and under local sponsorship there has been little apparent change. Work experience projects—jobs at minimum wages in the public or private nonprofit sector—were developed principally for youth and were usually administered by schools or community agencies. These were Neighborhood Youth Corps (NYC) types of projects and varied in quality, perhaps more widely than any other program. In some projects, participants were closely supervised; in others, they were not. Some provided related skill training; others did not. There was no single model; what is known about work experience projects comes from descriptions or studies of individual programs at various sites. One study commented that "NYC has never been popular in this city, its stipends typically being below that believed by many youth to be the minimum acceptable payment and having a reputation for makework."[15] A study on another community noted: "the projects might be divided between those . . . in the schools and public agencies where the experience has been sound . . . and those in community action

---

[14]U.S. Department of Labor, Employment and Training Administration, "Transmittal of Key Performance Indicators for Title I Programs," Field memorandum no. 209-77, March 21, 1977.

[15]Olympus Research Corporation, *Total Impact Evaluation of Manpower Programs in Four Cities*, Salt Lake City: Olympus Research Corporation, 1970.

agencies and youth groups, where the emphasis has tended to be on developing militancy."[16] A review of evaluations of youth work experience found little evidence that youth work experience contributes to positive attitudes, better work habits, or job skills for its participants. Nevertheless, conventional wisdom has assigned to work experience a value "as a combination income maintenance and maturation device to youth to stay out of trouble until they are old enough to get a sustaining job or to enroll in a training program."[17]

Although the bulk of summer funds comes from Title III, sponsors serve large numbers of youth under Title I through work experience programs. A comparison of sponsor enrollments in work experience programs with the proportion of school youth shows that sponsors with the highest proportion of full-time students also had the highest proportion of enrollees in work experience programs (see Figure 3).

A few of the sponsors studied have reduced or eliminated expenditures for youth work experience. Calhoun County dropped the NYC programs. This was a big shift—these programs had accounted for 30 percent of total fiscal 1974 funds—but the prime sponsor regarded youth work experience as nothing more than a handout, with negative effects on the attitudes of young people toward work. A similar sentiment was expressed by a field researcher at another site, who questioned the value of "being employed in meaningless unsupervised work which will eventually make it more difficult to enter the world of work. . . . In some cases students are cleaning up vacant lots and then no provision is ever made for trucks to haul the trash away."

Pasco and Middlesex counties reduced the youth work experience program; St. Paul reduced and reorganized the program. However, with these exceptions, the fundamental program concept of work experience for youth appears to continue more or less unchanged under local sponsors, with more of the same problems that it had under federal direction.

The major work experience program for adults before CETA had been "Operation Mainstream." Mainstream and equivalent work programs were in some cases temporary "parking lots" for persons awaiting entry into other programs. Principally, however, they were employment of last resort, providing income and some self-esteem for the elderly, adult residents of rural areas, and others unlikely to make it in the regular labor market. Under CETA, work experience for adults has expanded somewhat, made necessary, according to prime sponsors, by the

[16]*Ibid.*

[17]Perry *et al., The Impact of Government Manpower Programs,* pp. 449–450.

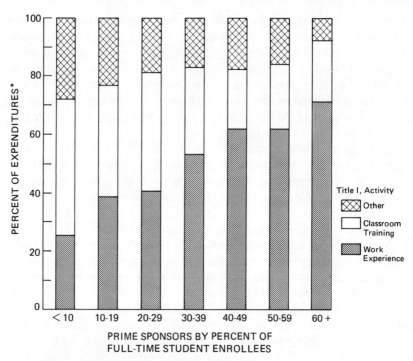

*Title I expenditures for first 3 quarters of fiscal 1976.

SOURCE: Based on Employment and Training Administration Data

FIGURE 3 Prime sponsors with high levels of full-time students in Title I spend more on work experience and less on classroom training and other activities.

recession. In one county, although work experience is regarded "more as makework and income maintenance than solid preparation for unsubsidized jobs" and despite negative sentiments expressed by the planning council, "the staff has, willy-nilly, been led into a large effort in this area." Another, however, regards work experience as a useful holding device for those who are unemployed but have a strong attachment to work. One sponsor in the study sample eliminated work experience as an independent activity; it is offered only as a means of income support to participants enrolled in classroom training, but this appears to be an exception to the prevailing practice.

ON-THE-JOB TRAINING

Changes in on-the-job training as a result of CETA were minor. Before

CETA, employers had a choice between participating in "high-support" programs, in which they provided supportive services for participants and were compensated accordingly, and participating in "low-support" programs, which involved fewer services, less money, but also less bother. In general it appears that the high-support option was most attractive to large employers. And, under CETA, there was a shift from large employers to smaller firms, and a corresponding movement from high-support to low-support contracts. Sponsors identified on-the-job-training more than any other activity as a preferred strategy, but in fiscal 1976 less than 10 percent of Title I funds was spent on OJT.

SUPPLEMENTARY SERVICES

Manpower jargon defines two categories of supplementary services as adjuncts to major program activities. "Manpower" services generally include outreach, intake, assessment, orientation, counseling, job development, and placement. Before CETA these services were usually provided by the employment service. "Support" services generally refers to services provided by other social agencies to overcome employment handicaps, such as health problems or the need for transportation and child care facilities. Before CETA, the usefulness of these social services and the extent to which they should be budgeted were frequently program issues. Recently, relatively little has been heard on the subject, in part because sponsors have been able to make cost-free referrals to other service agencies within their jurisdictions. The Cook County Title I plan for fiscal 1976 specified that no more than 5 percent of the cost of a slot was to be spent on support services; both Cook County and the Phoenix consortium indicated that they planned to reduce support costs by greater use of other community agencies. The Maine BOS Title I plan also called for expenditures for support services that averaged 5 percent of participant costs, but this was significantly more than was spent before CETA.

The principal change with regard to manpower services has been in delivery agents (see Chapter 6) rather than in the nature of the services. The delivery of "direct placements" has been a particular source of controversy. The Department of Labor insisted that placement of job-ready workers who have not participated in any other substantive CETA program be done exclusively by the employment service (ES). Prime sponsors viewed this as an intrusion on local autonomy, but DOL was concerned with buttressing the mandate of the ES and with reducing the duplication of functions.

Sponsors have justified their direct placement services on a number of grounds. Direct placement helps to ease the pressures generated by large numbers of eligible job applicants and conserves resources for others who need more assistance. It builds the image of the sponsor as an employment-oriented agency and broadens potential job prospects for CETA clients. Finally, it helps meet critical placement goals by serving persons who are relatively easy to place and makes the prime sponsor's general performance look better. This issue illustrates the collision between one CETA objective, local decision making, with another objective—the use of existing institutions. The question was finally resolved by having DOL encourage, but not mandate, the use of the ES.

SUMMARY

Under CETA, local sponsors were to have a chance to experiment with the manpower programs, shaping them to fit an individual's needs or the unique characteristics of a particular labor market. Change has occurred, but it did not take the direction that some had envisioned.

• Program change can be measured in terms of alterations in the nature of programs offered and in terms of shifts in the relative emphasis on various kinds of programs. The nature of program services and activities changed little under CETA. The overwhelming majority of prime sponsors surveyed indicated that their strategy in determining the kinds of programs to be offered under Title I was to retain the existing kinds of programs, using the established program operators. Only one sponsor in the study sample introduced a totally new program design; a few others introduced novel pilot projects.

• Contributing to the status quo were the legacy of past programming, the decentralization to smaller planning units for which alternatives are fewer, the recession that sponsors felt limited their options, and the state of the art—only the most sophisticated sponsor staffs were in a position to improve upon existing program models. Finally, the Department of Labor was preoccupied with getting the money spent and assisting sponsors to develop appropriate administrative and procedural structures.

• Traditional pre-CETA work experience programs for youth and adults have continued nearly unchanged under CETA. A few sponsors have eliminated work experience, but most have retained it and increased expenditures for adult programs in response to the recession. Work experience continues to absorb a major share of Title I funds, despite evidence even before CETA that for youth, at least, the quality of many such programs contributes little to positive attitudes, better work habits, or job skills.

• Sponsors have, however, shifted the balance of programs during the first 2 years. They did not at first plan significant changes in the distribution of resources among major program activities, but the effects of fiscal pressures in big cities, difficulties in getting programs going under new sponsorship, and the recession all contributed to a shift of funds away from classroom training and OJT (from 60 percent in fiscal 1974 to 40 percent of program budget in 1976 and 50 percent in 1977) to a greater emphasis on work experience and public service employment.

This shift, arising from external and contingent circumstances rather than from any sponsor conviction that it made the best balance to promote individual employability, has aroused concern, because it appears to mark a subtle but definite change in the character of manpower programs, away from preparation for economic self-sufficiency and in the direction of subsidized employment. This is especially true if funds provided under Titles II and VI are also considered: More than 80 percent of all CETA funds in the three titles has been used to maintain people in subsidized public sector jobs, often unaccompanied by significant efforts to move them into unsubsidized employment.

6 The Delivery of Title I Services

While CETA prime sponsors have tended to remain within the charted course in the programs offered, they have introduced far-reaching changes in the delivery system and program operators. One result of these changes was to dissolve the near monopolies of the employment service and the MDTA skill centers in their areas of service.

Structuring the delivery system and selecting the service deliverers are the two principal tasks of CETA sponsors that follow from decisions about who will be served and what services will be provided. The term "delivery system" describes the interrelationships of agencies and organizations that carry out the activities at entry, exit, and transfer points through which individuals pass as they receive manpower services. It was the former chaotic state of these arrangements that led to CETA. Before CETA, categorical program operators offered to applicants only their own services, as determined by legislative or administrative guidelines. Each recruited its own clients, and seldom were clients or services shared with another program.

Within the same community, some services might be duplicated by several agencies; others might not be available at all. Some agencies provided only part of the services for a single program package, others offered a whole program, and still others administered more than one program. Much of the criticism of the delivery of manpower services before CETA was directed to such fragmentation and lack of coordination.

Under the Manpower Development and Training Act, the employment service and local vocational education agencies played the leading roles in most communities, but various community-based organizations and other agencies also furnished services for activities stemming from the Economic Opportunity Act. For the most part, the greater the number of deliverers, the larger the number of separate delivery structures operating within the community. For example, a relatively small county, such as Stanislaus (population less than 200,000), had 10 different manpower programs operated by six different agencies. In large cities, it was not uncommon to find dozens of programs, many unknown to one another.

In addition to criticism of the process, there was dissatisfaction with the delivery agencies themselves: They did not reach or adequately serve certain segments of the community; they were not conveniently located; they spent too much on administration. CETA offered to sponsors the opportunity to structure the manpower delivery system and select the agencies through which manpower services were to be delivered.

There were two major expectations for CETA. One was that the jumble of categorical programs would be transformed into an orderly array of program activities in each community, a system with clearly designated entry points, each of which would have access to all services that the system provides. The second expectation was that under the eye of the local sponsor, delivery agencies would be obliged to become more efficient and effective—or be replaced. Discernible progress has been made in the former goal; the extent of improvement in the latter is not clear and needs further study.

SYSTEM DESIGN

At CETA's inception, there was no working model of a comprehensive delivery system for prime sponsors, although some approximations had been attempted. One was the Concentrated Employment Program (CEP), created in 1967 to coordinate service delivery within a limited geographic area, usually the low-income section of an inner city. For the most part, CEPs were sponsored by community action agencies. These agencies had difficulty in coordinating services among subcontractors; organizational conflict and lack of cooperation adversely affected the potential of CEPs.[1]

Another early effort was the Comprehensive Manpower Program (CMP), a pilot program anticipating CETA, which was established in nine

[1]Charles R. Perry, Bernard E. Anderson, Richard L. Rowan, and Herbert R. Northrup, *The Impact of Government Manpower Programs: In General, and On Minorities and Women,* Philadelphia: Industrial Research Unit, Wharton School, University of Pennsylvania, 1975, Ch. 13.

areas in fiscal 1973. The CMP experience highlighted some of the start-up problems that were later encountered, particularly among relatively inexperienced sponsors.[2]

The concept of comprehensive service delivery implied that all activities and services offered in one geographic area would be unified, and accountability for program outcome would be centralized. Manpower services would be coordinated; program participants would be exposed to a full range of training and service options; there would be continuity of responsibility for each client throughout his or her stay.

Of the 24 local prime sponsors studied in the first year, 4 were found to have a comprehensive delivery system, 11 to have a mixed system, and 9 to have retained a categorical configuration (see Figure 4). By the second year, 8 sponsors had adopted a comprehensive system, 6 a mixed system, and 10 retained a categorical system, as shown in the table below:

Comprehensive System	Mixed System	Categorical System
St. Paul	Gary	Philadelphia
Topeka	Long Beach	Pasco County
Chester County	New York	Stanislaus County
Lorain County	Calhoun County	Cleveland Consortium
Middlesex County	Balance of Cook County	Lansing Consortium
Balance of Ramsey County	Capital Area Consortium	Phoenix/Maricopa Consortium
Balance of Union County		Orange County Consortium
Kansas City/Wyandotte		Raleigh Consortium
		Pinellas/St. Petersburg Consortium
		San Joaquin Consortium

Those sponsors who tended to stay with a categorical system were large cities, which have long had an established manpower infrastructure and significant political pressures, and consortia, which consist of numerous separate jurisdictions. The larger and more urban areas with many ethnic groups may find a comprehensive system, in which a single agency controls program entry, less suited to their needs. Consortia prefer the categorical system, since it enables each jurisdiction in the alliance to control its own activities. Movement to a comprehensive model, then, has been most typical of small and medium-sized jurisdictions.

The 5 largest sponsors studied, each with a population of more than 1 million, have delivery systems that resemble their pre-CETA patterns (see Table 22). All 5—New York City, Cook County, Cleveland, Philadel-

---

[2]U.S. Department of Labor, Manpower Administration, *Manpower Report of the President 1974*, pp. 42–44.

| Type System | Client Intake | Program Activity | Job Referral |

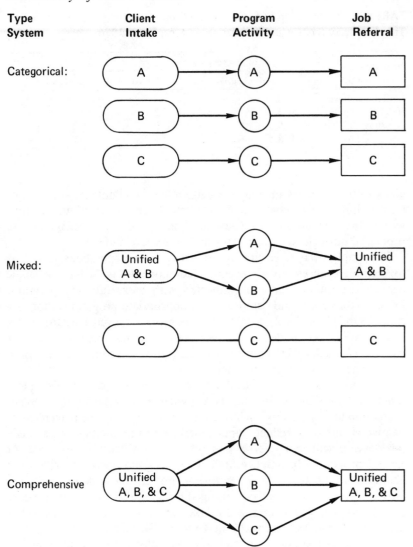

FIGURE 4   Client flow models.

phia, and Orange County—have many program operators that continue to maintain varying degrees of independence within the delivery system. Each, however, has organized parts of its entry and exit services under a single agency or organization. New York has a network of 26 city-funded neighborhood centers; Philadelphia, an in-house manpower center;

TABLE 22   Distribution of Sample Local Prime Sponsors by Type of CETA
Title I Delivery System and Population of Area, Fiscal 1976

Population of Prime Sponsor	Type of Delivery System		
	Comprehensive	Mixed	Categorical
1 million and over	0	2	3
300,000-500,000	3	2	4
Less than 300,000	5	2	3
TOTAL	8	6	10

Cook County is using the employment service for all intake; and Orange
County has a basic network of 6 recruitment centers run by jurisdictions
within the consortium. In Cleveland, many of the participants are
processed through Aims-Jobs—formerly the Cleveland CEP.

The simplest way to ensure control over program operations, as well as
to guarantee access to all program components, is to have a single
agency control the services connected with entry into the program:
intake, assessment, and referral to an appropriate program option. By
fiscal 1976, 11 of the 24 local prime sponsors surveyed had adopted a
centralized intake model, and 2 more were planning such a system for
fiscal 1977. Each of 11 sponsors with central intake controlled access to
an average of 8 major program activities.

There has not been quite as much movement toward centralizing exit
functions. Opinion is divided as to whether it is better to preserve
accountability by making each operator responsible for the placement of
its own clients or to reduce duplication of effort by establishing a single
job development and referral unit operating on behalf of enrollees of
several programs. In practice, individual program operators with good
channels for placing their enrollees are encouraged to continue.
However, some sponsors have arranged for centralized placement. Six of
the 11 sponsors with centralized intake have centralized placement, but
individual service deliverers also make some placements.

A centralized system does not automatically represent an improvement in the delivery of services, although in most instances this is
assumed to be the case. As one field researcher noted, "CETA target
groups from the rural and urban ghettos [may be] reluctant to enter a
large, shiny institutional 'one-stop' office. If the clientele are not being
reached, . . . integrated systems are largely an exercise in futility."

While they are more difficult to analyze, intermediate program
activities appear to have been even less centralized. Whether sponsors
have retained the same services and activities previously offered or

whether they have added, subtracted, or restructured the substance of programs is hard to trace because the labels of categorical programs have often disappeared. Therefore, it is nearly impossible to compare differences in programs before and after CETA.

Changes in the number of major service deliverers might be one clue. Of the 254 pre-CETA programs identified in 23 sample areas (other than New York City and the balance of states), in fiscal 1975 under CETA, one-third were either discontinued or were assigned to different operators. According to a Department of Labor study, there was a 35-percent increase in the number of service deliverers in the first year—from an estimated 1,440 under MDTA and EOA sponsorship in fiscal 1974 to 1,950 under Title I of CETA in fiscal 1975.[3] The number of subcontractors has continued to increase substantially.[4] In Cook County, the number of subcontractors shot up from 130 in 1975 to 235 in 1976 because of the listing as primary contracts of dozens of contracts on behalf of individual participants for classroom training and on-the-job training.

Some specific examples may indicate more clearly the types of change that have occurred. In Topeka, the following programs operated prior to CETA:

Delivery Agency	Program
Employment service	MDTA on-the-job training (JOPS)
Employment service and vocational/technical school	MDTA skill training
OIC	Skill training, placement
SER	Skill training, placement
Kansas Neurological Institute	Public service careers
Topeka school district	Neighborhood youth corps in-school Operation Mainstream
Shawnee County community action agency	Neighborhood youth corps out-of-school

In the first year, the Topeka school system and the community action agency were dropped as service deliverers, but there was no program change, as the prime sponsor took over the NYC and Mainstream programs. In the second year, OIC, SER, and the vocational–technical school were dropped as delivery agents, and all classroom training was assigned to the Kansas Neurological Institute. This shift in delivery agencies changed the kinds of courses offered in classroom training. There remained only three delivery agencies in fiscal 1976: the

[3]U.S. Department of Labor, Manpower Administration, *Manpower Interchange*, 1(1) October 1975.

[4]A GAO report refers to "50,000 or more" subgrantees under CETA, but the vast majority of these are grantees under Titles II and VI.

employment service, the Kansas Neurological Institute, and the prime sponsor. In that year, the employment service did all the intake and assessment and counseling; the institute did most of the classroom training; and the prime sponsor did everything else: a little classroom training and all of the work experience and OJT. Thus, all of the program options that had previously been available were still offered, but with far fewer service deliverers.

In Stanislaus County, which had a similar range of pre-CETA programs, the situation was very different. The Public Service Careers program was dropped; one deliverer, the National Alliance of Businessmen (NAB), was dropped; two activities have been added, each provided by a new agency. The teaching of English as a second language is one new activity; the other is a construction training program in which clients are learning carpentry skills by building new houses. Otherwise, the programs and agencies are the same.

The Phoenix–Maricopa area was served by 10 agencies before CETA. Under CETA these agencies remained operators, but most were relocated to one of three neighborhood centers. Two of these centers served Phoenix; at the third, serving Maricopa County, the county and other operators conducted work experience and other programs. In fiscal 1976, five small new projects were funded—the Phoenix Indian Center, a Basic Youth Project, a Black Theatre Troupe, and two union training programs. Each of these projects was to be conducted by a new agency to be located in one of the three centers. While these projects increased the number of deliverers by 50 percent, they accounted for less than 10 percent of Title I funds.

The foregoing illustrations demonstrate varying degrees of consolidation of the standard functions. Sponsors have been moving toward delivery systems that centralize intake and, to a lesser extent, consolidate the rest of the program. However, integration of services among titles has not occurred. While eight sponsors in the sample indicated that their intake centers processed applicants for all three titles, once applicants came through the door, interviewers simply sorted them into job-ready or not-job-ready groups and assigned them correspondingly to public service employment or Title I activities. There was little or no provision for the transfer of services from one to the other. There was only one instance in the sample of persons being trained under Title I and then assigned to a public service job under Title II or VI.

PROGRAM OPERATORS

Consistent with the stress on local autonomy, Congress placed the responsibility for selecting the agencies to provide manpower services with the prime sponsor. There were to be no "presumptive deliverers." CETA supporters anticipated that this would put pressure on existing agencies to become more efficient and responsive and that wasteful or ineffective agencies would be dropped. However, critics feared that this authority would lead to the extinction of the advocacy base built up over the 1960s by minorities and the disadvantaged. They were concerned that "public agencies such as the schools, personnel offices and vocational educators . . . [might] 'capture' the programs or squeeze out effective community groups which could serve as planning or delivery agents".[5]

In the face of such objections, Congress also stipulated that existing institutions of demonstrated effectiveness should be used to the extent deemed feasible. Having thus disposed of the issue, Congress left it to the federal and local administrators to sort things out. What followed was a struggle over turf.

PRIME SPONSORS

One of the most striking results of decentralization has been the emergence of a new agency for service delivery—the prime sponsor itself. This has come about as sponsors have attempted to coordinate and centralize the delivery system. Integration was accompanied by a reduction in the number of agencies controlling the basic operations and extension of the role of the local prime sponsor from administrative overseer to direct program operator. Prime sponsors cited additional reasons for moving into operations: unsatisfactory performance by existing agencies and a reluctance to choose among organizations competing for program contracts. Others have suggested that bureaucratic aggrandizement on the part of the sponsor's staff may also have been a motive.

Seventeen of 24 local sponsors in the sample reported that they were directly engaged in some aspect of program operations in fiscal 1976. Of the 11 sponsors with central intake, 6 operated that activity and 2 more planned to take it over (from the employment service) in fiscal 1977.

Results of a Department of Labor survey of the operating role of

[5]National Manpower Policy Task Force, *The Comprehensive Employment and Training Act: Opportunities and Challenges*, Washington, D.C.: National Manpower Policy Task Force, April 1974, p. 10.

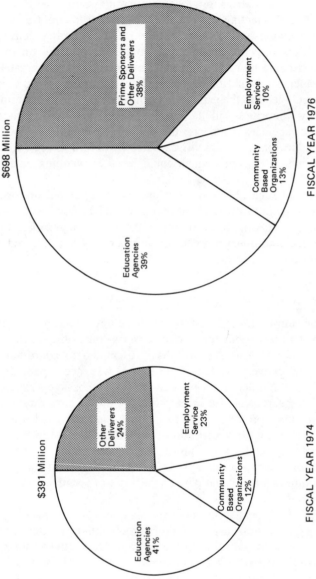

Expenditures for Service Deliverers*

Prime Sponsors and Other Deliverers 38%

Employment Service 10%

Community Based Organizations 13%

Education Agencies 39%

$698 Million

FISCAL YEAR 1976

Other Deliverers 24%

Employment Service 23%

Community Based Organizations 12%

Education Agencies 41%

$391 Million

FISCAL YEAR 1974

*Excludes allowances, wages, fringe benefits; 1974 figures for comparable programs.

SOURCE: Based on Data from Employment and Training Administration

FIGURE 5   Prime sponsors' roles as service deliverers under CETA are increasing.

sponsors in 1976 were similar. Prime sponsors were reported as operating the intake function in 61 percent of Title I programs and as being the primary deliverer of placement services in almost half of the Title I programs.[6]

An analysis of Title I expenditures provides another measure of the new importance of sponsors as program operators (see Figure 5 and Table 23). The employment service, education agencies, and leading community-based organizations accounted for about 75 percent of all expenditures in fiscal 1974 and about 62 percent in fiscal 1976. The prime sponsor shares the remainder with all other agencies, but the proportion now going to the prime sponsor is sizable.

COMMUNITY-BASED ORGANIZATIONS

Although funding of the major community-based organizations (CBOs) increased significantly during the first 2 years of CETA, the study found that these organizations express considerable uneasiness about their changed relationships and responsibilities and the expanding role of the sponsor as a direct deliverer of service. According to DOL national data, funds contracted to the three major community-based organizations— OIC, the Urban League, and SER—rose from $46 million in 1974 to $95 million in 1976 (see Table 24). However, their proportionate share of total Title I expenditures changed little from 1974 to 1976 (see Figure 5).

The local prime sponsor reduced CBO funding because of what it viewed as poor performance in some instances. A few organizations lost funds when political alliances shifted. But even where CBOs have retained their role as service deliverers, they do not necessarily control the flow of clients from entry to exit, but may provide only certain services within the total sequence. They frequently are required to serve all applicants rather than just their original constituency. CBOs believe their autonomy has been curtailed and see a potential challenge to the rationale for their existence.[7]

Such concerns prompted OIC to seek legislation for separate financial support for itself and the other community-based organizations. In a statement at a House committee's oversight hearings, a spokesman said

[6]U.S. Department of Labor, Office of Program Evaluation, Employment and Training Administration, "Report on CETA/SESA Linkages and Relationships, March 1976," p. 48 (unpublished).

[7]See, for example, Charles Krider's discussion of this issue in "Topeka, Kansas," In William Mirengoff, ed., *Transition to Decentralized Manpower Programs: Eight Area Studies*, Committee on Evaluation of Employment and Training Programs, Washington, D.C.: National Academy of Sciences, March 1976, pp. 14–15.

TABLE 23   CETA Title I Expenditures by Major Service Deliverers,
Fiscal 1974 and 1976[a] (millions of dollars)

Service Delivery Agency	FY 1974	FY 1976
Employment service[b]	90	67
Community organizations[c] (OIC, SER, NUL)	46	95
Education agencies[d]	162	271
Other deliverers[e]	93	265
Subtotal (expenditures for services)	391	698
Expenditures for wages, allowances, and fringe payments to enrollees[f]	477	892
TOTAL	868	1,590

SOURCE: Computed from Employment and Training Administration, U.S. Department
of Labor data.
[a]Includes 5 percent vocational education grants to governors.
[b]Sponsor expenditures on employment service estimated by using DOL data on number
of man years contracted and a rate of $15,000 per man year.
[c]Includes some wage/allowance expenditures.
[d]Calculated by using total Title I expenditures for prime sponsor classroom training,
subtracting Title I expenditures on allowances, and adding expenditures from the
5 percent vocational education grant.
[e]Calculated as residual.
[f]Estimated at 55 percent of total Title I expenditures for 1974.

TABLE 24   Federal and Local Funding of Community-
Based Organizations for Manpower Services, Fiscal
1974–1976 (millions of dollars)

Organization	FY 1974	FY 1975	FY 1976
OIC	23	42	55
Urban League	10	16	21
SER	13	19	19
TOTAL	46	77	95

SOURCE: Employment and Training Administration, U.S. Department of Labor.

that OIC was " . . . in danger of being fragmentized, divided, weakened
and possibly destroyed." He spoke of the need to preserve the OIC
training sequence from outreach through training and counseling to
placement: "the integrity of the OIC process . . . should be maintained. . . . "8

8Statement of Dr. Leon H. Sullivan, Chairman of the Board, Opportunities Industrializa-
tion Centers of America, in U.S. Congress, House, Committee on Education and Labor,
Oversight Hearings on the Comprehensive Employment and Training Act, Part 3, Before the
Subcommittee on Manpower, Compensation, and Health and Safety, 94th Congress, 2nd
Session, August 26, 1976, pp. 229–230.

The inclination of some prime sponsors to absorb rather than coordinate the work of other agencies has been noted. The Director of Human Resources and Economic Development for Cleveland indicated that agencies such as the employment service, the vocational education agency, the Concentrated Employment Program, and the National Alliance of Businessmen are generally reluctant to cooperate with each other or with the prime sponsor, and that the only way to create a truly comprehensive manpower system would be for the city to develop the capacity to deliver all manpower services. San Joaquin established a central intake, assessment, and referral center at Stockton in 1977 that consolidated many of the services then being furnished, not only by the employment service, but also by CBOs and the vocational education agency. In Kansas City, the employment service was at the outset replaced as service deliverer by a number of CBOs, including SER, OIC, the Urban League, and the local community action agency. The number of service deliverers was cut from 14 to 7 in fiscal 1977, and services were to become more highly centralized. One of the three city commissioners has already suggested publicly that the city take over "the whole thing" in order to end the annual "hassle" among service deliverers and provide better program coordination.

There are, of course, different ways in which sponsors can take over. In several areas sponsors have absorbed the staffs of the CBOs as well as their functions. To some, this appears to be an advantage in the long run, since service to the target group now becomes a part of the system rather than a function outside it. On the other hand, it may signal, as others fear, a decline in attention to those most in need.

In a letter to the National Association of Counties dated July 29, 1976, the Department of Labor stated that henceforth, if prime sponsors planned to make changes in delivery agents, these changes would have to be supported by a detailed documentation of the reasons for change, including data on "comprehensive costs, types of service and responsiveness of services." It remains to be seen whether regional offices will interpret this as a signal to discourage further changes in service delivery agencies, including CBOs.

COMMUNITY ACTION AGENCIES

Prior to CETA, community action agencies (CAAs) operated manpower programs in 21 of the 28 areas of the sample. In 1975, three sponsors (Topeka, Lorain County, and Stanislaus County) took over the CAA programs or assigned them to other agencies. While 18 sponsors retained CAAs in fiscal 1976, several (Union County, Kansas City, Orange County, and Raleigh) reduced their role. Precise data for fiscal 1976 are not available, but Community Services Administration officials estimate that, at the national level, the dollar value of DOL/CETA funding was about the same in 1976 as in 1975.

VOCATIONAL EDUCATION

While funds spent on classroom training (both by prime sponsors and from the supplemental 5-percent governors' grants for vocational education) increased 45 percent (from $360 million in 1974 to $524 million in 1976), they did not keep pace with the increase in total expenditures on Title I activities, which rose about 80 percent. DOL data also indicate an internal shift in the use of classroom training funds, with a relatively smaller proportion going for allowances and a greater share to the institutions themselves. The effect of this has been to sustain the proportion of total Title I expenditures actually going to educational institutions. The share of Title I dollars going to classroom training would have been smaller in 1975 and 1976 if not for the 5-percent money.

The 5-percent money has also been a factor in persuading prime sponsors to spend more on public education agencies than they otherwise might. Public vocational education is by no means monolithic. It is offered by both state and local systems; by high schools, community colleges, vocational–technical institutes, and other public sources. Under CETA there has been much greater opportunity for these institutions to compete directly for sponsor funding, and sponsors reported considerable shifting in the use of these sources.

In part, the shifts may be due to the tensions between prime sponsors and vocational education officials. Conflicts generally revolve around the selection of trainees, performance standards, and duration of courses. Education officials complain that trainees are not selected carefully. They also tend to favor longer, more broadly based, and career-oriented occupational preparation, in contrast to CETA sponsors, who frequently seek short, single-purpose courses to prepare trainees for specific entry-level jobs. Sponsors responded to these problems, in part at least, by moving to individual referrals and by using a much larger number of training facilities, which presumably offers a greater range of curriculum options. In the Orange County consortium, for example, where three community colleges had previously delivered all of the MDTA training, the prime sponsor is now contracting with four colleges, two regional occupational programs, two school districts, and some private schools.

The increase of individual referrals appears to be contributing to the demise of the skill centers—vocational education institutions established under MDTA to serve manpower enrollees exclusively. Of the 10 areas in the sample that had been using skill centers, 6 had abandoned them by fiscal 1976, citing reasons such as the limited range of courses, high costs, and poor performance.

Some of the conflict between vocational educators and CETA sponsors may arise from differences in strategy and outlook. In many cases, however, sponsors changed classroom training deliverers for other, more political considerations. One factor already mentioned is the propensity of sponsors to operate programs directly. For example, when the Cleveland consortium wanted a second skill-training center, it decided to operate the center directly.

To summarize, the prime sponsor appears to be exerting authority over classroom training of the established vocational agencies in somewhat the same way as it has with the community-based organizations. The result is a dissolution of the near-monopoly previously held by a few educational agencies. However, it seems unlikely that sponsors will attempt to provide technical training on a large scale themselves. For the most part, they are using more training agencies.

EMPLOYMENT SERVICE

CETA has had a greater effect on the organizational relationships of the employment service than on any of the other long-time service deliverers. In the first year of CETA, the employment service lost a significant number of staff jobs previously funded by manpower programs. But more important than its diminished position as one of the delivery agents is its loss of primacy as the manpower planner and the linchpin in manpower operations. Most significant in the long run may be the challenge that CETA presents in terms of the basic labor market mission of the employment service.

It is one of the ironies of public administration that Congress, in reacting to the multiplicity and duplication of manpower programs on the local scene, created a new federal–local system alongside the existing federal–state employment service network established by the Wagner–Peyser Act in 1933. Thus, the stage was again set for competition and duplication.

From its inception in 1933 until the early 1960s, the employment service occupied a major position in manpower affairs. Only in the mid-1960s, with the onset of the War on Poverty, did the hegemony of the employment service begin to be challenged. The Manpower Development and Training Act expanded and preserved the dominant position of the employment service. However, the Economic Opportunity Act of 1964 introduced the Office of Economic Opportunity (OEO) into the manpower arena, challenging existing institutions, including the employment service, for not being responsive to the needs of the disadvantaged. The 1960s were characterized by an explosion of social programs and by bitter bureaucratic struggle among DOL, HEW, and OEO over the manpower components of the Great Society programs. The DOL saw the world through "manpower-colored" glasses; the OEO viewed the same scene through glasses colored "poor" and made its claims accordingly; HEW's focus was practically all-encompassing.

The response of the employment service to the problems of the disadvantaged was mixed. Pressed by the Department of Labor to participate more strongly in manpower programs for the disadvantaged, the employment service found itself faced with a dilemma. If it did not give priority attention to the disadvantaged, it would be accused of being insensitive to those most in need; if it focused its resources on the disadvantaged, this emphasis would be at the expense of its basic mission of matching employer job orders with qualified job applicants. Some ES agencies perceive themselves in the same kind of quandary with CETA manpower programs.

As manpower programs proliferated, ES agencies became increasingly involved in them, until one in every four of their positions was funded from special manpower legislation. The impact of CETA upon the ES agencies as deliverers of manpower services varied considerably among regions and states. Although 80 percent of the prime sponsors used the employment service to some extent, state agency man-years funded for manpower programs declined from the 6,000 positions that had been allocated in fiscal 1974 for MDTA/EOA programs to 4,500 in fiscal 1976 for comparable CETA Title I programs (see Table 25).

In fiscal 1975, the first year of CETA, the level of ES participation in manpower programming under Title I declined about 30 percent from the 1974 level for comparable programs. Fiscal 1976 showed a modest gain, but the number of ES staff-years supported by agreements with prime sponsors under Title I was still about 25 percent below the 1974 level.

This loss was offset to a considerable extent by ES activity under CETA Titles II and VI. However, the gain was confined entirely to balance-of-state areas, in which the local offices were better integrated in the community and where there were fewer alternative deliverers (see Table 26).

TABLE 25 Man Years Contracted by State Employment Security Agencies for CETA Title I, II, and VI Manpower Activities and Payment of Allowances in Fiscal 1974–1976

Fiscal Year	Employment Service			Unemployment Insurance Service[b]	Total
	Title I[a]	Titles II and VI	Special Governor's Grant		
1974	6,002	–	–	678	6,680
1975	4,260	1,033	–	591	5,884
1976	4,543	1,385	338	463	6,729

SOURCE: Employment and Training Administration, U.S. Department of Labor.
[a]Fiscal 1974 includes man years contracted for MDTA and Economic Opportunities Act services; fiscal 1975 and 1976 for CETA prime sponsors.
[b]Payment of allowances.

TABLE 26 Employment Service Man Years Contracted with CETA Prime Sponsors, Fiscal 1975 and 1976[a]

	State/BOS Sponsors		Local Sponsors	
	FY 1975	FY 1976	FY 1975	FY 1976
Title I	2,039	2,253	2,221	2,290
Title II	278	368	85	43
Title VI	461	806	209	168
TOTAL	2,778	3,427	2,515	2,501

SOURCE: Employment and Training Administration, U.S. Department of Labor.
[a]Excludes man years contracted for unemployment insurance service or under state manpower services grants.

As they move toward a comprehensive delivery system and become familiar with the entry–exit functions previously performed by the employment service, prime sponsors have been assuming more of these responsibilities themselves. For example, in 20 of the 28 prime sponsor areas in the sample, the ES either has no role, has a diminished role, or is threatened with declining status and funds.

The explanations for the reduced role of the employment service vary with the respondents. Prime sponsors voiced three basic concerns: (1) limited effectiveness in job placement and OJT referrals, (2) inadequate service to minorities and disadvantaged clientele, and (3) excessive costs, especially for handling allowance payments.

Other respondents suggested additional considerations: (1) lack of interest on the part of some ES offices, (2) empire building by ambitious CETA staff, (3) the influence of other local agencies with politically effective constituencies, and (4) the operation by some sponsors of the entry and exit points of their manpower system as part of an effort to develop a comprehensive system.

There seems to be little doubt that costs have handicapped state employment security agencies in bidding to perform CETA services. The employment service has fixed costs that are often higher than those of private or nonprofit agencies. The cost for handling training allowances through the unemployment insurance system was frequently not competitive with charges made by other deliverers. It is not clear, however, that services are always comparable. Nevertheless, because of such cost differences, the number of man-years contracted for this activity dropped about 30 percent over 2 years.

State ES agencies used widely different cost approaches and different pricing strategies, depending upon whether they wanted to maximize or minimize their CETA involvement. To a considerable extent, their interest depended on their perception of how participation would affect their placement performance, upon which local ES budgets are allocated to a large degree.

The evidence on whether the ES has been diligent or effective in serving the disadvantaged is mixed. The diminished role of the ES was due in some measure to the decisions of sponsors to participate more in placement and on-the-job training. In four instances, the prime sponsor was dissatisfied with the quality of ES staff assigned to handle CETA placements. Dissatisfaction was also evident in other areas (Chester, Lansing, and Raleigh), where the sponsors took over the placement function, and six other sponsors seemed to be moving in the same direction. Similarly, several sponsors felt that they could do a better job of handling on-the-job training than the employment service.

However, not all sponsor placement activity is attributable to the ES inadequacies. In San Joaquin, for example, the employment service had the best performance of any program operator. In Ramsey, the sponsor added its own staff to work on placements with ES staff, not necessarily because the employment service performed poorly, but to do a "more coordinated" job. Transfers of responsibilities have occurred in the smaller counties, cities, and consortia. In larger urban areas, such as New York, Cleveland, Philadelphia, and Orange County, the ES role was limited from the beginning.

On the whole, the employment service has fared better with BOS prime sponsors than with local sponsors, but not as well as might have been expected. As the manpower agency with a statewide network of local offices, it could have been designated by the governor as the deliverer of manpower services in all of the BOS areas. In some instances, that has happened. But in other states several factors operate to inhibit the governors from using their authority to press for the use of the ES.

First, governors are inclined to be responsive to the wishes of local elected officials. Because the BOS programs are almost always decentralized, it is awkward for governors to insist on the use of the ES if local authorities prefer their own systems. Second, many ES agencies have used the unique character of the federal–state system to achieve a large measure of independence by citing federal law to the governor and state law to federal officials. As a consequence of this "arm's length" relationship, the state ES agency was frequently not part of the governor's immediate family and was treated accordingly. In Texas and North Carolina, for example, the governors bypassed the employment service in assigning responsibility for the statewide BOS program. Texas has, however, come to the aid of the ES at the local level through ingenious methods. In fiscal 1975, the state used its special state funds under Section 103(e) of the act to contract with the employment service to develop jobs for CETA clients. In 1977 the state was to use this money to finance the state ES agency to provide a free allowance payment system to all local sponsors in the state. This proposal was to free local prime sponsor administrative funds and, by taking advantage of economies of scale, provide checks weekly rather than biweekly. However, despite these services, CETA has been a losing game for the Texas employment service. CETA-funded man-years dropped from 368 in 1974 to 285 in 1975 and to 217 in 1976.

In Arizona, the state department of economic security moved aggressively to carve out a role for the local ES office. In 1976, it assigned responsibility to the employment service for all intake, assesment, selection and referral, placement, and follow-up. This arrangement was extended for fiscal 1977, but the decision ran into strong local opposition. One letter from a council of governments declared: "Our elected officials are opposed to the process that was used in the development of such a policy. . . . [T]o arbitrarily change from an existing system to a new one is not in the best interest of the clients or the sponsor. We have reviewed the Balance of State Manpower Planning Council minutes and can find no indication that this matter was ever discussed or considered."

There is little evidence to suggest that prime sponsors systematically employed objective performance criteria in choosing program deliverers. There was, in the first year, neither the time, the capability, nor reliable program data for making comparisons. It is clear, however, that the role of the ES in manpower programs has been seriously affected by the shift of authority from federal to state and local levels. The challenge is more serious now than it was during the antipoverty era of the 1960s. The issue is no longer limited to services for the disadvantaged and the challengers now are politically potent elected officials.

The erosion of the ES role in manpower programs is particularly awkward for the Department of Labor, which, as parent to both ES and CETA, must balance its responsibility to protect the autonomy of the prime sponsor and its obligation to ensure the maximum feasible use of the ES as an established manpower institution. Testifying at House oversight committee hearings on the employment security system in June 1976 and again at House oversight committee hearings on CETA in September 1976, then Assistant Secretary William Kolberg appeared to move toward re-establishing the position of the ES in this sphere of operations: " . . . in the long run, it is clearly not desirable, and resources will not permit, funding of the ES and CETA prime sponsors to provide the same services in the same area to the same individuals. Accordingly, we . . . [are making efforts] to identify areas for improvement in the ES, to avoid funding duplicative and overlapping services."[9] Kolberg stated that the department intended to examine sponsors' reasons for not using the employment service in order to rectify deficiencies and thus presumably eliminate any legitimate reasons for sponsors to choose other deliverers.

During the first year of CETA, the extent to which the Employment and Training Administration intervened on behalf of the employment service varied among regional offices. Some, mindful of the decentralizing thrust of CETA, assumed a "hands-off" attitude. Others, more concerned with the fate of the employment service, actively intervened, pushing reluctant ES agencies on one hand and nudging hesitant prime sponsors on the other. In the second year, there was much more consistent and concerted effort to buttress the employment service. In July 1976, regional administrators were requested to urge state agencies to offer "direct placement" services to sponsors at no cost and to review critically any

---

[9]Statement of William Kolberg, in U.S. Congress, House, Committee on Education and Labor, *Oversight Hearings on the Comprehensive Employment and Training Act*, Before the Subcommittee on Manpower, Compensation, and Health and Safety, 94th Congress, 2nd Session, September 29, 1976, p. 752.

prime sponsor plans that did not propose to accept the proffered services.[10]

Opposition to this approach was voiced by some ES agencies that did not see their best interests served by this kind of policy and, more importantly, by prime sponsors who viewed it as an intrusion on their freedom to select agencies to provide manpower services. A compromise was developed by an advisory committee of CETA directors, which recommended that "ETA should not restrict the types of services which prime sponsors may contract from ES, nor should it mandate an exclusive right to the ES for placement activity in a local area."[11]

The Emergency Jobs Programs Extension Act of 1976, which extended the public service employment programs under Title VI, afforded a new opportunity to increase ES participation in CETA. The ETA has proposed that the employment service furnish to the prime sponsor without cost: (a) a pool of potential applicants for the enlarged Title VI program (the ES is in a unique position to do this, since the eligibility requirements of the new legislation are tied to the welfare and UI status of applicants, and this information is in the UI and WIN records of the ES offices); and (b) certification of individual eligibility, including the application of the required family income test. Under this arrangement, the prime sponsor would not be held responsible for any errors in certification. In return, the employment service would receive from the prime sponsor all job orders for the newly created Title VI positions and receive budget credit for placements made. Although this proposal, too, infringed on the decision-making authority of prime sponsors, the majority of prime sponsors accepted the offer of cooperation by the employment service.

SUMMARY

Against the anticipation that earlier fragmented programs would be rearranged under CETA into a comprehensive system that would

---

[10]Telegraphic Message, Floyd E. Edwards, Employment and Training Administration, to All Regional Administrators, July 16, 1976. "Direct placements" are defined as participants placed in unsubsidized employment after receiving only outreach, intake, and job referral services from the CETA program.

[11]Directors' Work Group Meeting Synopsis, Notes on a meeting of the CETA Directors' Work Group, Washington, D.C., September 15, 16, 1976, Department of Labor (unpublished).

centralize responsibility, reduce duplication, and offer participants greater program options, the study finds that:

• One-third of the local sponsors studied have adopted a comprehensive delivery system for Title I programs; one-quarter have a mixed system; the remaining 40 percent have retained categorical delivery arrangements. In general, smaller cities and counties have been more likely to move to comprehensive systems; larger urban areas and consortia in particular have tended to retain the categorical structure or to adopt mixed systems. Categorical programs may permit better understanding of the special problems of a particular target group and continuity in handling clients; these must be balanced against the advantages of closer program control, uniform standards, and reduction of duplication and fragmentation that are inherent in integration and centralization.

• As part of the trend toward integration, almost half the local sponsors in the sample have moved to centralize the entry facilities for the Title I program and bring them under the control of a single agency. There has also been some movement, but not as much, to centralize exit functions. However, there is little or no coordination between employability development programs of Title I and the public service employment program under Titles II and VI. Nor is there movement of applicants between programs, even in areas where a common intake center registers applicants for both PSE and Title I.

• One of the most striking results of local decision making is the expanding role of the prime sponsor as a direct program operator. More than half of all sponsors are reported to be delivering intake and/or placement services in Title I programs. Within the sample, 16 of 23 local sponsors reported that they were directly operating some aspect of the program. Many of these sponsors have concluded that centralization of delivery services can best be accomplished through their own organizations.

• The funding of the major community-based organizations more than doubled from 1974 to 1976—more than the relative increase in total Title I funds. However, curtailment of some of their independence and range of services has given rise to a feeling of uncertainty about their future.

• The near-monopoly of skill training previously held by public vocational education agencies has been dissipated as sponsors have shifted decisively to the use of a larger number of different types of training institutions and to greater use of individual referrals.

• The ES role in manpower programs and, even more broadly, its basic mission have been challenged by the emergence of CETA as a federal–local manpower system with parallel and sometimes competing functions. Prime sponsors increasingly are performing some of the traditional labor exchange functions of the employment service, particularly applicant intake and job placement.

7 Public Service Employment

Since the Work Projects Administration (WPA) in the mid-1930s, the United States has had relatively little experience with programs under which the government assumes responsibility for creating jobs for individuals unable to obtain employment in the private economy. Until the early 1960s, direct government intervention in the job market had been deemed appropriate only in times of crisis. The federal government influenced the demand for labor only indirectly, through monetary and fiscal policies.

In the 1960s, a confluence of economic and social forces brought changes in this view. It became apparent that even in good times there were people and places that did not share in the general affluence. There was growing demand for government actions to revitalize the economy of depressed areas and to assist in the readjustment of workers displaced by automation. Pressures for civil rights and social equality focused attention on barriers in the job market for groups such as youth, women, minorities, older workers, and the poorly educated.

Identification of these structural problems led to special government efforts to supplement monetary and fiscal policies designed to stimulate economic growth. One remedy proposed was federally subsidized public employment. The public sector was viewed as a possible pacesetter for hiring those who have difficulty obtaining jobs. It was presumed that with supplementary training or other assistance those persons could eventually be absorbed into unsubsidized employment. Prospects for transferring into regular public employment seemed good since state and local government employment had been growing steadily. Another type of public employment—work experience, which involved tasks that could be performed by the least skilled at the minimum wage level—also afforded some preparation for regular employment.

EARLY STEPS

The programs of the 1960s were tentative in their approach to employment of the disadvantaged in the public sector. Through the Neighborhood Youth Corps (NYC) and Operation Mainstream programs, jobs created for low-income youth and for chronically unemployed workers served both economic and social purposes. Although the contribution of these programs in terms of employability development has been questioned, they achieved other objectives. The NYC programs were designed mainly to enable disadvantaged youth to stay in or return to school by offering them supplemental income as well as work experience and job market orientation. It was expected that NYC would also help to defuse tensions in the inner cities. Mainstream was a relatively small-scale program designed to give jobs to disadvantaged elderly workers. These programs became mainly vehicles for income maintenance. The Public Service Careers program attempted to provide training and develop career ladders for the disadvantaged in the public sector, but this small program proved expensive, difficult, and not very successful in securing commitments from employing agencies.

In the 1970s, there was renewed interest in job creation programs on a large scale as a countercyclical strategy. An attempt in 1970 to include such programs in a comprehensive manpower act was vetoed by President Nixon, who described public service employment as "dead end jobs in the public sector."[1]

However, in the following year, the Emergency Employment Act (EEA) was passed and approved by the President, with the understanding that jobs created would be "transitional," that is, temporary jobs leading to unsubsidized employment. The EEA, which became known as the Public Employment Program (PEP), authorized $2.25 billion for a 2-year period. Rapidly mounted and effectively managed, this program created 175,000 jobs at its peak.

When attention turned to the need for a comprehensive reform of the manpower system in 1973, the earlier differences between Congress and the administration reappeared. There was general consensus on the need

[1]Roger H. Davidson, *The Politics of Comprehensive Manpower Legislation,* Policy Studies in Employment and Welfare no. 15, Baltimore: Johns Hopkins University Press, 1972, p. 66.

for manpower reform legislation. However, Congress insisted on the inclusion of a significant public service employment component and the administration opposed it on the grounds that it would result in make-work jobs.

CETA LEGISLATION

CETA was a compromise. Through it, manpower programs were decentralized, and only that section of the EEA that provided for public service jobs in areas with lingering pockets of high unemployment (6.5 percent or more) was incorporated into the act (Title II). A program participant was expected to use a CETA job as a stepping-stone to unsubsidized employment. Like its PEP predecessor, Title II was open to all unemployed, although it urged special consideration to those most disadvantaged in terms of duration of unemployment and employment prospects.

But the modest funding of Title II was inadequate to deal with the deepening recession and the highest unemployment rates in more than 30 years. In December 1974, Congress hastily passed the Emergency Jobs and Unemployment Assistance Act. This law authorized a $2.5 billion countercyclical public service employment program (CETA Title VI).[2]

Title VI differed from Title II in several respects. It extended public service employment programs to all areas, not just those with substantial unemployment. In addition to those who were given preference in Title II (Vietnam veterans, former manpower trainees, and the long-term unemployed), persons who had exhausted unemployment insurance or who were not eligible for UI benefits were to receive preferred consideration. To encourage rapid implementation, Congress relaxed the requirement that sponsors attempt to find jobs for participants in unsubsidized employment. Placement was to be considered only as a goal that could be waived; indeed, more than 90 percent of all sponsors requested and received waivers. With a decline in the growth of employment, sponsors argued, they could not ensure openings in unsubsidized government or private sector jobs. Thus, one of the major objectives of public service employment—to provide a bridge to permanent employment—was sacrificed to encourage speedy implementation.

[2]The Emergency Jobs and Unemployment Assistance Act also authorized special unemployment assistance benefits for unemployed workers not eligible for unemployment compensation and a 1-year program of financial assistance to create jobs through public works in areas of severe unemployment.

Title VI was originally authorized for 1 year, with the expectation that unemployment would recede and the program could be phased out. A Department of Labor spokesman appearing before a Senate subcommittee in April 1976 stated that the recession had hit bottom and a substantial recovery was under way.

Because a supplemental appropriation for Title II enacted at the end of fiscal 1976 was expected to carry both titles through fiscal 1977, no new funds were requested for PSE for fiscal 1977. However, by fall 1976, it was apparent to the administration and Congress that the pace of economic recovery would be slower than expected.

With unemployment again on the rise, in September 1976 Congress passed the Emergency Jobs Programs Extension Act, which extended Title VI through fiscal 1977. With that act, Congress also attempted to correct some shortcomings in the public service employment program. It attempted to contain substitution of federal for local funds by directing that funds allocated above the amount needed to sustain existing levels of Title VI enrollment be used for special projects, i.e., activities of limited duration that are not part of the regular public service structure. It also sought to redirect the program toward those people most in need by requiring that half of any Title VI vacancies, as well as all project-created jobs, be filled with long-term, low-income unemployed persons or welfare recipients.

The Title VI extension also raised the proportion allowable for administrative costs from 10 to 15 percent, making it easier for sponsors to acquire equipment and materials and to rent suitable facilities. These provisions, however, were not accompanied by additional funds; Congress appropriated only enough money to sustain until early 1977 the Title II and VI PSE employees already on board.

The Carter Administration's economic stimulus legislation of May 1977 drastically altered the situation by providing an additional $6.6 billion for fiscal 1977 and fiscal 1978, most of which was to be used for special projects. The number of jobs funded under Titles II and VI was expected to rise from the fiscal 1976 level of about 300,000 to 725,000 by early 1978. In its sixth year, the public sector job program was expanding again, with broadened objectives.

Other legislation affecting public sector employment included the Public Works Employment Act of 1976, which authorized funds for public works projects. That act also made available antirecession funds to help local governments maintain public services. With special revenue-sharing funds to sustain their regular employment levels, localities were expected to use CETA funds to create additional positions.

IMPLEMENTATION

The initial Title II grants were funded during summer 1974, but only about 56,000 persons were enrolled at the end of the second quarter in December 1974—far below the level needed if both fiscal 1974 and 1975 Title II appropriations were to be spent before the end of the fiscal year.[3] The buildup was hampered by confusion over transition requirements as well as the newness of the CETA system. Local governments were eager for funds but concerned about the commitments the funds entailed.

However, Title VI, enacted in December 1974, was implemented speedily. By the end of January 1975, 98 percent of the initial grants had been signed and hiring had begun in about 70 percent of the jurisdictions. Combined employment under the two titles rose rapidly, reaching over 275,000 by June 1975 (see Figure 6).

However, prime sponsors still carried over into fiscal 1976 almost half ($750 million) of available Title II and VI funds. Under DOL prodding, enrollments rose to about 340,000 in spring 1976 and many sponsors exhausted their Title VI allotments. Since the initial 1-year authorization for Title VI funds had expired and the administration was not, at that time, seeking renewal, those sponsors were permitted to shift enrollees to Title II to avoid layoffs.[4]

Their difficulties were aptly summarized by one CETA administrator: "The problem is that the federal government is undecided about whether to continue PSE or not—and so local governments don't know which way to jump." Some jurisdictions feared that they might become too dependent on the federal government and began planning to phase out their program. Others, plagued by fiscal problems, embraced the CETA public service employment program wholeheartedly, hoping to embed CETA so deeply in their revenue structure that it would be difficult to extract.

PUBLIC SERVICE JOBS

The regulations implementing Title VI encouraged prime sponsors to share job allotments with other governmental and private nonprofit agencies within their jurisdictions.[5] One of the early decisions that a sponsor had to make was how many of its allotted job openings to retain

[3]Much of the information in this section is derived from the *Employment and Training Report of the President*, 1976, p. 97, and the *Manpower Report of the President*, 1974, pp. 152–153.
[4]See Chapter 4 for a discussion of this period.
[5]This section deals with local prime sponsors only.

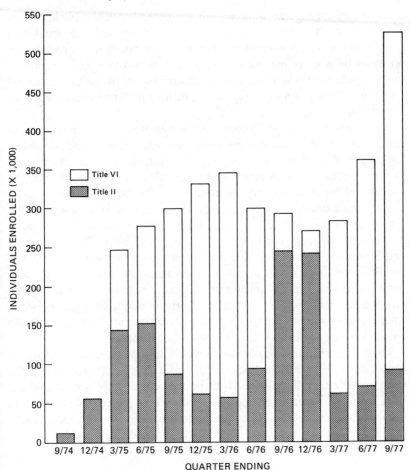

SOURCE: Based on Data from Employment and Training Administration

FIGURE 6 Trends in public service employment under CETA, 1974–1977.

and how many to distribute to other organizations. Assigning slots to outsiders had both advantages and disadvantages. Sponsors that limited additions to their own payroll minimized the need for firing participants or the difficulties of absorbing the PSE activity when the program ended. On the other hand, assigning slots elsewhere could mean foregoing fiscal relief and/or the local governmental services that PSE participants could provide.

CETA jobs allotted to other groups were thought to be less likely to be used to replace regular workers. On the other hand, the likelihood of obtaining unsubsidized jobs for enrollees was considered to be smaller in private nonprofit agencies than in public agencies. The distribution of positions between public sector and private nonprofit agencies assumed more significance when the Carter Administration more than doubled the level of the program through the economic stimulus legislation of May 1977.

The study found that decisions to assign positions to public or to private nonprofit agencies were associated with three related variables: the degree of fiscal pressure, the size of the jurisdiction, and the identity of the principal CETA decision maker. As discussed in Chapter 3, the greater the fiscal stringency, the more likely the elected official is to be the principal decision maker; and fiscal pressure is most severe in the largest urban areas. Thus, in New York, Philadelphia, and Cleveland, elected officials make CETA decisions; while in Topeka, Chester County, and Stanislaus County, areas that had relatively little fiscal pressure, PSE decision making was left largely to the CETA staff. During fiscal 1976, large jurisdictions in the study sample gave less than 15 percent of the allotted positions to federal, state, and private nonprofit agencies, while smaller, more affluent areas, where decisions are more likely to be made by CETA staff, gave away nearly one-third (see Table 27).

These patterns are also consistent with findings concerning the use of Title I funds for public service employment. Ten local sponsors in the study sample used Title I funds for public service employment in fiscal 1976; of these, seven were in jurisdictions where the elected official was the sole decision maker. All of the largest jurisdictions and those under extreme financial pressure used Title I funds for public service employment.

UNION CONCERNS

Organized labor has been an influential and consistent supporter of public service employment legislation, insisting, however, on adequate job safeguards for regular public sector employees. As a consequence, the legislation prohibits the use of CETA participants if regular employees have been laid off from the same or similar positions; it also limits PSE jobs to entry-level positions.

The issues that have most concerned public service employee unions are layoffs and rehires. In New York City, the union exerted considerable pressure to change the sponsor's policies so that regular

TABLE 27 Percentage of CETA Title II and Title VI Positions Allotted
to Federal, State, and Nonprofit Agencies, Sample Local Prime Sponsors,
Fiscal 1976

Selected Characteristics of Prime Sponsor Jurisdictions	Average Percent of CETA Positions Allotted by Local Sponsors to Federal, State, and Nonprofit Agencies[a]
Degree of fiscal pressure[b]	
Extreme (N = 3)	3
Moderate (N = 14)	18
Little or none (N = 4)	35
Identity of principal decision maker	
Elected official alone (N = 9)	13
Elected official and CETA staff (N = 6)	18
CETA staff (N = 6)	29
Size of jurisdiction	
Large (1 million population and over) (N = 4)	5
Medium (300,000 to 1 million) (N = 8)	15
Small (under 300,000) (N = 9)	29

[a]Average of percents of the sponsors in each group.
[b]Fiscal pressure refers to the financial position of the major unit of government, based on revenues, expenditures, and other relevant information.

workers would receive preference over CETA employees in layoffs and rehires.[6] The unions in Philadelphia did not intervene in CETA operations unless layoffs were involved, and in Cleveland the unions were satisfied with the sponsor's policy under which regular public service employees were rehired.

There were scattered union complaints in other survey areas. In Phoenix, union representatives on the planning council protested to the DOL regional office that plans for Titles II and VI had not been submitted to the council and that the sponsor was not making adequate efforts to facilitate the transition of CETA employees to regular positions. In St. Paul and in Middlesex County, union representatives were concerned that some CETA enrollees were being hired above entry level. In other places, unions complained that existing standards were being undercut. By contrast, unions in some jurisdictions welcomed CETA, because it provided an opportunity to enlarge their membership.

Membership on the planning council offers public sector unions the best position from which to monitor PSE activities, but for the most part

[6]See David R. Zimmerman, "The Impact of Public Sector Employment on Public Sector Labor Relations," In James L. Stern and Barbara D. Dennis, eds., *Proceedings of the Twenty-Eighth Annual Winter Meeting, December 1975*, pp. 171–178, Madison, Wis.: Industrial Relations Research Association, 1976.

TABLE 28 Percentage Distribution of Public Service Employment by Function: CETA, Emergency Employment Act, and Total State and Local Government Employment

Function	CETA FY 1975 Title II	CETA FY 1975 Title VI	Emergency Employment Act FY 1972-1973	Total State and Local Government Employment, October 1975[a]
Education	17	10	20	49
Public works and transportation[b]	19	25	22	11
Law enforcement[c]	12	11	12	7
Health and hospital service	8	7	9	11
Parks and recreation	9	8	8	2
Social services[d]	9	6	6	3
Environmental quality[e]	3	3	4	2
Fire protection	2	1	2	2
Administration and miscellaneous[f]	21	29	17	13
ALL FUNCTIONS	100	100	100	100

SOURCES: Employment and Training Administration, U.S. Department of Labor (unpublished data); U.S. Bureau of the Census, *Public Employment in 1975*, GE 75 No. 1, page 3.

[a] Full-time equivalent.
[b] Highways, sewerage, sanitation, water supply, and other local utilities.
[c] Police protection and corrections.
[d] Public welfare.
[e] Natural resources.
[f] General control, financial administration, employment security, and all other.

union representatives on the councils tended to come from unions in the private sector. Relationships between these two groups are not necessarily close. In Middlesex County, for example, a representative of a steelworkers' union district office was chairman of the public employment subcommittee, but no public service employee union had approached him to discuss the sponsor's CETA plans.

Even in Lansing, where a large percentage of government workers are covered by collective bargaining, the four union representatives on the council represent workers from the private sector. A public sector union representative who was not on the planning council handled negotiations with employing establishments to give PSE workers the same protection as employees under collective bargaining agreements with respect to probationary period, seniority, promotions, reductions in force, and other provisions.

TYPES OF JOBS

The key decision maker generally selected the agencies to receive PSE positions, a process that in turn identified the kinds of jobs to be filled. Table 28 compares the distribution of CETA enrollees by function with that of regular public sector employment. The most dramatic difference is in education, which employed 49 percent of all state and local government workers but only 15 percent of CETA workers. The opposite was true of public works and transportation and parks and recreation activities. Here the proportion of CETA jobs was much higher than the corresponding proportions of all state and local public sector employment. These are activities with a lower claim on local government resources and therefore more readily expanded when extra funds become available. The proportion of CETA jobs in administration and miscellaneous activities was also higher and includes some positions assigned to CETA staff, a category that has no parallel in the regular public sector. Many sponsors also allocated slots to subcontractors, a practice that helped them to reduce administrative costs.

The pattern of CETA–PSE jobs by function resembled closely that created under EEA. The principal differences are comparatively fewer jobs in education and more jobs in administration and miscellaneous services.

Some sponsors had a definite strategy in distributing slots among agencies (and indirectly among job categories); others did not. For example, the Phoenix–Maricopa consortium and Ramsey County distributed dollars widely. St. Paul, on the other hand, concentrated on the "have not" agencies and assigned proportionately more slots for such human services as health and recreation. Topeka adopted a distribution policy calculated to encourage transition; initially, each employing agency received a few positions, but only those that absorbed the participants into regular employment were given additional CETA employees.

Calhoun and Lorain counties reported an emphasis on low-wage, low-skill jobs, which they believed would be easier to terminate when funds were exhausted. Gary and Philadelphia, on the other hand, assigned slots within a broad range of services to relieve fiscal pressures.

Most participants were engaged in activities ordinarily performed by the employing agency. The original CETA regulations for Title VI encouraged prime sponsors "to develop large, labor intensive employment projects which provide immediate jobs for a maximum number of participants." Projects were defined at that time as activities of limited duration that would use participants to meet "additional" community needs. Some sponsors in the sample tended to refer to any seasonal or short-term maintenance activity as a project. Others considered a new service to be a special project—drug diversion, for example, although, once adopted, it might be expected to continue.

Despite national policy, project activities in fiscal 1975 and 1976 were few and modest except for maintenance work and some new services. The most common of these were bicentennial projects that employed one or two persons to serve as local staff. The Maine BOS cooperated with the Community Services Administration in supporting a project to winterize homes of low-income families. CETA participants in other projects rehabilitated public or low-income housing. In St. Paul, unemployed union construction workers were hired for this purpose; CETA paid the first $10,000 of their wages, and the public housing agency provided the rest.

Sponsors reported other PSE activities that had some noteworthy features. Union County used Title I funds to train persons as drivers who were then hired by the Red Cross under its allocation of Title VI funds. This is the only example of linkage between Titles I and PSE programs that surfaced in the study. In the Lansing consortium, in fact, the Urban League complained that their Title I trainees were being denied access to Title II or VI jobs.

In several instances, PSE participants helped to increase local revenues. For example, the district attorney's office in one jurisdiction was using PSE participants to locate fathers of AFDC families who might be able to provide family support.

Under CETA, the original emphasis was on placing participants in occupations likely to expand within the private or public sector. However, the jobs were to be at the entry level and not more than one-third were to be in professions. The $10,000 yearly salary ceiling also limited the range of occupations. A broad spectrum of occupations was reported in the sample, with the heaviest concentrations in the laborer, clerical, and semiskilled categories.

Kansas City estimated its PSE jobs as 30 percent unskilled, 50 percent clerical or semiskilled, and the balance as skilled, professional, or technical. The Pinellas–St. Petersburg occupational mix was described as 50 percent unskilled, 40 percent semiskilled, and 10 percent professional. Jobs in Topeka were "mostly in the laboring and clerical categories." Gary reported that virtually all jobs were low-pay, low-skill jobs, because few of the participants in Gary possessed advanced skills. In Union County, clerks and laborers comprised the bulk of the PSE work force, with a few professionals in education and social services. Lorain County reported 35 percent laboring jobs, 25 percent clerical, 20 percent semiskilled, 10 percent protective services, and the rest professional. San Joaquin used CETA participants in a wide range of jobs "from laborers to attorneys," with about 20 percent in the professional and skilled categories.

Seventy-five percent of the CETA participants filling these jobs had at least a high school education. Many had college degrees. Unpublished data from the continuous longitudinal manpower study sample shows 16 percent of all CETA participants in public employment had 4 or more years of education after high school.

WORK EXPERIENCE

CETA permits the use of Title II and VI funds for employability development activities normally provided under Title I. Initially, some prime sponsors used Title VI funds to support work experience programs in order to take advantage of the less stringent requirements governing work experience. Ten percent of all Title II and VI slots at the end of June 1976 were categorized as work experience. Some sponsors were attracted by the lower wage rates, others by the freedom to use a larger proportion of the budget for administrative costs.

In the early months of the PSE program, some DOL regional offices encouraged sponsors to take the more rapid work experience route, when it looked as though hiring for regular PSE jobs might be bogged down.

The DOL subsequently required that these jobs be switched over to regular public service employment.[7] Some sponsors in the sample reported that Title II and VI funds were still used occasionally for work experience in private nonprofit agencies and in public sector activities employing youth and senior citizens. One consortium classified its Title VI jobs as work experience in order to avoid liability for unemployment compensation. In the Austin (Capital Area) consortium, work experience funds were shifted to public sector on-the-job training. Employing agencies paid the total wage and CETA paid only the training costs. In all, 4 of the 24 local sponsors in the sample reported that they used work experience under Titles II or VI in fiscal 1976.

WHO GETS SELECTED AND HOW

Since funds for public service employment under CETA are limited, only a fraction of the unemployed and underemployed can be accommodated. There are social arguments in favor of selecting applicants who would have poor prospects of obtaining employment on their own because of personal limitations such as lack of skill or inadequate education or because of external barriers. Indeed, an objective of both Title II and Title VI is to improve the participants' employability and access to jobs. Moreover, the inflationary effects of federally subsidized public employment may be mitigated and pressure on the wage structure reduced if less skilled, lower paid workers are selected, rather than the more highly qualified, who are likely to be in greater demand in the private sector.

During the first 2 years of CETA, however, three-fourths of the participants had at least a high school education and most were of prime working age. Some of the reasons are obvious. First, the types of jobs available controlled selection of participants to some degree. Second, employing agencies selected the most desirable applicant whenever they could. Public officials in small communities were even more selective, because they had few jobs to fill. In a small town in Maine, for example, CETA funds paid for one position, a full-time police officer for a third shift, and, as an observer noted, "one person symbolizes the entire CETA program."

The program structure also affects the kinds of people selected for public service employment. The coexistence of an employability development program (Title I) and a job creation program (Titles II and

[7]In spring 1977, DOL again encouraged sponsors to use the work experience approach in planning the projects required under the act that extended Title VI.

VI) has resulted in the prime sponsors' commonly referring the more qualified unemployed to PSE jobs and the less advantaged to Title I programs. A comparison of the characteristics of Title I with Title II and VI participants suggests how pervasive this practice is.

HIRING PROCEDURES

As might be expected, the nature of the hiring procedure influences who gets hired. Early in the implementation stages of Title II, sponsors selected participants carefully with the likelihood that many would have to be absorbed into regular employment. During the big push in the spring of 1975, shortly after enactment of Title VI, the pressure for rapid hiring was so great that employing agencies were permitted considerable freedom in recruiting and hiring. Several sponsors reported that the use of job fairs enabled them to fill their openings in a very short time. The large numbers of job seekers attending provided employing agencies with a wide selection opportunity.

Once the 1975 recruitment crisis passed, most sponsors centralized Title VI intake, screening, and referral procedures. This enabled them to exercise more control. Among local sponsors in the sample, only Cook County and Lorain County still permitted employing agencies and subjurisdictions to do their own recruiting and screening as well as hiring in fiscal year 1976. Typically, the intake system was operated by the prime sponsor or the employment service. Applicants were screened for eligibility and then referred to the local government personnel office or directly to the employing agency. However, even if an outside agency such as the employment service received, screened, and referred applicants, there were charges that employing agencies were preselecting employees.

A central intake system was used in some cases as a means of controlling the types of enrollees under Titles II and VI. Middlesex County kept a roster of potential candidates; CETA staff selected applicants for specific job orders in accordance with significant-segment and affirmative-action criteria and matched job specifications with the qualifications of applicants. If an employing agency rejected the candidate referred without good reason, no further referrals were made.

In other places, a central intake procedure was used in the selection and referral of participants, but final selection was left to the employing unit. In Pasco County, ES referral slips accompanying the applicant indicated to the employer the rating of the applicant in terms of priority for service. New York City reported that it recruited initially through its CETA neighborhood centers, using the same selection criteria as those for

Title I. Lansing continuously monitored the characteristics of participants, and, if one target group was underrepresented, employers were asked, although not required, to consider more applicants from that group. San Joaquin developed a point system of rating applicants that incorporated factors such as veteran status, eligibility for unemployment compensation, income, education, and age. However, agencies still selected the best qualified referrals. At two sites, staff reported an interest on the part of public sector employers in adding minority (though not necessarily otherwise disadvantaged) persons to their rolls to improve their affirmative-action positions.

No sponsor in the sample indicated that merit or civil service systems presented obstacles to hiring. Many of the smaller jurisdictions used no merit system. Larger jurisdictions with civil service systems hired employees as temporary or provisional workers or as trainees. This usually meant that they received the same or similar wages and fringe benefits as regular workers but did not acquire civil service status.

Overt political intervention in the hiring process did occur, but not often. In one large city, there were allegations of political intervention in hiring, and four other places reported minor patronage incidents. The nature of the hiring procedures made it fairly easy to exercise political influence in the regular hiring process. Sponsors who used their own staff rather than the employment service to determine eligibility and make referrals may have been more susceptible to this type of pressure. However, one CETA administrator reported, "It's so clean here it squeaks."

On the whole, the evidence suggests that the individuals hired were relatively well qualified. There were several reasons: The nature of the jobs attracted well-qualified people, the employing agency usually had a choice of several persons for each job, and sponsors did not insist on priority to those with relatively greater needs. For the most part, jurisdictions simply hired as they would have in the absence of CETA, with similar procedures, standards, and results.

DURATION OF EMPLOYMENT

One of the advantages of public service employment is the experience and work history that continuous employment confers on the participant. But incentives for both the worker and the employer frequently result in the retention of participants in subsidized employment for longer than necessary to develop such experience. Although the average

TABLE 29   Labor Force Status of Terminees by Time
Spent in the Public Employment Program

	Percent Employed 1 Month Post-PEP		
Months in PEP	Total	Public Sector	Private Sector
Less than 2	55	17	38
2-3	65	31	34
4-6	71	40	31
7-9	73	45	28
10-12	78	54	24
13-18	77	59	18

SOURCE: Unpublished data from a sample survey of PEP
participants conducted by Westat, Inc., 1972-1973.

stay is about 8 months, according to the DOL, some PSE enrollees date
back to the "PEP generation" of 1971–1973.[8]

Limited resources in relation to the universe of need suggest that PSE
participants should move into unsubsidized employment as rapidly as
possible, but there are at present no limits on the length of time a person
remains in the program.

The PEP experience suggests that the longer an individual stays on a
subsidized job, the less likely he or she is to move into private sector
employment and the more likely to be placed in the public sector (see
Table 29). Information has not yet been accumulated for a corresponding analysis of postprogram labor force experience of CETA participants.

JOB CREATION

The effectiveness of a public service employment program lies in its
ability to create job opportunities, over and above the number that state
and local governments would have maintained without federal funds.
Hence the CETA legislation includes a maintenance-of-effort provision
that prohibits prime sponsors from substituting federal for local funds.
Since considerable confusion surrounds the concepts of "maintenance of
effort," "substitution," and "job creation," these terms are defined below
for purposes of the discussion that follows.

[8]The average length of stay of terminees in the PEP program was reported to be 13.4
months. See U.S. Department of Labor, Office of Manpower Program Evaluation,
*Longitudinal Evaluation of the Public Employment Program and Validation of the PEP Data
Bank*, PB-242 779-SET/ST (1 vol., 9 vols. appendixes), Prepared by Westat, Inc., Rockville,
Md., April 1975 (available from NTIS).

Maintenance of effort refers to the act's requirement that local governments, as a condition for receiving federal grants to hire CETA employees, must maintain the level of regular public service employment they would have had without CETA. Maintenance of effort is not identified simply by changes in employment levels. If local public service employment would have increased because of greater demand for services or more local revenues, the rise in employment should equal what would have occurred, plus CETA employees. On the other hand, if local employment would have decreased, the decline should be less than what would have occurred by an amount equal to the number of CETA participants.

Substitution is the converse of maintenance of effort; it implies the use of federal funds to pay the salaries of state or local public service employees who, in the absence of CETA, would have been paid from local revenues. Substitution may take two forms:

1. *Direct Substitution.* The most obvious is the replacement of regular workers with CETA participants in order to reduce local expenditures: e.g., (a) laying off regular employees who would not otherwise be terminated and replacing them with CETA workers doing the same or similar work, (b) laying off regular employees and rehiring them on the CETA payroll, (c) using CETA employees for work normally performed by contractors, or (d) filling vacancies with CETA employees rather than with regular employees. Rehiring laid-off regular employees with CETA funds is not in itself evidence of substitution. It depends on whether the separations were caused by inadequate revenue or whether they were "paper layoffs" in anticipation of receiving CETA funds. The former case is justified; the latter would be a violation of the maintenance-of-effort requirement.

2. *Budget Substitution* can occur through (a) reducing tax effort (or failing to increase it) in order to use CETA funds to maintain the existing level of public service, (b) failing to budget for expenditures normally supported by local taxes and using CETA to replace these funds, or (c) juggling local funds among accounts to create the appearance of maintaining effort in some departments in order to justify the use of CETA funds.

Net job creation refers to employment generated by CETA above the normal complement of workers. It occurs where the local government maintains or increases the number of regular public service employees and hires CETA employees as well. It may also occur in a contracting situation, where layoffs or a hiring freeze are unavoidable. In such case, the use of CETA funds to rehire regular employees or to fill vacancies that may not otherwise have been filled would constitute job creation, even if local public employment levels have not increased.

LEGAL REQUIREMENTS

Congress sought to protect the integrity of public employment programs by requiring that a CETA program "result in an increase in employment opportunities over those opportunities which would otherwise be available." CETA enrollees may not be used to displace employed workers or to do work that would normally be performed under contract. These provisions were carried over from the Emergency Employment Act of 1971 and new rules to tighten maintenance of effort were added: (a) Sponsors must assure the DOL that CETA participants will not be used to fill vacancies resulting from layoffs made in anticipation of hiring CETA employees; (b) applicants for jobs must have been unemployed for 30 days or more prior to enrollment, except for Title VI applicants in areas with 7 percent or more unemployment (this provision was intended to prevent paper layoffs); and (c) a CETA employee may not be hired when a regular employee has been laid off from the same or a substantially equivalent job. In 1976, when Title VI was extended, a clause was added prohibiting private nonprofit agencies from using CETA employees in performing services customarily provided by a unit of government.

The conference report on the Emergency Jobs and Unemployment Assistance Act of 1974 underscored the prohibitions on substitution and paper layoffs. However, it did indicate that the reemployment of persons who had lost their jobs due to a bona fide layoff was not illegal.[9] The fine distinctions between "paper" and "bona fide" layoffs and between "substantially" and "not substantially" equivalent jobs have returned time and again to haunt federal and local administrators.

The law's maintenance-of-effort provisions were further refined by DOL regulations. One dealt with reductions in force and required that where such reductions were necessary, CETA participants in equivalent positions be terminated first or transferred to positions unaffected by the layoffs. Similarly, the sponsor may not retain CETA employees in positions equivalent to regular positions that become vacant due to a legitimate hiring freeze.

[9]U.S. Congress, House, Committee of Conference (on the disagreeing votes of the two houses), *Public Service Employment*, Conference Report to Accompany HR 16596, House Report 93-1621, 93d Congress, 2d session, December 17, 1974. The report states that rehires are in a category that is to be given "preferred consideration" by reason of ineligibility for unemployment insurance.

The regulations regarding layoffs and rehires have been particularly controversial. The Department was faced with a dilemma. If the rehire of regular workers was unconstrained, CETA funds might be used solely to recall regular employees, to the exclusion of all other unemployed workers, including the long-term unemployed and other groups targeted for service. On the other hand, hiring new employees is difficult to justify in terms of merit systems and efficiency of service when regular workers have been laid off. DOL adopted a middle course by limiting rehires to the percentage of unemployed public service workers to total unemployment in an area.[10] This position was based on the proposition that all long-term unemployed should have equitable access to CETA positions.

The Department's rule was challenged in Detroit, where large-scale staff reductions had occurred. The Detroit case stimulated an amendment to the act that prohibits any quota on the number of Title VI public service workers who may be rehired, provided that the layoffs are bona fide.[11] The amendment opened up the possibility of greater use of CETA funds for rehires and may make it more difficult to enforce maintenance-of-effort regulations.

Concern over substitution was a major reason for two changes in Title VI when the act was extended and amended in 1976: (a) Most new hiring must be for projects of limited duration in activities clearly separate from those normally supported by the local government, and (b) eligibility for most Title VI CETA positions was limited to the long-term, low-income unemployed and to welfare recipients—persons not likely to qualify for regular public service openings.

EMPLOYMENT IMPACT

One approach to assessing the job creation effort of CETA is to examine trends in state and local government employment before and after the implementation of CETA's public service employment programs. For a period of about 25 years, from 1945 to 1970, state and local government employment rose steadily at a 4.7 percent annual growth rate. The rate then slowed to 3.9 percent between 1970 and 1974. Just before CETA became operational in June 1974, the number of state and local government employees was 11.4 million. Two years later, the total was 12.2 million, including some 300,000 CETA employees—a gain of only 3.6

[10]This regulation applied only to Title II. However, Field Memorandum 109-76, dated March 31, 1976, extended the rule to all public service employment.
[11]PL 44-444 Section 5(d), October 1, 1976, amended Title VI of CETA, prohibiting the Department of Labor from setting limits on rehires under Title II or Title VI, provided that maintenance-of-effort requirements are observed.

percent a year. The decline in the rate of growth coincided with a slowdown in the rate of growth of state and local government revenues and an increase in wage costs. Between 1970 and 1972, real state and local revenues increased at a rate of 4.5 percent per year; between 1972 and 1974, the rate of increase averaged 1.1 percent; while between 1974 and 1976, revenues increased at a rate of less than 1 percent annually. Thus, it is not clear from employment trend data what the effect of CETA has been without taking into account the influence of revenues and labor costs.

Observers have noted that federally subsidized job creation erodes over time because of the increased possibilities of adjusting state and local budgets to the availability of PSE positions. One method used to assess the effectiveness of the public service employment programs at various time intervals is the job creation ratio. This ratio is usually defined as the number of new jobs resulting from a federally financed public service employment program divided by the number of federally financed positions. Thus, a ratio of 0.6 would mean that 60 percent of the CETA employees represent new employment generated by CETA.

A study of the PEP experience by the National Planning Association (NPA) based on direct observation of 182 units of government in 12 sites arrived at a net job creation ratio of 0.54 after 1 year.[12] The NPA analyzed two groups of governmental units—a demonstration group with high levels of PEP employees and a comparison group with low levels. An expected level of public employment for 1972 was projected for each unit in the demonstration group as follows:

1. The historical difference between the demonstration group and the comparison group was determined.
2. The difference in the two groups was forecast for 1972.
3. The actual employment in the comparison group was observed for 1972, and the forecast difference was added to obtain the 1972 expected employment for the demonstration group if PEP had not existed.
4. The difference between the actual and the expected 1972 employment in the demonstration group was attributed to PEP.
5. This difference, divided by the number of PEP employees in the demonstration group, yielded the net job creation ratio.

---

[12]U.S. Department of Labor, Employment and Training Administration, *An Evaluation of the Economic Impact Project of the Public Employment Program,* vol. I, PB-236 892/ST, Prepared by National Planning Association, Washington, D.C., May 1974 (available from NTIS), Chapter III. The High Impact Project was an experimental design to test the consequences of a large-scale public employment program.

The NPA direct observation estimates have been criticized on the grounds that the comparison group used to measure job creation also included some PEP jobs.[13] Correction for this resulted in a recalculated estimate of up to 0.7, instead of 0.54. However, in view of the differences in the economic climate when PEP and CETA were operative and the vastly increased scope of CETA, unqualified application of PEP results to CETA may be inappropriate.[14]

George E. Johnson and James D. Tomola have written several papers examining the job creation effect of public service employment based on an econometric approach using national data. Their published estimates of the job creation ratio for PEP and CETA range from 1.0 in the first quarter after implementation to 0 after six quarters. These estimates were based upon a regression analysis which measured the degree of association between the level of state and local government employment and a number of explanatory factors. The explanatory variables in the model are: personal income to represent the revenue-raising capacity of the governments; employee compensation to measure the effect of wage increases; age (the proportion of the population 5 to 19 years of age) to reflect demand in the education sector; and the number of PEP and CETA public service employees. The coefficient of the PEP and CETA employment variable obtained from this estimating procedure was used to calculate the job creation ratio.[15] The authors conclude that subsidized public service employment may be a very effective counter-recession tool in the short run (the first one or two quarters after introduction of the program), but not over longer periods of time. They acknowledge, however, that the results "are subject to a fairly wide error band" and should be used with caution.

[13]Michael Wiseman, "Public Employment as Fiscal Policy," In Arthur M. Okun and George L. Perry, eds., *Brookings Papers on Economic Activity I*, pp. 67–114, Washington, D.C.: Brookings Institution, 1976.

[14]See also U.S. Congress, Congressional Budget Office, *Employment and Training Programs*, Staff working paper, Washington, D.C.: Congressional Budget Office, May 1976, and *Public Employment and Training Assistance: Alternative Federal Approaches*, Budget issue paper, Washington, D.C.: Congressional Budget Office, February 1977.

[15]George E. Johnson and James D. Tomola, "The Fiscal Substitution Effect of Alternative Approaches to Public Service Employment Policy," *The Journal of Human Resources* 12(1):3–26, Winter 1977.

JOB CREATION: NATIONAL ESTIMATE

The study reported on here, using a regression model, arrived at an average net job creation ratio of 0.65 for the first 10 calendar quarters of CETA.[16] The net job creation ratio for each quarter was estimated using the following formula:

$$\text{Net Job Creation Ratio} = \frac{\text{Actual} - \text{Forecasted State and Local Government Employment (in absence of CETA)}}{\text{CETA Public Service Employment}}$$

To arrive at the forecasted value of state and local government employment in the absence of CETA, it was hypothesized that state and local government employment tends to grow steadily over time due in part to an increased taste for public services. A number of factors push employment above or below the secular trend. It was assumed that state and local government employment is primarily determined by the purchasing power available to state and local governments. Real purchasing power is a function of the availability of revenue and the cost of labor, and these are measured by state and local revenues, federal grants-in-aid, and state and local public employee wage levels. Estimates of the parameters for each of these variables were made, based on the 54 quarters prior to implementation of CETA. These estimates were then used to forecast what employment would have been without CETA (see Appendix B).

State and local government employment (minus instructional personnel in the education sector), without CETA employment, was projected in this model to rise from 8,178,000 in the fourth calendar quarter of 1974 to 8,598,000 by the fourth quarter of 1976—a gain of 420,000. The actual growth was 494,000, according to BLS reports. CETA employment rose from about 71,000 to 306,000 during that time, then declined to 246,000 by the tenth quarter. The net job creation ratio fell from 0.82 in the fourth quarter of 1974 to 0.59 in the fourth quarter of 1975, after which the rate of decline diminished. In the tenth quarter, the job creation ratio was estimated to be 0.54 (see Figure 7). In this analysis, CETA employment was reduced by 15 percent to adjust for jobs allocated to private nonprofit agencies. However, some of these jobs may also have represented net additions to employment.

[16]In making the calculation of average job creation ratio, the first calendar quarter was omitted, since the number of CETA public service employees was too small to arrive at a meaningful job creation ratio. The job creation ratio for nine quarters, beginning with the second quarter, averaged 0.65. The job creation ratio, including the first quarter, was 0.62.

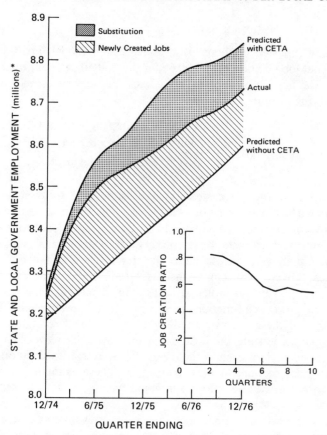

FIGURE 7   On average, 2 out of 3 CETA positions were net additions to state and local government employment.

The pattern of gradual decline in the net job creation ratio over time
suggests that the impact of public service employment is most significant
in the first five quarters. The decision in spring 1977 to increase the level
of public service jobs from 300,000 to 725,000 as part of the economic
stimulus package should have increased the job creation ratio initially,
especially if the jobs were in projects that are not normally public service
functions.

NET IMPACT ON UNEMPLOYMENT

The 344,000 CETA public service enrollees in the peak month of March 1976 represented nearly 5 percent of the 7 million unemployed that month (seasonally adjusted). Expressed in another way, if Titles II and VI had not been enacted, the nation's unemployment rate in March 1976 might have been 7.8 percent instead of 7.5 percent. Furthermore, this estimate does not take into account job creation in the private sector through the indirect or secondary effect of the added income of PSE participants. As the money that CETA participants earn is spent, it becomes income for others who in turn spend a portion. This multiplier effect implies that the increase in aggregate demand from a PSE program is larger than the initial PSE grant. Consequently, a PSE program will result not only in public sector jobs but also in private sector jobs in response to rising aggregate demand. Because a large proportion of CETA participants are drawn from low-income families, believed to have a high propensity to consume, these indirect effects are probably quite large. Even for those who were receiving welfare or unemployment insurance before CETA enrollment, the difference between CETA income and AFDC or UI payments represented a net increase in potential demand; for others the entire CETA salary minus taxes might be added to aggregate demand.[17]

The effectiveness of job creation in reducing unemployment was somewhat mitigated by two factors: First, not all participants were unemployed prior to enrollment. Second, some CETA employees were substituted for regular PSE workers who would otherwise have been employed and paid from state and local resources.

According to the Department of Labor, 78 percent of PSE participants in 1977 had been unemployed prior to enrollment; the remainder were designated as underemployed (4 percent) or "other" (18 percent).[18] The

[17]For a discussion of the aggregate demand stimulation effect, see Charles C. Killingsworth, "CETA and Manpower Program Evaluation," In James L. Stern and Barbara D. Dennis, eds., *Proceedings of the Twenty-Seventh Annual Winter Meeting, December 1975*, pp. 203–215, Madison, Wis.: Industrial Relations Research Association, 1976; Charles C. Killingsworth, "The Role of Public Service Employment," Paper delivered at Spring meeting of the IRRA, March 1977; Martin N. Baily and Robert M. Solow, "Public Service Employment as Macroeconomic Policy," In Vol. III of National Commission for Manpower Policy, *Job Creation Through Public Service Employment*, pp.21–88, Washington, D.C.: National Commission for Manpower Policy, March 1978.

[18]According to a Westat, Inc., report, only 48 percent of CETA public service entrants were unemployed before entry in fiscal 1976, 35 percent were employed, and 17 percent were not in the labor force. However, the Westat study used a different concept of labor force status than the DOL uses, a fact that may account for part of the difference. Westat classified

"other" category includes persons who were out of the labor force or who had been employed. CETA enrollees reported as having been out of the labor force included some discouraged workers who had given up the search for jobs, as well as reentrants and new entrants. Some of those listed as employed were in fact transfers from one program to another, e.g., from Title VI to Title II, and were actually unemployed before entering CETA. But even those CETA participants who moved directly from jobs in the private sector to CETA employment left behind vacancies to be filled by others. To that extent, there could still be a net job creation effect.

The second mitigating factor, substitution, is more serious. But, in this case, too, the possibility of indirect job creation exists. Savings to state and local governments resulting from the use of federal funds in place of local resources could be used for other government expenditures or to defer local tax increases. In either case, the savings would be expected to boost demand and stimulate employment. But with these kinds of program dynamics, the public service employment components of CETA more closely resemble general revenue sharing than a direct job creation program.

OTHER SOCIAL AND ECONOMIC BENEFITS

The man-year cost of a CETA PSE position was about $7,900 in fiscal 1976 and $8,400 in fiscal 1977. This cost is partially offset by savings in welfare and unemployment insurance payments, by gains in income and social security taxes, and by the value of the goods and services produced by CETA employees. About 14 percent of CETA public service enrollees received unemployment insurance prior to enrollment, and over 13 percent were in families receiving AFDC or other welfare payments in fiscal 1976.

An analysis of costs and benefits of CETA PSE must include an assessment of social benefits. One such benefit is the access to temporary CETA government jobs afforded to disadvantaged and minority workers who might not otherwise be considered and, for some, transition to unsubsidized public sector positions. Even where substitution occurs, the

respondents by "primary activity." The DOL definition of an unemployed person is one who is out of a job (or in a welfare family) and available for work. Some participants counted by both DOL and Westat as employed prior to CETA may have been transferred from other CETA public service titles. See U.S. Department of Labor, Employment and Training Administration, "Characteristics of New Enrollees in CETA Programs During Fiscal Year 1976," Report no. 6 of the Continuous Longitudinal Manpower Survey, PB-272 950/ST, Prepared by Westat, Inc., Rockville, Md., 1977 (available from NTIS).

effect of targeting the program may tend to change the composition of the public sector work force.

CETA PSE shares with other programs the objective of providing income to unemployed persons. But in addition, it provides to the participant the opportunity for employment and to the community the resources to maintain services or to offer new services. On the debit side, the introduction of CETA employees with lower skills or experience than regular public service workers could affect the quality of service.

JOB CREATION IN THE STUDY AREAS

In addition to developing national estimates of job creation, the study examined the job creation effects of CETA in 24 of the areas in the NRC sample. In assessing the job creation effects of CETA in the sample areas, the study not only examined public sector employment trends from 1971 to 1975 for indications of job creation attributable to CETA, but also analyzed these trends in the context of program and economic developments in each area. Field research associates gathered information on the fiscal and budgetary position of the sponsors' jurisdictions, indications of maintenance of effort and substitution, views of local officials on the objectives of Title II and Title VI, and the extent to which private nonprofit agencies and special projects were used for PSE activities. The principal sources of information were CETA administrators, chairmen of the planning council, and, in some cases, regional office representatives and union officials.

Of the 24 nonstate jurisdictions in the sample, 14 experienced substantial net job creation in the first six quarters of CETA; 5 had moderate job gains, and 5 appear to have had little gain. The extent of job creation took into account trends in local government employment but was not computed as a numerical ratio for specific areas. The 5 areas with little gain were difficult to classify, because some may have used CETA resources to alleviate further cutbacks or to replace workers whose positions would not otherwise have been filled. On the whole, information from the sample, when weighted by the number of PSE jobs, reinforces national data indicating that CETA public service employment, in the short run, results in moderate job creation.

Job creation varied with fiscal pressure in prime sponsor areas.[19] A local government with little or moderate budget constraint was more

---

[19] The degree of fiscal pressure (extreme, moderate, relatively little) was gauged by field research associates, taking into consideration information on tax revenues, local government expenditures, the budget situation, layoffs of regular employees, and other local circumstances.

TABLE 30 Net Job Gains Resulting from CETA Titles II and VI, by Degree of Fiscal Pressure, Sample Local Prime Sponsors, October 1975

Increases in Public Service Employment Attributable to CETA[a]	All Areas	Degree of Fiscal Pressure[b]		
		Little	Moderate	Extreme
Substantial	14	5	9	0
Moderate	5	1	4	0
Little apparent job gain	5	0	1	4
TOTAL	24	6	14	4

[a]Increases in local government or in private nonprofit agencies.
[b]Fiscal pressure refers to the financial position of the major unit of government, based on revenues, expenditures, and other relevant information.

likely to use a substantial part of its CETA funds to create new jobs that would otherwise not exist (see Table 30).

Areas with Substantial Job Gains

The 14 jurisdictions with substantial net employment opportunities resulting from CETA public service positions generally had moderate or little fiscal pressure. Most are small or medium-sized consortia or counties. They increased employment opportunities in several ways. Some used CETA jobs to supplement staff in regular departments; others established new categories of activities not performed previously; and a number relied heavily on agencies outside government to expand employment possibilities.

The Kansas City–Wyandotte consortium, classified as having moderate fiscal pressure, illustrates the first approach. CETA employees were used mainly to supplement existing staff, especially in the highways and parks departments. A few workers were employed on projects, one of which provided interns to help the planning department reduce a backlog of record-keeping. A number of positions were allotted to community-based organizations. Public employment in Wyandotte County (including Kansas City) rose 10 percent between October 1974 and October 1975, compared with a 1971–1974 annual average growth rate of 1.2 percent (including PEP jobs). The total growth of 600 between 1974 and 1975 was largely in education and unrelated to CETA, but gains were also reported in functions in which CETA participants were employed. It appears that a significant proportion of the 215 CETA employees represents additional employment that would not have existed otherwise.

San Joaquin is an example of a prime sponsor using CETA positions mainly for new activities. The sponsor concentrated on using positions for "getting people off the streets," largely through labor-intensive, environmental jobs. No complaints from public employee unions or other sources were reported, and the DOL regional office representative was confident that the area was fulfilling its requirements for maintenance of effort. According to Census reports, public employment in the county rose about 1,200 between October 1974 and October 1975, a gain of more than 10 percent. This gain compared with an average yearly increase of 2 percent for the 3 preceding years.

Phoenix–Maricopa allotted almost a third of its CETA jobs to state, federal, and private nonprofit agencies—including the Red Cross, a black theater troupe, a Baptist children's home, and Catholic social services. Public service employment generally expanded at a greater rate in that consortium between 1974 and 1975 than in previous years.

Areas with Moderate Job Gains

The areas with moderate CETA job gains for the most part experienced only slight growth in total public service jobs. Some CETA positions have been used to fill vacancies, while others were clearly in new government activities or in private nonprofit agencies.

In Middlesex County, for example, the net increase in public service employment between 1974 and 1975 was slight. CETA public service employees were scattered through regular county or city departments, but some were in new projects that normally would not have existed. One such project created a systematic control for vehicle maintenance. The county also centralized all document reproduction and microfilming with CETA help. About 20 percent of the county's CETA public service positions were assigned to state agencies, including a state university, and to such private nonprofit agencies as the YMCA, the Urban League, the Red Cross, and Catholic Welfare and Social Services.

The Lansing consortium used CETA positions for both regular public service and project-type jobs. Although its public sector employment continued to grow, the question of budget substitution was raised by the press, which quoted local officials as acknowledging that CETA employment reduced some of the budget expansion that might otherwise have taken place.

Other Areas

In the remaining five areas—four with over 1 million population—public employment declined or was relatively stable. All but one were in dire financial straits and have been dependent on CETA to maintain essential services. Whether what occurred in those situations is defined as substitution depends on what might have happened without CETA. CETA funds may have permitted the diversion of local funds to other uses and reduced pressure on local governments to raise taxes, or, on the other hand, they may have prevented further cutbacks in employment.

Public employment declined sharply in New York City from 396,000 in October 1974 to 356,000 (including CETA employees) the following year; 20,000 CETA participants had been slotted into regular government jobs to maintain those essential municipal services that were cut back most severely. Approximately 2,100 of the 20,000 were former city workers, rehired largely because of union insistence. Moreover, nearly 10 percent of fiscal 1976 Title I funds was used for public service employment, including some for CETA employees who had been scheduled to be terminated because they were in positions deemed to be substantially similar to those of laid-off regular civil service employees. Despite the city's fiscal crisis, about 8 percent of CETA positions were assigned to state and private nonprofit agencies, and to that extent CETA may have contributed to net job creation.

The number of employees reported by the Census Bureau in all the jurisdictions of the Cleveland consortium was virtually the same in October 1975 as in the previous year, although some 2,400 Title II and VI participants were on the public payrolls and over 50 percent of Title I funds was also used for public service employment. Well over half of the Title I, II, and VI participants in the city of Cleveland were rehired regular employees, and questions were raised as to whether their separations were bona fide. The DOL regional office ordered a reduction in the number of public service employees rehired under CETA, and the city has been gradually reabsorbing some of them on its own payroll.

Gary, Indiana, the smallest of the five areas that had little or no job gains, ranks among the most hard-pressed cities in the country. Without CETA, some of its essential services would probably have been discontinued. At the time of the survey, the city was using revenue-sharing funds to maintain a number of public service positions, but was planning to use CETA to rehire regular employees as the squeeze between rising costs and dwindling revenues intensified. According to local respondents in the survey, there has not been substitution of CETA for regular funds, although CETA employees were performing work that is customarily paid from local funds in other cities.

Philadelphia's fiscal situation was less critical. That city had attempted to honor its no-tax-increase pledge until spring 1976, an attempt that had resulted in an extremely stringent budget. There had been no large-scale layoffs, but public service employment declined between October 1974 and October 1975, despite the employment of 2,800 CETA workers. The city has come to depend on CETA to meet staff shortages; over 1,000 were employed in the sewer and sanitation departments. None of the CETA positions was given to nonprofit organizations, but a few were assigned to the state employment service.

Between 1971 and 1974, public employment in the Orange County consortium expanded at an average rate of more than 6 percent per year, according to the Census Bureau. However, between October 1974 and October 1975, public employment stabilized, despite the addition of 1,285 CETA workers and the fact that its jurisdictions face only moderate fiscal difficulties. County and city officials say that the need for additional services that had been associated with growth in parts of the county is now diminishing. Some cities were holding the line on employment, while in others public employment was declining through attrition and layoffs. There was reluctance to seek additional revenues to maintain or expand public services. CETA workers, for the most part, were being slotted into regular vacancies and were used as a pool for filling regular jobs, instead of being placed in new jobs. This, according to local officials, increases their chances for being selected for permanent employment. The Orange County experience illustrates the trade-off between the transition and the maintenance-of-effort objectives of CETA.

MAINTENANCE OF EFFORT

The maintenance-of-effort requirements in the Department of Labor regulations on direct job substitution are carefully spelled out. They prohibit displacing currently employed workers; abrogating existing contracts for services; substituting CETA resources, using CETA positions, for jobs financed by other federal programs; and hiring CETA personnel when regular workers in equivalent jobs have been laid off. Where a layoff of regular employees is planned or a hiring freeze is in effect, the sponsor must certify that the action is due to a budgeting crisis and the DOL regional office may request supporting documentation. Rehiring of regular workers with CETA funds is permitted if the layoffs are bona fide. The regulations, however, do not deal with more subtle maintenance-of-effort violations, including indirect budget or fiscal substitution. This is not strange, considering the general lack of understanding of the nuances of substitution.

The DOL relies mainly on assurances in the grant document, limited monitoring and auditing, and complaints to enforce maintenance-of-effort requirements. A General Accounting Office study of the rehire situation in Toledo, where 100 permanent city employees were laid off and rehired with CETA funds, showed that information provided by the city did not justify the action.[20] The report pointed out the difficulty of properly assessing the financial picture in the various accounts in a typical city. The Department of Labor would have to increase vastly its auditing capability to monitor maintenance of effort effectively.

A more extensive GAO report based on visits to 12 sponsors in 5 states cited maintenance-of-effort violations, including the use of CETA participants to fill budgeted positions that presumably would have been paid for from local funds to replace temporary, part-time, or seasonal workers who would have been hired anyway and to fill jobs normally contracted out.[21]

Several maintenance-of-effort problems were reported in the 28 areas in the sample. The experience of two of them demonstrates the major issues in layoff–recall situations. The issue in New York City was whether, in a reduction in force, CETA employees in "substantially equivalent" positions should be laid off before regular employees. About 20,000 CETA Title II and Title VI employees were on the payroll in municipal agencies that were cutting back regular employees. The controversy embroiled the city, CETA employees, one of the unions representing city workers, the Department of Labor, members of Congress, and, ultimately, the courts. The Department of Labor decided that 1,400 CETA positions were substantially similar to those held by regular employees who were laid off and ordered the city to terminate (or transfer) CETA employees in those positions and rehire the regular employees with CETA funds. A court ruling upheld the Department's action and denied that it violated the equal protection rights of CETA participants. The effect of the ruling was to give laid-off public service workers preference over other unemployed (including the disadvantaged and long-term unemployed) in filling CETA jobs, provided the municipal workers were not laid off with the intent of rehiring them under CETA.[22]

[20]U.S. General Accounting Office, *Using Comprehensive Employment and Training Act Funds to Rehire Laid-Off Employees in Toledo, Ohio*, Washington, D.C.: General Accounting Office, March 19, 1976.

[21]U.S. General Accounting Office, *More Benefits to Jobless Can be Obtained in Public Service Employment*, HRD-77-53, Washington, D.C.: General Accounting Office, April 7, 1977.

[22]Daniel L. Persons, "A Union View of the Impact of Public Service Employment on Public Sector Labor Relations," In James L. Stern and Barbara D. Dennis, eds., *Proceedings of the Twenty-Eighth Annual Winter Meeting, December 1975*, Madison, Wis.: Industrial Relations Research Association, 1976; and Lois Blume, "Rehiring of Laid Off Municipal Workers Under CETA: The Law, the Regulations and Congressional Intent," *Adherent* 3(1), April 1976.

In Cleveland, the issue was the Department of Labor's regulation that limited the percentage of rehires of regular employees under CETA to a number consistent with their proportion among the unemployed. This policy appears to have the opposite effect of the New York decision—it limits the recall rights of laid-off regular employees and provides equal opportunity to other unemployed people.

In a similar case, Detroit brought suit against the Department of Labor, charging that the formula limiting rehires was contrary to the intent of CETA and a threat to the city's ability to deliver adequate fire and police protection. The fact that the majority of the laid-off employees were members of minorities and women, identified as "significant segments" in the city's CETA plan, complicated matters. The case was settled in an agreement on a number of rehires within the context of the DOL regulations.

Overt substitution gets public attention, but indirect displacement may be more widespread. This may take the form of slotting CETA workers into existing vacancies or using them to meet expansion needs where such jobs would otherwise have been filled from local resources. Local officials who were reluctant to request funds for new positions in the economic climate of 1974–1976 found CETA a convenient way to pay for them. This subtle form of replacement is difficult to deal with through compliance procedures and could become more pervasive as the program is extended. Public officials might be tempted to limit or curtail normal tax effort if they were sure that the program would continue.

POLICY ISSUES

Federally subsidized local public service employment, eschewed for many years, is now widely accepted as a countercyclical instrument and a major component of national manpower policy. The change is due in part to looser labor market conditions of the 1970s and in part to widespread fiscal difficulties in local governments. Both federal and local officials view Titles II and VI as constructive legislation, although sometimes for different reasons. The federal focus is on reducing unemployment. However, many local officials see subsidized public service employees as a means of maintaining public services and providing fiscal relief as well.

Despite objections to the public service employment concept, President Nixon did finally sign the Emergency Employment Act of 1971. The Ford Administration supported the enactment of Title VI as a major program in CETA, although it expected the economy to improve so that the program could be phased out. The Carter Administration, confronted with a persistent recession, doubled the public service employment programs as part of its economic stimulus strategy.

Currently, the public service employment program is caught up in the debate on the reauthorization of CETA, the jobs component of welfare reform, and the revitalization of urban areas. The administration's planning presumes that improvements in the economy will permit phasing out most of the CETA PSE positions and the use of these resources and others to employ welfare recipients instead. There is, however, significant congressional support for retaining public service employment as an identifiable component of CETA. It is therefore timely to consider some of the broad issues of public service employment in the context of the early years of CETA operations.

SUBSTITUTION

Congressional concern with the operation of Title VI was focused on three problems: substitution of federal for local funds, clientele, and political improprieties. Of these, substitution was the most worrisome. This is understandable, since it threatened the validity of the premise upon which the program rested—job creation. In 1976, in the legislation to extend Title VI, the Emergency Jobs Programs Extension Act, Congress redesigned the program by mandating projects of limited duration and by encouraging the assignment of part of Title VI funds to private nonprofit organizations. The intent was to employ most Title VI participants in activities that are not part of the regular public service structure and therefore less likely to lead to substitution. The key element was the tight definition of a project. However, the original definition of a project, which stressed its "non-incremental" character, was subsequently loosened to permit projects that are extensions of existing activities. It remains to be seen whether the results that Congress anticipated will be realized.

TARGETING PUBLIC SERVICE JOBS

A second major congressional concern is the extent to which public service jobs programs should be used for the economically disadvantaged or for other groups with special employment handicaps. The CETA public service employment program was not originally viewed as an antipoverty program; eligibility criteria were purposely left loose and vague. The act suggested that consideration be given to Vietnam veterans, the long-term unemployed, former manpower trainees, unemployment insurance exhaustees, persons not eligible for UI, and "significant segments" of the unemployed population—but not specifically to the poor. As the program unfolded, it became clear that the economically disadvantaged were participating only to a limited extent. When Congress extended Title VI, it took the occasion to modify its original position. The Emergency Jobs Programs Extension Act limited participation in most of the new PSE positions to the long-term unemployed who are also low-income persons or welfare recipients. This change has created an anomalous situation. Title VI, which is basically the countercyclical program of CETA, has more stringent eligibility requirements than Title I, which was designed for those most in need. The issue is whether a public service jobs program should primarily serve structural or countercyclical objectives or both. If the objective is to deal with "structural" problems, is it appropriate for the public sector be the major vehicle for the readjustment of persons with various drawbacks to employment? What would the effect be on the structure and nature of public service? These questions are likely to become more pertinent if welfare reform and CETA are linked.

EROSION OF THE TRANSITION OBJECTIVE

Transition, the entry of PSE participants in regular unsubsidized jobs, was, in the beginning, a major objective. It was the central theme in the PEP program and a major objective when CETA was enacted. Congressional intent was clearly expressed in a 1973 report on CETA of the House Committee on Education and Labor: "First, it is agreed that, to the extent feasible, persons employed on public service jobs funded under this Act should be absorbed into the regular workforce of the employer, or, alternatively, assisted in securing other suitable employment not subsidized under this Act."[23] However, with the enactment of Title VI of CETA and the Department of Labor's overriding concern with speedy implementation, the emphasis on transition was sacrificed. Prime sponsors, faced with the prospect of having ultimately to absorb significant numbers of their PSE participants proceeded cautiously until the transition goals were waived by the DOL.

The 1976 amendments to Title VI, with its emphasis on temporary projects outside the mainstream of public service activities, will affect the entry of PSE participants into regular public sector jobs. In its effort to contain substitution through the use of projects, Congress has, in effect, traded off the transition possibilities in the public sector.

[23]U.S. Congress, House, Committee on Education and Labor, *Comprehensive Manpower Act of 1973*, House report no. 93-659, November 21, 1973, pp. 12–13.

Another possible consequence of the new Title VI legislation is the development of a dual public service employment system: one for persons employed in positions equivalent to regular public service jobs with potential for obtaining permanent positions; the other, for persons lower on the socioeconomic ladder, assigned to temporary project jobs.[24]

THE QUALITY AND UTILITY OF JOBS

The WPA stereotype of public service jobs as make-work lingers on. However, during the first 2 years of CETA, most public service employment participants held productive jobs comparable to those of the regular work force. But the present emphasis on temporary projects, the pressure on prime sponsors to absorb large numbers of enrollees in a very short time, and the focus on the long-term, low-income unemployed may indeed result in some activities of marginal usefulness.

INSTITUTIONAL FRAMEWORK OF CETA

The expansion of countercyclical public service employment programs within a framework designed primarily for programs dealing with structural problems raises a number of institutional issues. For example, what effect has the grafting of the large-scale public service employment program had on the administrative structures of its prime sponsors? On the relative importance of employability development programs? On local interorganizational relationships? There undoubtedly will also be new issues rising from the widespread use of private nonprofit organizations to administer CETA projects.

SUMMARY

The study finds that:

• In the short run, CETA has a positive impact in creating new jobs, but this effect tends to erode over time. Over the first 10 quarters, the job creation ratio in the public sector ranged from 0.82 in the second quarter to 0.54 in the tenth. On the average, it is estimated that for every 100 CETA positions, there were 65 new state and local government jobs. Total job creation is actually higher, as a result of CETA funded jobs in the private nonprofit sector. In addition, CETA exerts a multiplier effect on

[24]However, DOL regulations have tended to water down the project concept by permitting projects that are in effect extensions of normal public service employment.

employment by stimulating the demand for goods and services, but there is no reason to expect this effect to be any different from the stimulative impact of other federal government programs.

• The degree of job gains in local areas in the sample varied with the fiscal pressure on local governments. Those with the greatest gains were jurisdictions with little or moderate fiscal pressure. They tended to be small and medium-sized areas. Those with the least amount of apparent job gains were generally areas experiencing the most fiscal sringency. In some of these hard-pressed jurisdictions, however, CETA may have forestalled possible reductions in the public sector work force.

• Several maintenance-of-effort problems arose in the NRC study areas, including two major controversies. One involved the limitation imposed by the Department of Labor on the use of CETA funds for the rehire of regular public service workers. The other dealt with the use of CETA employees in positions substantially equivalent to those of laid-off regular workers.

• There is an inherent trade-off between the "transition" and the "job creation" objectives of the act. Sponsors concerned about transition sometimes used CETA employees to fill regular vacancies. This may help to place CETA enrollees in permanent jobs, but it may also contribute to a form of budget substitution. Similarly, the use of temporary projects as a device for controlling substitutions may make it difficult for persons in such projects to move into regular unsubsidized jobs in the public sector.

• The functional areas in which CETA enrollees were employed resembled the pattern set under EEA in 1971–1972. Most were employed in activities ordinarily performed by the employing agencies; some were absorbed into the administrative structure of CETA.

• Despite the emphasis on projects in the Title VI regulations, the study uncovered few such projects prior to the enactment of the Emergency Jobs Programs Extension Act of 1976. There was some confusion over the exact nature of a project, and sponsors tended to describe some of their regular short-term public service jobs as projects.

• Local sponsors in the study areas allocated 20 percent of their Title II and VI funds to private nonprofit organizations and to state and federal agencies operating within their jurisdictions. The extent of such allocations appears to be related to the size and fiscal situation of the sponsors. Large jurisdictions, those experiencing fiscal pressure, and those in which elected officials made decisions gave away fewer positions.

8 Clientele

Who benefits from the billions of dollars now spent on manpower programs? Are the available services directed to the disadvantaged, or is CETA becoming a countercyclical program for the unemployed but ready-for-work person? Are the types of participants changing under CETA? What factors are associated with such changes? Do these developments call for a closer focusing of manpower programs in line with national objectives?

Over the years, manpower programs have reached out to different groups in the population as changes in economic conditions and social policy have developed. The Area Redevelopment Act of 1961 set out to retrain unemployed persons in depressed areas. This strategy, it was hoped, would attract industry and would contribute to economic development. The major manpower training initiative, however, came in 1962 with the Manpower Training and Development Act. The primary concern at that time was to retrain persons who were expected to be displaced by automation and technological change and to help them rebuild their skills to meet the new occupational demands of the labor market. At that time, there was no specific emphasis on the poor or disadvantaged, and, when the expected displacement did not occur, MDTA became a program in search of a constituency. In 1963, the act was amended to place greater emphasis on the retraining of youth unable to qualify for jobs because of inadequate vocational preparation. Reorientation of MDTA toward the disadvantaged occurred in the mid-1960s, after the start of the War on Poverty.

In the second half of the 1960s, a number of categorical programs were initiated under the aegis of the Economic Opportunity Act. Each program had a specific clientele and approach, but the general purpose was to aid poor persons who were unemployed or underemployed. The primary focus of manpower programs was to provide remedial skill training and work experience to those who had difficulty in competing in the job market, despite the generally strong demand for labor.

Several major programs—the Neighborhood Youth Corps, the Job Corps, and the summer youth employment programs—were geared to poor youth. Operation Mainstream was for older workers, primarily in rural areas with few employment opportunities. The Job Opportunities in the Business Sector (JOBS) program enlisted private employers in efforts to hire and train the disadvantaged unemployed—young and older workers, handicapped, and others with special obstacles. The Public Service Careers program similarly attempted to improve the access of the disadvantaged in the public sector through on-the-job training. In addition, ethnic-oriented organizations such as OIC, the Urban League, and SER received grants to expand counseling and training for minorities.

The picture began to change again in the early 1970s. With the winding down of hostilities in Vietnam, unemployment began to rise, and growing concern about the level of joblessness and the employment prospects of Vietnam veterans led to the passage of the Emergency Employment Act (EEA) of 1971. Because its aim was countercyclical, with emphasis on creating new jobs in essential governmental services, it was not directed exclusively toward the disadvantaged. Public sector employment often requires persons with qualifications not frequently found among workers with lower skills and less education.

With the EEA program about to be phased out, on the eve of the passage of CETA most manpower programs were predominantly for the disadvantaged. EOA programs were almost exclusively for the unemployed and underemployed in poor families, and MDTA policy was to select two-thirds of the participants from the disadvantaged population.

LEGISLATIVE FRAMEWORK

The Comprehensive Employment and Training Act incorporates some elements of earlier legislation, but in keeping with its basic objective of decentralization, it permits considerable local flexibility in identifying the groups to be served. The preamble of the act states that its purpose is to provide training and employment opportunities to the "economically disadvantaged"—a reference to its EOA antecedents—but also to "unemployed and underemployed persons"—reminiscent of MDTA and EEA. Since the original act was passed, several amendments have focused on rising unemployment, as discussed in earlier chapters. They have introduced client preference categories in public service employment, and the most recent are directed specifically to the long-term, low-income unemployed.

Concern for the protection of especially vulnerable groups was expressed during the deliberations leading to the enactment of CETA. In order to reconcile this concern about serving specific clientele categories with the administration's emphasis on maximum local autonomy, a compromise was reached. Title I decategorizes programs, and its language pertaining to clientele is loose. Title III, however, authorizes special programs to be administered by the federal government outside the block grant package for Indians, migrant and seasonal farm workers, youth, offenders, older workers, persons of limited English-speaking ability, and other groups. The Job Corps, for disadvantaged youth, was also continued under federal direction (Title IV). Prime sponsors are free to include any of these groups in local programs as well, but the act ensured that a significant proportion of funds would be set aside nationally to be used for the disadvantaged (see Chapter 2).

Unlike categorical programs, which limited and defined eligibility narrowly, Title I operates as a block grant program, allowing prime sponsors to choose groups to serve and assign priorities according to their own perception of local needs. The legislative history of CETA suggests that the administration opposed language that would have required special consideration for particular client categories or for organizations that had previously concentrated on ethnic communities and the disadvantaged, on the grounds that such language could lead to a legislative mandate for categorical programs.[1] However, some vestiges of categorization remain, even in Title I. Sponsors must give assurances in Title I plans that they will serve those "most in need," including "low income persons of limited English-speaking ability." There is also an oblique reference to the use of community-based organizations. Assurances that "programs of demonstrated effectiveness" will be continued are standard requirements. But the vagueness of Title I language invited broad local interpretation.

Title II, which authorizes public service employment in areas of substantial unemployment, is more specific than Title I in designating groups to be given consideration. Eligibility is limited to unemployed

[1]Testimony of William Kolberg, in hearings before the Senate Subcommittee on Employment, Poverty, and Migratory Labor of the Committee on Labor and Public Welfare on S. 1559 and S. 1560, February–March 1973, p. 282.

and underemployed persons living in areas of substantial unemployment who have been jobless for 30 days or more. Prime sponsors are required to give consideration to the most severely disadvantaged in terms of length of unemployment and their prospect for finding employment without assistance, to Vietnam veterans, and to former manpower trainees.[2] To the extent practicable, they are to share public service employment opportunities on an equitable basis among "significant segments" of the unemployed population. Congressional intent was clarified in a later House committee report: "The Conferees' intention was to urge the Secretary to use his discretion and judgment to see that, wherever practicable, minorities, youth, the elderly, women, and other groups who have been traditional victims of job discrimination had equal access to jobs created under CETA."[3] As defined in DOL regulations, "significant segments" are locally determined groups that generally experience unusual difficulty in obtaining employment and who are most in need of the services authorized in the act. The difference in interpretation between the committee report, which implies proportional treatment of various disadvantaged groups, and the Department of Labor regulations, which imply preferential treatment, has been a source of confusion in implementing the act.

Since CETA was passed, several developments have moved the program in the direction of recategorization. The passage of special appropriations for summer programs under Title III set up, in effect, a new categorical program. The administration's intent had been that such programs could be supported by sponsors from their regular Title I allotment as one of a number of options, but Congress has appropriated summer funds each year over and above the Title I appropriation.[4] Title VI, enacted in 1974, was a categorical program created in response to the developing recession. In mid-1975, Congress passed a law requiring state employment security agencies to interview persons receiving Federal Supplemental Benefits and, if appropriate, to refer them to an approved manpower training program.[5]

These amendments to CETA have tended to emphasize the long-term unemployed as candidates for public service jobs. Under Title VI,

[2]The Emergency Jobs and Unemployment Assistance Act of 1974 amended this requirement to cover any veterans discharged within the last 4 years.
[3]U.S. Congress, House, Committee on Education and Labor, *Emergency Job Programs Stop-Gap Extension*, House report no. 94-1019, 94th Congress, 2d session, April 8, 1976.
[4]The fiscal 1977 budget request was the first in which the administration asked for summer funds for youth (see Chapter 2).
[5]The Emergency Compensation and Special Unemployment Assistance Extension Act of 1975, June 30, 1975. This act extended Federal Supplemental Benefits for 13 additional weeks to persons who have exhausted 39 weeks of benefits.

sponsors were to give "preferred consideration" to those unemployed who had either exhausted their entitlement to unemployment insurance or who were never eligible (except for persons lacking work experience), and to those who have been out of work for 15 weeks or longer. However, Title VI stopped short of mandating eligibility for the long-term unemployed.

To summarize, the original concept of CETA—broad local discretion—was gradually diluted (at least for public service employment) by the establishment of preference categories. CETA amendments, while not strongly worded, signify the intent of Congress to direct the attention of local sponsors to recently separated veterans and the long-term unemployed.

But it was not until the Emergency Jobs Programs Extension Act of 1976, which continued the Title VI program for another year, that Congress took the additional step of requiring prime sponsors to limit eligibility for new public service projects to long-term unemployed persons (or AFDC recipients) with low household income.[6] This step marks a change in philosophy: It incorporates a major structural objective in programs that have been primarily countercyclical. Under the new Title VI, funds available to sponsors greater than the amount necessary to maintain their existing level of public service employment must be used for special projects, to be staffed exclusively by persons who have been unemployed for 15 weeks or more and who are members of low-income or welfare households. The purpose of this provision is to ensure that the new jobs go to the long-term, low-income unemployed with substantial attachment to the labor force. A secondary purpose is to reduce the cost of public service employment by offsetting cash payments from unemployment insurance and public assistance. Half of the vacancies resulting from attrition below the June 1976 level must also be reserved for the long-term unemployed with low household income.

In mid-1977, Congress added a youth employment title to CETA (Title VIII) and increased appropriations for veterans and for other youth programs under Title III.

What started out to be an effort to reform manpower legislation into a

[6]Emergency Jobs Programs Extension Act of 1976, October 1976, Sections 607 and 608. Funds above the sponsor's June 1976 level of PSE employment, plus part of the funds reserved for vacancies in regular CETA PSE positions, must be reserved for members of families with an income of 70 percent or less of the lower living standard. U.S. Congress, Senate, Committee on Labor and Public Welfare, *Emergency Jobs Programs Extension Act of 1976*, Senate report no. 94-883, May 14, 1976; U.S. Congress, House, *Emergency Jobs Programs Extension Act of 1976*, Conference report, House report no. 94-1514, September 13, 1976.

relatively simple block grant program with only a few general provisions for selecting clients has gradually become more complex and specialized as the nation has attempted to deal with a recession longer and deeper than any since the Depression. What is unfolding is a trend towards establishing discrete national programs as the federal government sets new national objectives to meet emerging needs. Inherent in this process is a larger degree of national control in determining categories of clients to be served and in specifying the kinds of services to be provided.

CHARACTERISTICS OF CETA PARTICIPANTS

In its short life, CETA has reached a level of enrollment that greatly exceeds the level of pre-CETA programs. The number of persons in need of manpower services—the unemployed, the discouraged, the working poor, and part-time workers seeking full-time jobs—has been conservatively estimated at 10 to 12 million on a given date (see Chapter 2). The number of individuals requiring such services in the course of a year is much higher. In 1976, with 7.3 million unemployed in an average month, nearly three times as many people were jobless at some time during the year; over 8.5 million of these people had sought work for 15 weeks or longer according to the Bureau of Labor Statistics.

Manpower programs reach only a fraction of those in need. In fiscal 1976, 2.5 million persons were served in Title I, II, and VI programs. This is a significant increase over the 1.5 million in 1975 and about 1 million in comparable programs before CETA (see Table 31). However, CETA figures are not entirely comparable with those for 1974 for several reasons. The CETA count includes clients who receive only minimal services—outreach, intake, and assessment (a tighter definition was introduced in fiscal 1977). About 5 percent of the people served by CETA are placed directly in jobs without participating in any employment or training program. Finally, there is an unknown amount of double counting resulting from the shift of enrollees from one title to another.[7] If one corrected for the looser definition and for the double counting, the number served would be far lower than the reported figure. According to the Department of Labor's continuous longitudinal manpower survey (CLMS), there were 500,000 fewer new enrollees in Titles I, II, and VI in fiscal 1976 than were reported by the ETA for that year.[8]

[7]For example, in some cases in fiscal 1975, summer enrollees began under Title I and then were shifted to Title III when funds became available. In fiscal 1976, due to the exhaustion of Title II funds, enrollees were transferred to Title VI; when a supplemental appropriation was received, Title VI enrollees were switched to Title II.

[8]The estimated total number of new participants enrolled by CETA prime sponsors

TABLE 31 Participants in CETA Titles I, II, and VI, Fiscal 1974–1977 (thousands)

	Cumulative Participants				New Enrollments			Peak Number of Participants		
	FY 1974[a]	FY 1975[b]	FY 1976[c]	FY 1977[c]	FY 1976	FY 1977		FY 1975	FY 1976	FY 1977
Title I	796	1,126	1,732	1,416	1,250	1,119		571	575	367
Title II	{183	227	256	353	116	165		156	57	92
Title VI		157	495	593	372	432		123	287	431

SOURCE: Employment and Training Administration, U.S. Department of Labor.

[a]Programs comparable to Title I: MDTA institutional, JOP, JOBS, SER, OIC, Urban League, Public Service Careers, Hometown Plans, Operation Mainstream, NYC in-school, NYC out-of-school, CMP, CEP. Program comparable to Titles II and VI: PEP, exclusive of PEP summer youth enrollees.

[b]Excludes 247,000 enrollees in categorical programs and 43,000 in PEP in 1975, as many of these were transferred to CETA.

[c]Figures for FY 1976 and FY 1977 include carry-over from previous years.

200

Because it excludes double counting and for other reasons, the number served in all three titles on a given date may be a more useful measure of the magnitude of the program. The peak in fiscal 1976 was 919,000. Discounting the nearly one-third of Title I enrollees who were in school, there were about 700,000 members of the labor force in all three programs. Counting Indians, migrants, and Job Corps youth, the total would be 800,000—about 1 out of 15 persons who were estimated to be in need of service.

The demographic characteristics of CETA participants have undergone changes compared with those in pre-CETA training and employment programs. The shift toward public service employment programs, which have been oriented largely to the cyclically unemployed; the spread of resources into suburbs, which have different types of populations from cities; and the deteriorated economic climate, which broadened the groups seeking assistance, all contributed to the change.

The number of youth, persons with less than high school education, the economically disadvantaged, and minorities in CETA Titles I, II, and VI combined is greater than that in similar pre-CETA programs. In relative terms, however, the clientele being served under CETA includes more people of prime working age, more with high school education and beyond, and fewer poor people. The proportion of whites served rose in 1977 (see Figure 8 and Table 32). To some extent, increases in Title III national programs for such groups as Indians, migrant farm workers, and youth may offset some of the changes in clientele under other titles.

TITLE I PARTICIPANTS

With a limited penetration rate of service, the question of who receives services is critical. Congress intended that the remedial and employability services of Title I be directed to those "most in need," presumably those who have the most difficulty in obtaining employment without assistance. During the transfer of control from federal to state and local government, however, new forces and considerations have tended to result in service to a different clientele.

For the most part, Title I participants are still the economically

(excluding summer youth) during fiscal 1976 was 1,219,600 in Titles I, II, and VI according to the CLMS; the Department of Labor reported 1,737,600 new enrollees; U.S. Department of Labor, Employment and Training Administration, "Characteristics of New Enrollees in CETA Programs During Fiscal Year 1976," Report no. 6 of the Continuous Longitudinal Manpower Survey, PB-272 950/ST, Prepared by Westat, Inc., Rockville, Md., 1977 (available from NTIS); U.S. President, *Employment and Training Report of the President*, 1977, Table F-2, p. 262.

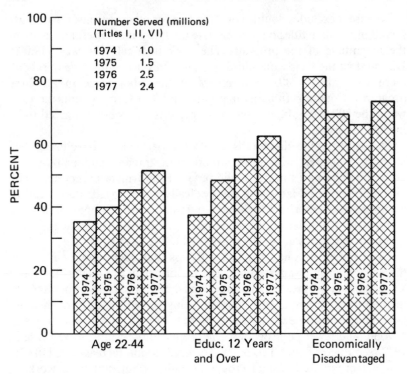

SOURCE: Based on Data from Employment and Training Administration.

FIGURE 8 CETA participants are older, better educated, and less disadvantaged than those in pre-CETA manpower programs.

TABLE 32 Percentage of CETA Participants by Selected Characteristics, Titles I, II, and VI Combined, Compared with Pre-CETA Manpower Programs, Fiscal 1974–1977

Characteristics	FY 1974[a]	FY 1975	FY 1976[b]	FY 1977
Age: 22-24	36	39	45	41
Education: 12 years and over	38	47	54	50
Race: White	56	70	58	61
Economically disadvantaged	81	58	66	71

SOURCE: Computed from Employment and Training Administration, U.S. Department of Labor data.
[a]Includes MDTA Institutional, JOP-OJT, NYC in-school, NYC out-of-school, Operation Mainstream, Concentrated Employment Program, JOBS, and PEP.
[b]Excludes transition quarter.

disadvantaged, members of minority groups, and the young and poorly educated. About half are either black or Spanish-American. In fiscal 1977 more than three-fourths were disadvantaged, one-half were less than 22 years of age, and one-half had not completed high school, including a large proportion who were full-time students participating in school programs (see Table 33). According to the CLMS report, 38 percent of enrollees in adult-oriented employability development programs in 1976 had completed 11 grades or fewer of school.[9]

However, a comparison of the characteristics of CETA participants with a composite of enrollees in categorical programs for fiscal 1974 shows a decided shift. Although youth still are in the majority, the proportion who are age 18 and younger is declining (from 46 percent in fiscal 1974 to 31 percent in fiscal 1977), and the number of persons with less than a high school education is also declining. Particularly significant is the decrease in those identified as economically disadvantaged (from 87 percent in 1974 to 78 percent in 1977), despite the looser definition of economically disadvantaged and the fact that the 1974 composite figures used in this comparison exclude the programs with a heavy emphasis on minorities and the disadvantaged operated by the OIC, SER, and the Urban League.[10] On the other hand, the proportion of clients on welfare prior to enrollment has increased.

The decrease in the proportion of poor persons enrolled under Title I, compared with those in previous programs, may be related to the declining number of school-age youth—most of whom come from poor families. But there is some evidence that CETA adults also have come from higher-income families recently. The CLMS showed that 63 percent of CETA enrollees in adult employability development programs in fiscal 1976 were disadvantaged, compared with 78 percent reported by the Department of Labor for comparable pre-CETA programs.[11] According to that study, 56 percent of adult CETA enrollees were from families with annual incomes of $4,000 or more, compared with only 30 percent of

[9]U.S. Department of Labor, Employment and Training Administration, "Characteristics of New Enrollees in CETA Programs During Fiscal Year 1976," Table 5-4, p. 5-12.

[10]The term "disadvantaged" used before CETA implied a combination of poverty plus some other disadvantage (school dropout, member of minority, less than 22 years of age, 45 years of age or more, or handicapped). Under CETA, "economically disadvantaged" refers to a member of a welfare family or a family whose income is below the accepted poverty level and does not necessarily imply additional disadvantage.

[11]U.S. Department of Labor, Employment and Training Administration, "Characteristics of New Enrollees in CETA Programs During Fiscal Year 1976," Table 5-19, p. 5-54. The data may not be comparable since the pre-CETA figure comes from client records, while the CETA figure was obtained through the Westat survey of a national sample of participants.

TABLE 33 Percentage Distribution of CETA Title I, II, and VI Participants, by Selected Characteristics, Compared With Pre-CETA Programs

Characteristics	Manpower Programs[a] FY 1974	PEP Program FY 1974	CETA Title I			CETA Title II			CETA Title VI		
			FY 1975	FY 1976	FY 1977	FY 1975	FY 1976	FY 1977	FY 1975	FY 1976	FY 1977
Sex: Female	42	34	46	46	48	34	36	40	30	35	36
Age:											
22 and under	63	23	62	57	51	24	22	20	21	22	20
22-44	31	67	32	36	41	63	64	64	65	64	65
45 and over	6	11	6	7	8	13	14	15	14	14	15
Years of school:											
Less than 12	66	23	61	55	50	27	26	27	26	26	27
12 or more	34	77	39	45	50	72	74	78	73	74	73
AFDC and public assistance	23	10	27	26	26	16	15	13	14	13	18
Economically disadvantaged	87	34	77	76	78	48	47	48	44	44	66
Race: Black	37	23	39	37	35	22	27	23	23	23	26
Spanish-speaking	15	13	13	14	14	16	12	8	13	10	8
Vietnam veterans	NA	NA	5	4	3	11	10	7	13	9	6
Full-time student	NA	NA	33	31	25	3	2	2	3	2	2
Labor force status:											
Unemployed	NA	90	62	70	74	84	77	74	88	82	81
Receiving unemployment insurance	5	7	4	6	6	12	13	14	15	14	16

SOURCE: Employment and Training Administration, U.S. Department of Labor.
[a]Includes MDTA-Institutional, JOP-OJT, NYC in-school, NYC out-of-school, Operation Mainstream, CEP, and JOBS.

pre-CETA enrollees at that level. CLMS data indicate a higher proportion of welfare recipients under CETA, however.

The proportions of women and of workers of prime working age increased noticeably from fiscal 1974 to fiscal 1977. This trend is related to changes in program activities, as discussed below. The proportion of blacks was lower in 1977 than before CETA, and that of Spanish-speaking participants remained virtually unchanged, although programs have expanded into localities with relatively smaller minority populations.

TITLE I PARTICIPANTS COMPARED WITH PERSONS IN NEED

To the basic question of whether CETA sponsors are reaching the population groups most in need of service under Title I, there is no ready answer, since there is no set of statistics that satisfactorily describes the unemployed and low-income group that Title I programs are intended to serve. However, an approximation can be made by comparing the characteristics of CETA Title I enrollees in adult-oriented employability development activities with those of persons who have been unemployed for 15 weeks or longer. Table 34 shows a good record for reaching

TABLE 34 Percentage Distribution of CETA Title I Employability Development Participants by Selected Characteristics, Compared with Long-Term Unemployed, Fiscal 1976

Characteristics	Percent of Persons Unemployed 15 Weeks or More	Percent of New CETA Employability Development Participants	Targeting Ratios[a]
Sex: Female	44	46	1.05
Race: Black	18	33	1.83
Age:			
16-21	26	29	1.12
22-44	52	61	1.17
45 and over	22	10	0.45
Education:			
8 years or less	15	11	0.73
9 to 11 years	24	27	1.12
12 and over	61	62	1.02

SOURCE: Computed from Bureau of Labor Statistics, *Work Experience of the Population in 1976*, Special Labor Force Report 201, and *Educational Attainment of Workers*, March 1976 data. Westat, Inc., *Continuous Longitudinal Manpower Survey*, Report No. 6, Aug. 1977, Table 5-4.

[a]Percent of CETA participants in employability development activities, fiscal 1976, to percent of persons unemployed for 15 weeks or more in U.S. labor force, calendar year 1976.

females, blacks, youth in the 16–21 age-group, and persons with some high school education—groups that normally need assistance in obtaining employment. However, the targeting ratios are low for persons 45 and over and for those with 8 years or less of school.

SHIFTS IN PATTERNS OF THOSE SERVED

Many diverse and often opposing trends account for the shifts in the types of people enrolled in Title I programs. On one hand, there are built-in stabilizers that resist change, such as the continuation of pre-CETA programs and operators. On the other hand, the funding process, program mix, procedures for selecting clients, and decisions regarding groups to be served do tend to affect manpower program clientele. Although it would be useful to compute the relative effect of each of these factors on changes in clientele, available data are not specific enough for this purpose. Seven major factors affecting the choice of participants:

1. *Funding process.* Before CETA, funds for most manpower programs were channeled toward the disadvantaged and to areas with concentrations of people with low incomes. Since the CETA formula provides for a universal distribution of resources, relatively greater shares are going to suburban counties that had few, if any, manpower programs in the past (see Chapter 2). Because of the demographic and economic characteristics of the suburban counties, clients with different racial, ethnic, and socioeconomic backgrounds are necessarily drawn into CETA.

The effect of shifting funds from cities to suburbs is shown in Table 35. Manpower programs in counties that are prime sponsors tend to attract a higher proportion of people of prime working age and high school graduates. But counties have relatively fewer blacks and Spanish-speaking clients, economically disadvantaged, and welfare recipients. Of course many counties are serving a disproportionate number of clients who are disadvantaged and members of minority groups in relation to their representation in the population. But the demographic and economic features of county populations almost inevitably result in a different racial and economic mix of clients than that of central cities.

The mostly rural counties in the balance of states, which receive approximately the same share of Title I funds as before CETA, have a high proportion of youth, persons with less than high school education, full-time students, and the economically disadvantaged. This effect results from the nature of the program. Balance-of-state sponsors spend a much larger proportion of their manpower resources on work experience

TABLE 35 Percentage Distribution of CETA Title I Participants by Selected Characteristics and Type of Sponsor, Fiscal 1976 (cumulative to third quarter)

Characteristics	City	County	Consortium	Balance of State
Sex: Female	49	47	45	45
Age:				
Less than 22	59	52	55	59
22-44	36	40	37	34
Education:				
Less than 12 years	56	48	54	59
12 years and over	44	52	46	41
Economically disadvantaged	79	71	75	79
AFDC or public assistance	31	27	26	22
Race: Black	60	27	40	25
Spanish-speaking	17	15	16	8
Full-time student	32	25	28	36
Vietnam veteran	3	5	4	4
Unemployed prior to CETA	76	73	71	59
Receiving unemployment insurance	5	9	6	5

SOURCE: Employment and Training Administration, U.S. Department of Labor (unpublished data).

programs than other types of sponsors. These programs characteristically involve activity viewed as appropriate for younger, more disadvantaged individuals. Balance-of-state programs enroll the lowest proportion of black participants (25 percent), due in part to their demographic makeup.[12]

2. *Decisions on program.* Local decisions on program have a considerable bearing on the kinds of clientele selected and, to some extent, these decisions are influenced by the skill level, education, and extent of job readiness of the available applicants.

Generally, classroom training and work experience are supply-oriented, i.e., the nature of the activity is geared to the characteristics of the available applicants. However, on-the-job training and public service employment tend to be demand-oriented; employers stipulate their needs and usually influence the kinds of clients selected for openings. To illustrate, in one jurisdiction where nearly half of Title I funds were used in 1976 for public service employment, 57 percent of the Title I

[12]In 1970, blacks constituted 9.1 percent of the nonmetropolitan population, 12.0 of metropolitan areas, and 20.6 percent of central cities.

TABLE 36   Percentage Distribution of CETA Title I Participants by Selected Characteristics and Program Activity, Sample Local Prime Sponsors as of December 1975

Characteristics	Classroom Training	On-the-Job Training	Work Experience	Public Service Employment
Sex: Female	56	26	50	38
Age:				
Under 22	38	34	71	34
22-44	56	59	20	54
Education:				
Less than 12 grades	43	28	66	27
12 grades or more	58	72	34	74
Economically disadvantaged	70	66	71	45
Public assistance recipients	37	10	42	7
Race: Black	43	26	42	31
Spanish-speaking	14	9	11	10
Vietnam veterans	4	7	2	5
Full-time student	4	2	59	19
Unemployed prior to CETA	84	87	43	50

SOURCE: Prime sponsor records. Percentages are averages of percentages in 16 prime sponsor jurisdictions.

participants had 12 years or more of education, compared with a U.S. average of 46 percent.

The dichotomy between those in demand-oriented and those in supply-oriented activities is reflected in Table 36. Classroom training and work experience programs have higher proportions of the economically disadvantaged, minorities, persons with less than a high school education, and public welfare recipients. (Work experience, moreover, is largely for youth—full-time students and dropouts.) In the two demand-oriented activities—on-the-job training and public service employment—more of the participants are men of prime working age and are relatively better educated; fewer are members of minority groups or poor.

The higher socioeconomic level of participants could in part be accounted for by those participants who are placed in employment directly, with only minimal services. These persons, about 6 percent of the Title I enrollees, are generally ready for jobs, and they have a minor influence on the statistical profile of CETA clients. One sponsor, responding to a firm's request for workers, recruited over 200 participants, gave them a few hours of orientation, and referred them to the employer the same day. Most were white women of prime working age.

The characteristics of those referred directly to jobs is corroborated by the CLMS of 1976 CETA participants. Adults receiving direct placement only were generally older (and presumably more experienced) than those referred to employability development activities. They were more likely to be men, with a high school education or more, white, and not economically disadvantaged.

3. *Community influences.* In decentralizing the control of manpower programs, CETA has also shifted the point of pressure from regional and national offices of the federal government to more accessible local officials. Congress requires that clients be represented on local advisory councils, and many councils now have members representing women's organizations, Indians, blacks, Spanish-speaking, and other minorities. At a minimum, this representation reinforces sponsor awareness of client needs. For example, two ministers in Lorain County who charged the county with being insensitive to the needs of minorities were awarded contracts for outreach and job development.

Media pressure is not uncommon. The *Santa Ana Register* in Orange County attacked CETA on the grounds that the poor and especially the Spanish-surname population were not being served as effectively as they had been under pre-CETA categorical programs. In Lansing, *The State Journal* reported critics as saying that public service employment funds were not being used to serve the hard-core unemployed. CETA officials denied both charges. Even where accusations are ill-founded, adverse publicity is a threat that public officials are anxious to avoid. The tendency to spread resources to newly identified client groups, particularly in areas receiving more funds than in the past, is often a response to implied or open criticism.

The growing proportion of females in Title I activities is partly related to the increased activism of women in local manpower planning councils. Women as a client group were represented on 10 planning councils in the sample, usually by the League of Women Voters, NOW, or local groups concerned with the status of women. Changes in program mix, less on-the-job training, and preferences of service deliverers are also factors in the greater proportion of women.

4. *Planning for priority groups.* In theory, the selection of groups to be served was to reflect local needs. Supply and demand forces were to be compared, groups in need of services identified, and the segments of the population to receive services listed in the plan. In practice, the relationship between groups identified in plans and those served is tenuous.

Sponsors described significant segments in widely differing terms; there is no common nomenclature. Nevertheless, it was clear that

TABLE 37   Significant Segments by Rank Order in CETA Title I, II, and VI Plans, Sample Prime Sponsors, Fiscal 1976

Rank[a]	Title I	Title II	Title VI
1	Household heads	Household heads	Unemployed
2	Youth	Women	Veterans
3	Women	Veterans	Women
4	Economically disadvantaged	Economically disadvantaged	UI Exhaustees
5	Minorities	Minorities	UI Ineligibles

[a]Ranked by frequency of listing among top three significant segments.

priorities were perceived quite differently by different sponsors in the sample. There were also sharp differences between the Title VI lists featuring the unemployed, veterans, and UI exhaustees and those for Title I. The latter more frequently give top billing to "heads of households," youth, women, and the economically disadvantaged (see Table 37). Priorities for Title II are more similar to Title I than to Title VI, a fact that may reflect a difference in emphasis in the early days of CETA that has since become obscured.

Under Title I in particular, there is a tendency to serve those who apply rather than to seek out those most in need. Under Titles II and VI, the preferences of employing agencies are often the determining factor. In a number of plans, lists of significant segments were treated perfunctorily to fulfill grant application requirements. They were drawn up to respond to groups mentioned in the legislation and regulations. In other areas more efforts were made, including objective point systems used to select those who most nearly conform with preferences listed in the act.

5. *Choice of service deliverers.* The type of clientele is affected by the choice of delivery agencies, particularly those responsible for intake and referral. The control that sponsors exercise over the client selection process varies considerably, depending on the degree to which the manpower system is integrated. But even in a comprehensive system, the dynamics of the labor market, pressure from individuals in need of service, and preferences of organizations furnishing service influence the selection process.

Typically, sponsors inherited a number of service deliverers, many of whom were committed to one or another client group. To the extent that sponsors continued to rely on them for intake, the likelihood of radical change in clientele was minimized. Modifications were more likely to occur where changes were made in assigning intake responsibilities. In

Kansas City, for example, the sponsor contracted with two community-based organizations for core services of intake, assessment, orientation, counseling, job development, and placement. In 1977, however, one operator (the Economic Opportunity Foundation) was assigned this responsibility in order to streamline the delivery system. By contrast, Philadelphia has a typical independent delivery system with little control over selection by the prime sponsor. Except for the JFK Center, whose intake is done through the employment service, all service deliverers do their own intake, and there is little coordination.

The effect of the ethnic orientation of program operators in the selection of manpower trainees can be demonstrated by the New York City CETA structure. The CETA administrator there contracts with numerous private and public organizations within specific ethnic and racial communities. The OIC is the largest, but a number of other agencies arrange for training within the black, Puerto Rican, Jewish, or other community groups.

In several jurisdictions studied, changes in service deliverers significantly affected the profile of clients. In Raleigh, the entry of the OIC, with its emphasis on low-income, black, and female trainees, has had an effect on the composition of clients. In the San Joaquin consortium, the choice of the Filipino Bayanihan and El Concilio, two community-based organizations, for outreach services in rural sections of the county is bringing in more males, adults, high school dropouts, migrant and seasonal farm workers, and Spanish-speaking persons. In Topeka, a decrease in minority participants in 1976 was associated with a shift of responsibility for intake from community-based organizations to the employment service.

The location of service centers and the allocation of funds to specific communities within a prime sponsor's jurisdiction also heavily affect selection of clients. Cook County's high proportion of blacks in Title I activities in fiscal 1975 (60 percent) compared to the low proportion of blacks in the population (4 percent) was attributed to the location of intake and service offices in black communities. In the Orange County consortium, where the allocation of funds and services within the county is determined by a "fair share" formula based on the number of unemployed in each of the constituent communities, program operators complained that they must turn away applicants in some communities with large minority and poverty populations while training opportunties are unused elsewhere.

6. *Administrative effect.* Pressure on local sponsors to meet goals, competition among program operators for contracts, and emphasis on performance evaluation encourage selection of the applicants most likely

to succeed. These pressures are reinforced by the difficulty in finding jobs for manpower trainees, who compete with better qualified candidates in a loose labor market. Program operators prefer trainees who have some chance of being placed rather than those whose employability is minimal.

7. *The economic effect.* The recession brought in a class of participants who would normally be expected to make their own way in the labor market. In some areas, the number of applicants was so much greater than available openings for training or employment that it was impossible to adhere to plans. Concern for the recently unemployed has led to the practice of referring the more disadvantaged and less educated to remedial programs under Title I, while those with better preparation are placed in Titles II and VI slots.

CHANGES IN CLIENTELE IN THE AREAS STUDIED

Reports from the sample show considerable variation in clientele from area to area, but generally reflect national trends between fiscal 1975 and fiscal 1976 (fiscal 1974 data not available). In 26 areas for which data were available for fiscal 1975 and fiscal 1976, there was a trend toward serving a smaller proportion of youth (20 of 26 areas) and, associated with that, a greater proportion of persons of higher educational attainment (21 of 26). There was a less distinct trend with respect to serving economically disadvantaged persons: 14 of the 26 areas reported a higher percentage in the second year than in the first; 12 reported a lower proportion. Most of the areas also reported fewer blacks during the second year.

The availability of public service employment options, changes in outreach and intake activities, and changes in program were noted as reasons for these trends. The availability of more money in nearly all of the areas studied in fiscal 1976 (including carryovers from the previous year) made it possible to serve more persons and to expand to groups that had not been served before. This, too, affected the profile of the CETA participants.

The Federal Supplemental Benefits program implemented in fiscal 1976 had an insignificant effect on selection of clients in the sample. That program made extended UI benefits conditional on willingness to accept referral to training where appropriate. Referrals were few and only a fraction of those referred were enrolled in programs. Despite the commitment of the Department of Labor, the program failed, due to complicated procedures, delays in implementation, communication gaps between the employment service agencies and sponsors, competition for available openings, and, in many cases, a lack of enthusiasm on the part of unemployment insurance recipients.

TITLE II AND VI PARTICIPANTS

In designing the Comprehensive Employment and Training Act, the Senate proposed that it incorporate provisions of the Emergency Employment Act, with a sharper focus on Vietnam veterans (50 percent of openings) and on the economically disadvantaged unemployed and underemployed.[13] However, the less rigorous House version prevailed, with "special consideration" for Vietnam-era veterans, the most severely disadvantaged in terms of length of unemployment who have poor prospects for competing successfully in the labor market, and "due consideration" for former manpower trainees. Title VI later added "preferred consideration" for unemployment insurance exhaustees, those not eligible for UI, and persons unemployed for 15 weeks or more. Thus the act itself did not clearly give top priority for public service employment to the disadvantaged, except for the exhortation to treat significant segments equitably "to the extent practicable"—an apparent reference to minorities and other vulnerable groups. Moreover, emphasis on transition of participants to regular jobs in the public and private sectors gave added incentive to select those most likely to succeed, rather than the unskilled and the disadvantaged. Despite later relaxation of transition from a "requirement" to "goal," public service employment programs continued to be demand-oriented. Employers preferred to fill essential public service jobs, even on a temporary basis, with well-qualified applicants.

Title II and VI participants as a whole are a different group than those in Title I (see Table 33). Title I programs enrolled a much higher proportion of participants with characteristics associated with a disadvantaged status than did Titles II and VI. Public service employment participants in fiscal 1976 were predominantly adult, white, nondisadvantaged men who were high school graduates at least. Differences are partly due to the concentration of programs for school-age youth in Title I. The higher proportion of Vietnam veterans under Titles II and VI compared with Title I is explained by the emphasis of the act. This emphasis may have resulted in a smaller proportion of females in PSE programs.

[13]U.S. Congress, Senate, Committee on Labor and Public Welfare, *Emergency Employment Amendments of 1973*, Senate report no. 93-305, July 6, 1973, p. 2.

Table 33 also shows a higher proportion of disadvantaged, minorities, and welfare recipients and a lower proportion of persons who were unemployed prior to entry under Title II than under Title VI in fiscal 1976. This is due in part to the start of Title II in areas of substantial unemployment before the flood of new applicants under Title VI. (A marked change occurred in fiscal 1977 with the stricter elgibility requirements under Title VI.) Relatively more public service employment participants were reported to be unemployed prior to entry in CETA than enrollees under Title I. Labor Department statistics for fiscal 1976 show about 80 percent of Title II and Title VI participants to have been unemployed prior to enrollment in 1976, compared with 70 percent under Title I. About 16 percent of Title II and 12 percent of Title VI participants were reported to have been out of the labor force or employed. These figures are questioned by the CLMS, showing that 35 percent of those enrolled in CETA public service employment in 1976 had been employed just before entry, 17 percent had been out of the labor force, and only 48 percent had been unemployed.[14]

COMPARISION WITH PEP PARTICIPANTS

Clients selected for Title II and VI public service employment programs are generally similar to those in the PEP program in fiscal 1974 (see Table 33). This fact is not surprising, since PEP was the first manpower program operated directly by state and local governments and many prime sponsors and program agents use former PEP administrative staff to operate the CETA program. There are, however, some significant differences, the most important being a trade-off between veterans and the disadvantaged. PEP emphasized Vietnam-era and other veterans whose joblessness was more in the public consciousness at that time; under CETA, the proportion of veterans is smaller and the proportion of disadvantaged and former welfare recipients is higher. Second, under CETA, relatively fewer enrollees are unemployed and more are either out of the labor force or employed prior to entry. A third difference is the larger share of CETA enrollees that formerly were unemployment insurance recipients, a reflection of the emphasis that CETA places on the long-term unemployed and persons who have exhausted UI benefits.

---

[14]U.S. Department of Labor, Employment and Training Administration, "Characteristics of Enrollees in CETA Programs During Fiscal Year 1976," Table 6-1, p. 6-3. See also Chapter 7, Footnote 18.

TABLE 38 Percentage Distribution of CETA Title II and VI Participants by Selected Characteristics, Compared with Long-Term Unemployed, Fiscal 1976

Characteristics	Percent of Persons Unemployed 15 Weeks or More	Percent of CETA Participants		Targeting Ratios[a]	
		Title II	Title VI	Title II	Title VI
Sex: Female	44	36	35	0.82	0.80
Race: Black	18	26	23	1.44	1.28
Age:					
16-21	26	22	22	0.85	0.85
22-44	52	64	64	1.23	1.23
45 years and over	22	14	14	0.64	0.64
Education:					
8 years or less	15	8	8	0.53	0.53
9 to 11 years	24	18	18	0.75	0.75
12 and over	61	74	74	1.21	1.21

SOURCE: Computed from Bureau of Labor Statistics, *Work Experience of the Population in 1976*, Special Labor Force Report 201, and *Educational Attainment of Workers*, March 1976 and Employment and Training Administration data.
[a]Percent of CETA participants, fiscal 1976, to percent of persons unemployed for 15 weeks or more in U.S. labor force, calendar 1976.

CETA PSE PARTICIPANTS AND THE LONG-TERM UNEMPLOYED

CETA requires prime sponsors to give consideration to the long-term unemployed in selecting participants for Title II and Title VI. The characteristics of the long-term unemployed—those out of work 15 weeks or longer—differs from short-term jobless in two respects: they tend to be older and less educated. Table 38 shows that CETA had a mixed record in selecting those groups who have the poorest prospects of obtaining employment in the private sector. The targeting ratios—the percentage of CETA participants compared with the percentage among the long-term unemployed—are low for persons with less than a high school education, for persons less than 22 or more than 45 years of age, and for females. On the other hand, the percentage of blacks on the CETA PSE rolls is higher than their proportion among the long-term unemployed.

DIFFERENCES BY TYPE OF SPONSOR

As in Title I, the characteristics of public service employees vary by type of sponsor, with differences between cities and counties particularly marked (see Table 39).

TABLE 39 Percentage Distribution of CETA Title II and VI Participants by Selected Characteristics and Type of Sponsor, Fiscal 1976 (cumulative to third quarter)

Characteristics	City Title II	City Title VI	County Title II	County Title VI	Consortium Title II	Consortium Title VI	Balance of State Title II	Balance of State Title VI
Sex: Female	39	36	36	37	39	36	34	33
Age:								
Less than 22	22	20	24	24	21	22	21	19
22-44	66	67	63	63	66	66	62	64
Education:								
Less than 12 years	27	26	20	21	20	22	31	29
12 years or over	73	74	80	79	80	78	69	71
Economically disadvantaged	44	43	38	37	46	43	49	48
AFDC or public assistance	20	17	14	13	10	13	12	12
Race: Black	53	49	19	19	24	24	11	13
Spanish-speaking	14	13	10	8	13	11	3	10
Full-time student	2	1	3	3	2	2	2	1
Vietnam veteran	11	11	10	9	10	10	9	8
Unemployed prior to CETA	85	83	82	76	81	84	79	82
Receiving unemployment insurance	10	12	15	14	13	14	14	15

SOURCE: Employment and Training Administration, U.S. Department of Labor (unpublished data).

The differences in pattern by types of sponsors are related to the characteristics of the applicant pool and the nature and requirements of jobs established by sponsors. Not surprisingly, counties, which include suburban areas, have better educated and less disadvantaged participants. The proportion of minorities is also much lower in counties that are prime sponsors in their own right and in consortia, which include counties as well as cities.

A comparison of balance-of-state sponsors (largely rural counties) with other types of sponsors also shows a significant difference: more men, more older workers (45 and above), more persons with less than high school education, and more economically disadvantaged, but a smaller proportion of minorities.

In the study sample, too, characteristics of participants varied within each category of sponsor (see Appendix D, Table 8). This fact indicates that local considerations—priorities, types of openings, procedures for selecting applicants, the extent to which nonprofit agencies receive enrollees, and relationships with program agents and other subjurisdictions—have more to do with the kinds of clients than the type of sponsor.

For example, among cities in the sample, the percentage of economically disadvantaged persons in Title VI ranged from 25 percent in Long Beach to 99 percent in Gary. These two cities were also at opposite extremes in terms of educational attainment of participants—89 percent with 12 years or more of education in Long Beach, compared with 63 percent in Gary. Among counties, the range of economically disadvantaged was similarly wide; from 24 percent in Middlesex to 71 percent in Calhoun.

Sponsors confirm that a major basis for the selection of qualified participants for Titles II and VI is the preference of employers. One reason for the low proportion of economically disadvantaged participants in some places is a policy of referring applicants who are likely to meet employer requirements for public service jobs, while those considered to be in need of remedial education or skill training are referred to Title I openings. Several prime sponsors reported that their concern over the transition of PSE workers to permanent jobs impelled them to refer the more skilled and experienced applicants to employing agencies. About half the prime sponsors indicated that Titles II and VI were handled as one program, resulting in little difference in the kinds of clients served.

In some areas, the existence of civil service, literacy requirements, and job specifications tended to favor the best qualified applicants, giving the employing agency a pool of fully qualified persons to draw from in filling vacancies. For example, in San Joaquin, although applicants have been rated at intake by a point system that gives weight to veteran status, length of unemployment, exhaustion of UI benefits, and low family income, the employing agencies have the last word. Selection of applicants from those referred takes into account merit service standards and minimal education requirements. Thus, the CETA office rates applicants based on categories expressed in the act, but the employing agencies select the best qualified from among those referred. In Phoenix, the personnel office draws up requirements and stipulates standards of selection. In St. Paul, during fiscal 1975 local government units made a particular effort to attract recent college graduates with an eye toward eventual integration into their staff.

SUMMARY

The major objective of manpower policy has been to improve the employability of those segments of the labor force who cannot successfully compete, because of lack of appropriate education and skills or because of artificial barriers to employment. Rising joblessness in the 1970s generated an additional thrust to manpower policy and programs—the use of public service employment as a countercyclical measure. CETA now incorporates a combination of these two objectives, implemented within a framework of local rather than national determination of the groups and individuals to be served. With these dual objectives, there is growing concern over the balance between services to the poor and disadvantaged and assistance for the more recently unemployed. However, until the amendments of 1977, the legislation did not explicitly prescribe the groups to be served. After 2 years of experience, Congress refined its position on the clientele to be served (at least in public service programs) and in this process moved toward more categorical constraints attached to additional funds.

The record of the first years of managing manpower programs under local control indicates the following developments with respect to the people in the program:

• The number of individuals served by manpower programs (under Titles I, II, and VI) is significantly greater than before. However, with about 40 percent of participants in public service employment, there has been a marked relative change in the composition of the groups served compared with earlier programs. Participants under all three titles combined are older, better educated, and less disadvantaged than those in fiscal 1974.

• Title I programs, which more closely represent training and employability programs traditionally directed toward the disadvantaged, are primarily oriented to the young, minorities, and the disadvantaged. However, there has been a shift toward a broader economic group of clients, first noted in fiscal 1975 and reinforced by data for fiscal 1976 and by related studies. Factors associated with these changes are the spread of programs to the suburbs, changes in the mix and content of programs, conscious decisions to broaden the client base in response to community pressure, emphasis on selecting those most capable of succeeding, and a shift toward enrollment of heads of households in response to the economic decline. On the other hand, institutional factors—the continuance of pre-CETA programs deliverers with commitment to the disadvantaged and minorities and the purposeful decisions of some sponsors—have tended to restrict changes.

• On the whole, public service employees, influenced by employer requirements, are more likely to be male, better educated, white, and less disadvantaged than those enrolled under Title I. Clients enrolled in public service employment are similar to those under PEP, although CETA enrollees include a higher percentage of economically disadvantaged and welfare recipients and a lower percentage of veterans. More of the CETA participants formerly received unemployment insurance, reflecting the emphasis on this group under Title VI. Although PSE is intended for persons who are unemployed, a significant proportion were either employed or out of the labor force prior to enrollment. (Some of these were transfers among CETA titles.)

With new amendments to Title VI, a three-tier system seems to be evolving: (a) employability programs (Title I) largely for the severely disadvantaged, (b) public service employment for those higher on the socioeconomic ladder, and (c) project-type public service employment for the long-term unemployed in families above the poverty level but below the low-income level. The possibility of a fourth tier for welfare clientele at the minimum wage is under consideration. This trend will have implications in public service employment if CETA is extended for a number of years. It may lead to a secondary labor market in the public sector for employees who do not qualify for employment in the regular civil service structure.

9 Program Effectiveness

During the early years of CETA, emphasis understandably has been on developing the necessary organizational structure to handle manpower programs at the local level and to absorb new programs that have been added in rapid succession. Less attention has been paid to the broader question of whether manpower programs, as administered by local sponsors, have accomplished the underlying objectives of the act.

Common to all titles of CETA is the objective of enhancing the employability of clients and easing their adjustment in the labor market. Basically, the programs are aimed at increasing the ability of the unemployed and underemployed to obtain suitable employment. The central question is: Has CETA made a difference for those it has served and is this difference sufficient to justify the costs?

Some of the information needed for assessing the long-term effects of CETA on individuals served is expected from the continuous longitudinal manpower survey (CLMS) being conducted for the Employment and Training Administration. Other studies of CETA have concentrated on interorganizational relationships and processes rather than results. The kinds of evaluative research that accumulated under categorical programs, based on long-term analysis of costs and benfits, have not begun to emerge for CETA.

This chapter is concerned with the immediate postprogram experience of those enrolled in Titles I, II, and VI. CETA's premise is that a locally designed system serves clients more effectively than a federally run program because of the greater flexibility of local sponsors to adapt programs to local circumstances. The validity of this assumption is examined by comparing short-term outcomes with those of pre-CETA programs.

It is important to note, however, that the placement experience is only one measure of program outcome. Some sponsors are more concerned with strategies for employability development that may not necessarily yield immediate payoffs. Youth programs, for example, are designed mainly to keep youngsters in school and provide some potentially useful experience as well as support, rather than to launch them immediately into the job market.

The record of CETA programs compared with those of pre-CETA programs is disappointing. More people have been served, but the rate at which persons obtain unsubsidized jobs has fallen below expectations. This study raises questions as to whether the lower job entry rates under CETA are attributable to the economic downturn or whether other factors, such as the inexperience of sponsors, decreases in program services most likely to lead to jobs, and the downgrading of the transition objective by Congress, are also responsible.

LIMITATIONS OF MEASURES OF EFFECTIVENESS

Quantitative measurement of program results is seriously hampered by limitations in the CETA reporting system. The Employment and Training Administration restructured and unified the system to streamline and reconcile the separate reporting systems of a number of individual programs. As a result, it is impossible to isolate CETA data with sufficient detail to make comparisons with pre-CETA programs or even to fully analyze CETA outcomes.

CETA data are aggregated by function rather than by program. Programs for youth and adults of the same general nature are combined as one reporting item. Since the objective of most youth programs is to provide some work experience while strengthening the attachment to school and the objective of adult programs is to impart skills necessary for obtaining employment, the combining of youth and adult data obscures important differences and makes outcome analysis difficult. Other reporting problems are:

- The loose definition of "participants," which includes persons who receive only minimal services, may result in duplications in counts. Participants routed from one service component to another may be counted more than once, making it impossible to compare the service load from 1 year to another. The wholesale shifting of participants back and forth between Title II and Title VI for administrative reasons affected the validity of enrollment and termination figures. A person who is shifted from one title to another was counted as a "termination" and as a "new enrollment," although there was no substantive change in status.[1]

• Lack of data on preference groups listed under various titles of the act. There is no way of tracking the enrollment, services provided, or results for such categories as former manpower trainees; UI exhaustees; persons not eligible for UI; long-term, low-income clients; or Federal Supplemental Benefit referrals.

• Lack of separate data on terminations and placements by activity. It is not possible to determine from the standard reporting system which Title I program components yield best results.

• The questionable validity of outcome data—placements, expected duration of jobs, and wage changes from before to after CETA. The reporting system does not require validation of placement figures (particularly for those who obtain employment on their own or through outside channels). Moreover, there is no information on whether jobs obtained by participants are training-related, and no data are reported on job retention.

• Although there is a considerable amount of monitoring and evaluation in local areas, most is closely related to operations. There is very little overall assessment of or follow-up on trainees at the local level.

The weakness of the regular information system is demonstrated by the findings of the CLMS that reported decidedly different figures from those reported by ETA for such items as labor force and economic status of enrollees prior to entry into programs.[2] But even if the data were completely reliable and valid, operating statistics are not detailed enough for useful analysis. Given the low priority assigned to the data function and the many pressures on prime sponsors in launching and maintaining programs, it is not surprising that there are reporting problems.

In summary, the present data system, built up from prime sponsor reports on a limited number of items, has advantages for simplifying

---

[1]Reporting revisions effective in fiscal 1978 are designed to correct for double counting by indicating the number who terminate from one title and transfer to another.

[2]U.S. Department of Labor, Employment and Training Administration, "Characteristics of New Enrollees in CETA Programs During Fiscal Year 1976," Report no. 6 of the Continuous Longitudinal Manpower Survey, PB-272 950/ST, Prepared by Westat, Inc., Rockville, Md., 1977 (available from NTIS), Table 5-17, p. 5-48. The report shows that 58 percent of new enrollees under Titles I, II, and VI were economically disadvantaged, compared with 66 percent reported by the Employment and Training Administration in fiscal 1976.

program administration, but it has gaps in essential data, a lack of flexibility for making cross-tabulations, and poor quality control. Conversion to a reporting system based on central or regional data processing of individual client records would relieve local program operators and sponsors of tedious reporting, would make the entire system more flexible for analytical and management purposes, and would eliminate duplication.

Another quantitative approach to assessment would compare performance against standards of what might reasonably be expected. The Employment and Training Administration issued guidelines for reviewing grant applications that would be convenient if the standards were acceptable.[3] Although these guidelines, based on experience in the first 18 months of CETA, were intended to be used flexibly, they have been severely criticized because: (a) They represented broad averages that were not applicable to individual areas, especially since there is wide variation in program content; (b) they did not include some basic measures that, though difficult to quantify, are important, i.e., improvement in the earnings potential of clients and in job stability; and (c) the indicators tended to favor programs that produce immediate placement results rather than raise the employability of clients. These guidelines have been replaced with more flexible measures for the review of 1978 grants.

Quantitative methods do not tell the whole story. Less measurable benefits include such considerations as the range of options for enrollees, the quality of training and work experience programs, and the adequacy of counseling and other services provided. Programs can also be judged by how well they reach targeted groups, their effect in removing barriers to employment, and their links to the private sector. For lack of better data, the remainder of this chapter relies mainly on quantitative measures and on the judgment of informed local observers.

TITLE I JOB ENTRY EXPERIENCE

In the second year of CETA, 1.7 million individuals were in Title I programs. Of these, 1.6 million were enrolled in some specific program activity.[4] The rest were persons who received only minimal services or

---

[3]Primary indicators were: entered employment rate, indirect placement, "nonpositive" termination rate, and unassigned participant rate. Secondary indicators were: cost per participant in classroom training, on-the-job training, and work experience; cost per individual enrolled in program activities; and turnover rate.

[4]Peak enrollment in March 1976 was 574,000. Title I enrollments in 1977 were reported as 1.4 million, of whom 1.1 million were enrolled in program activities.

TABLE 40 Individuals Served, Terminations, and Job Entries, CETA Titles I, II, and VI, Fiscal 1975–1977 (numbers in thousands)

Item	Title I			Title II			Title VI		
	FY 1975	FY 1976	FY 1977	FY 1975	FY 1976	FY 1977	FY 1975	FY 1976	FY 1977
Total individuals served[a]	1,126.0	1,731.5	1,415.6	227.1	255.7	352.9	157.0	495.2	592.9
Total terminations	553.3	1,226.2	1,048.4	70.9	161.2	260.6	33.8	289.3	161.7
Entered employment	176.0	380.4	408.6	16.6	27.7	46.2	9.8	77.5	55.0
Percent of terminations	100.0	100.0	100.0	100.0	100.0	100.0	100.0	100.0	100.0
Entered employment	31.8	31.0	39.0	23.4	17.2	17.7	29.0	26.8	34.0
Direct placements[b]	11.4	9.1	6.5	1.4	0.7	0.4	1.0	1.3	0.6
Indirect placements[c]	15.3	16.2	24.5	13.7	11.2	12.0	12.3	15.3	19.3
Obtained employment[d]	5.2	5.7	7.9	8.3	5.3	5.4	15.7	10.2	14.2
Other positive terminations[e]	30.9	37.0	31.3	30.9	58.6	65.8	16.6	34.6	20.5
Nonpositive terminations[f]	37.3	32.0	29.7	45.7	24.3	16.5	54.4	38.6	45.5

SOURCE: Computed from Employment and Training Administration, U.S. Dept. of Labor data.
[a]Figures for fiscal 1976 and fiscal 1977 include carryover from previous years.
[b]Individuals placed after receiving only intake, assessment, and/or job referral service.
[c]Individuals placed after participation in training, employment, or supportive services.
[d]In fiscal 1975 this figure was self-placements; in fiscal 1976 and fiscal 1977 it included persons obtaining employment through means other than placement of sponsors.
[e]Individuals not placed in jobs but who left to attend school, to participate in other manpower programs, or to join the armed forces.
[f]Individuals who left for reasons unrelated to obtaining employment or training.

were in a holding status. Although these totals include some duplication, the number of persons served is substantially higher than the 800,000 enrolled in comparable activities before CETA. The increase is due to a 50 percent rise in funding levels.

Turnover in manpower programs is fairly quick. Seventy percent of the 1976 participants were reported to have terminated during that year, including both persons who completed a program unit and those who quit before completion. Many were youth who were counted as "terminees" when the program ended, although most returned to school and might have been reenrolled and counted again. Others were enrolled in short-term training or orientation courses, while still others may have received only counseling and orientation services. The average length of stay in a Title I program has been estimated at 4.3 months (compared with 8.1 months in a public service employment program).[5] Differences in length of stay are significant in terms of costs and the characteristics of clients served. CETA spends more on the less disadvantaged public service program participants than on the most disadvantaged served under Title I.

About 29 percent of those who terminated from Titles I, II, and VI in fiscal 1976 were reported to have entered employment; the rate climbed to 35 percent of terminees in fiscal 1977 (see Table 40). Job entry rates under CETA are low compared with rates of 50 to 60 percent of terminees for MDTA and other pre-CETA categorical programs (see Table 41). To a significant degree, this difference is due to the inclusion of CETA programs that are not aimed at immediate job placement (i.e., in-school youth programs). If programs for school youth were eliminated from both CETA and pre-CETA programs, the respective placement rates would be 42 percent for Title I and 57 percent for the adult-oriented categorical programs (see Table 42).[6]

Only 16 percent of the Title I terminations (or about 11 percent of all Title I enrollees) were listed as "indirect" placements in fiscal 1976. The indirect job entry rate rose to 25 percent of terminees in fiscal 1977, or about 18 percent of enrollees. This is the rate of participants placed in jobs by the sponsor after being enrolled in training, work experience, or other substantive activity or receiving support services. It is considered

---

[5]Employment and Training Administration data for 1976 (unpublished).

[6]The estimate of 57 percent for fiscal 1974 is a composite figure calculated from terminations and placements for the following programs: MDTA institutional, MDTA–JOP, JOBS, Public Service Careers, Comprehensive Manpower Programs (CMP), and CEPs. The CETA estimate of 42 percent is calculated from fiscal 1976 (first three quarters) Title I terminations and placements for the 79 prime sponsors with fewer than 10 percent of enrollees reported as full-time students.

TABLE 41   Enrollments, Terminations, and Placements, Selected Department of Labor Manpower Programs, Fiscal 1974

Program	Enrollees	Terminations	Placements[a] Number	Percent of Total Terminations
MDTA Institutional	152,800	106,800	65,100	61
MDTA On-the-Job Training (JOP)	52,500	37,100	20,400	55
Job Opportunities in the Business Sector (JOBS)	42,200	32,200	18,400	57
Public Service Careers (PSC)	29,700	24,600	15,600	63
Comprehensive Manpower (CMP)	44,900	16,900	9,800	58
Concentrated Employment (CEP)	95,800	72,400	37,100	52
TOTAL	417,900	290,000	166,400	57

SOURCE: Employment and Training Administration, U.S. Department of Labor.
[a]Placements in CEP are defined as those participants who entered unsubsidized jobs prior to completion or termination. In JOP, JOBS, and PSC, placements and completions are the same. In MDTA institutional, placements were recorded at the time of placement or within 30 days.

TABLE 42   CETA Title I Job Entry Rates by Percentage of Full-Time Students and Percentage of Economically Disadvantaged, Fiscal 1976 (cumulative to third quarter)

Rates	Prime Sponsors by Percent of Full-Time Students		Prime Sponsors by Percent of Economically Disadvantaged	
	Less Than 10%	60% or More	Less Than 60%	90% or More
Percent of terminations				
Entered employment	42	19	39	29
Direct placement	17	9	16	8
Indirect placement	19	8	16	17
Obtained employment	6	2	7	4
Other positive terminations	18	66	26	44
Nonpositive terminations	40	15	35	27

SOURCE: Computed from Employment and Training Administration, U.S. Department of Labor, unpublished data.

to be a more significant measure of program performance than the gross placement rate. The low indirect rates are influenced by such factors as the selection of trainees, duration of training, and types of courses offered, as well as the extent to which jobs are available.

The direct placement rate, 9.1 percent of Title I terminations in fiscal 1976 and 6.5 percent in 1977, is more controversial. Direct placements require no service to the client other than intake, assessment, and job referral. Since sponsors are under pressure to achieve planned placement and cost estimates, there is a tendency to concentrate on direct placements—the easier and more economical route to success. Reservations with regard to direct placement are that it tends to divert attention from the more fundamental task of enhancing the capabilities of those most difficult to place, encourages selection of the most job-ready clients, and tempts sponsors to place participants in low-wage, unstable jobs. Sponsors, on the other hand, maintain that direct placements are necessary because many of their clients are job-ready; but, as members of minority groups, they need all the help they can get to make their way in the job market. In several of the areas studied, a high direct-placement rate was attributed to the tie-in with the employment service, which stations employees in CETA manpower centers. These sponsors believe that, far from being a problem, direct placements fulfill a necessary function.

A small percentage of Title I participants obtain employment on their own or through other agencies shortly after terminating. One sponsor stated that this rate should be regarded as the most important, as an indication of the degree to which the objective of encouraging self-sufficiency is realized. There is little information about this group. It is not known whether they obtain suitable and stable employment leading to permanent jobs or whether they drift into low-wage, intermittent employment.

POSITIVE AND NONPOSITIVE TERMINEES

A large proportion of terminees are listed as "other positive." These are mainly youth who terminate from an in-school program but intend to continue their education. Others may leave for the armed forces or for other training. They may also be persons who transfer to another service component and are not in a real sense either "terminees" or completions. Intertitle transfers tend to distort the termination and placement rates.[7]

[7]Revised reporting instructions effective in fiscal 1978 separate "transfers to other titles" from "other positive" terminees.

Close to one-third of those leaving Title I programs were "nonpositive" terminees—persons who either dropped out of programs or completed them but entered neither employment, training, nor the armed forces. Some undoubtedly left the labor force. A high nonpositive rate may indicate poor planning and selection of participants, inappropriate training, lack of supervision, or the need for better counseling or supportive services. It may also be due to participant withdrawals for unrelated reasons. In one electronics course, for example, which failed because of the diverse background of enrollees, 16 of 24 enrollees were nonpositive terminations.

VARIATIONS IN TITLE I PLACEMENT RATES

The wide variation in job entry rates among individual areas is due to many circumstances. The employment situation in an area obviously has some influence on decisions on whom to serve and what types of services or programs to stress, and these factors are more directly associated with program outcomes.

Adult-oriented programs had higher job entry rates than those whose clientele are largely made up of full-time students. Sponsors with less than 10 percent full-time students had rates that were more than twice as high as sponsors whose clientele consists mainly of school youth, since students normally return to school (see Table 42).

Similarly, there is a striking difference in the experience of sponsors with large percentages of economically disadvantaged participants compared with sponsors with relatively few. Where fewer than 60 percent of Title I participants were disadvantaged, job entry rates averaged 39 percent. Where 90 percent or more of the participants were economically disadvantaged, the average placement rate was 29 percent.[8] Sponsors with high proportions of youth are commonly those with high proportions of economically disadvantaged persons, since programs for youth have traditionally been almost exclusively oriented to the disadvantaged.

There is a strong association between job entry results and the type of program activity offered (see Table 43). Rates were highest for on-the-job training, which is understandable, since the employer often commits himself in advance to hire the trainees. As expected, rates for work experience programs were lowest (primarily because of the preponderance of school-age youth). Classroom training rates varied from area to area. The classroom training category is a mixture of many different

[8]The placement experience of the economically disadvantaged is lower than for other clients. Three-fourths of Title I terminees but only two-thirds of those who got jobs were economically disadvantaged in fiscal 1976.

TABLE 43 CETA Title I Job Entry Rates, by Type of Activity, Sample Local Prime Sponsors, Fiscal 1976 (cumulative to second quarter) (*N* = 18)

	Classroom Training	On-the-Job Training	Work Experience
Total enrolled	14,371	3,585	19,795
Terminations	6,484	2,078	12,046
Percent of terminations			
Entered employment	31	51	9
Direct placement	1	–	–
Indirect placement	25	48	6
Obtained employment	5	3	2
Other positive terminations	20	10	57
Nonpositive terminations	49	38	34

SOURCE: Prime sponsor records.
NOTE: Details may not add to totals due to rounding.

kinds of courses; it includes everything from skill training to general education and English as a second language, which in themselves do not lead to immediate job placement. Among the sponsors in the study sample, those with the highest proportions of enrollees in work experience programs had significantly lower overall placement and indirect placement rates than those with smaller proportions in work experience. The highest placement rates are found among those participants who are not enrolled in any activity but are placed directly in jobs.

Among the various types of sponsors, the lowest overall job entry rates as well as the lowest indirect placement rates were found in cities; the highest were found in counties (see Table 44). The higher proportion of minority enrollees in cities has a bearing on lower placement rates. Surprisingly, balance-of-state areas had higher placement rates than cities and higher indirect placement rates than other types of sponsors. This is contrary to what one might expect, since a high proportion of balance-of-state funds are expended on work-experience programs.

Unemployment rates during 1975 and 1976 were high in most areas; 22 of the 28 sample areas had rates of 7 percent or more, ranging up to 13 percent. Contrary to expectations, however, there was little correlation between placement rates and unemployment rates. Even in areas with less than 6 percent unemployment, the relationship between the unemployment rate and placement rate was not clear, indicating that other factors had a bearing on job entry rates. Nevertheless, about one-third of the sponsors interviewed believed that the lack of employment opportunities had an important effect on outcomes. In some cases, emphasis was placed on training the most disadvantaged or giving them

TABLE 44   CETA Title I Job Entry Rates by Type of Sponsor, Fiscal 1976 (cumulative to third quarter)

Rates	City	County	Consortium	Balance of State
Percent of terminations				
Entered employment	26	37	32	31
Direct	10	12	12	4
Indirect	13	18	14	21
Obtained employment	3	7	6	6
Other positive terminations	50	29	33	40
Nonpositive terminations	24	34	35	29

SOURCE: Computed from Employment and Training Administration, U.S. Department of Labor, unpublished data.

an opportunity to acquire a work record rather than on attempting to find jobs for them.

Some respondents regard placements as decidedly secondary in a generally loose labor market. The short-run objective in their view is to attract participants and improve their employability. In St. Paul, major stress is placed on improving the employability of participants rather than finding jobs for them. Other sponsors stated that it is more important for the present to establish viable CETA institutions than to build up a good placement record.

When sponsors in the sample compared their placement rates with goals set forth in their own plans, most acknowledged that they had not achieved their job placement goals. Even sponsors with the highest job entry rates were often dissatisfied, because judgments are based on their self-imposed standards as expressed in grant applications and not on an absolute criterion. In addition to economic conditions, sponsors offered a variety of reasons for low placement rates: the mix of programs, emphasis on youth or on the hard-core unemployed, selection of participants poorly qualified for jobs, reluctance to refer clients to low-paying temporary or seasonal jobs, and discriminatory hiring practices.

In one consortium, there was virtually no Title I placement associated with any of the substantive manpower programs in the first half of fiscal 1976. Of 3,000 terminated from classroom and on-the-job training, work experience, or public service employment—only about 120 (4 percent) were able to get jobs, and almost all of these found jobs on their own. About one-half were listed as "nonpositive" terminees. After allowing for youth and the hard-core unemployed among participants and for poor labor market conditions, there is still a question as to whether the strategies and efforts to find suitable employment for participants in that consortium were adequate.

Discussion of placement activities with sponsors and other survey respondents brought out conflicting views on the appropriate measures of effectiveness for Title I. While there was general acceptance of placement rates as a convenient indicator, respondents viewed them as only one aspect of performance. They pointed to retention of jobs, increased earnings opportunities, enhancement of skills, and motivation as important considerations.

Sponsors also disagreed on the merits of direct versus indirect placement. In nine survey areas, direct placement rates were higher than indirect (see Appendix D, Table 9). Topeka, with relatively low unemployment, had a Title I job entry rate of 55 percent but an indirect rate of only 14 percent. Few participants were placed as a result of training or employment programs. In another area, the job development and placement function has been shifted from the OIC and SER to another community-based organization because of a disagreement on placement emphasis. The sponsor believed that indirect placements were a better indication of effectiveness; those placed directly might well have been able to obtain employment without CETA assistance.

TITLE II AND VI JOB ENTRY EXPERIENCE

As originally enacted, one of CETA's key features was a requirement that public service jobs lead to unsubsidized employment. The regulations stressed that sponsors should take definite steps to ensure that those hired for Title II would receive an opportunity for employment either in the public or private sector. Concern over this transition requirement was one of the reasons for the slow progress in filling Title II openings in the first half of 1975. Sponsors were doubtful of their ability to place CETA participants and wary about hiring the disadvantaged for fear they would have to absorb them into the regular public service structure. When Title VI was passed the following year, transition was downgraded to a goal and waivers of the goal were authorized when justified by stringent budget situations.

Department of Labor reports show that only 17 percent of Title II terminees and 27 percent of those who left Title VI programs entered employment in fiscal 1976. But placement rates are not reliable for that year because the termination figure, which is the denominator in calculating the rate, is overstated due to intertitle transfers of participants. The effect of this is to lower the job entry rate. As many as one-fourth of the Title II terminees did not leave the program, but merely

232   CETA: MANPOWER PROGRAMS UNDER LOCAL CONTROL

transferred to Title VI positions. Similarly, there was some shifting back from Title VI to Title II. Adjusting for these transfers, placement rates for both titles were approximately 30 percent. In fiscal 1977, the DOL reported job entry rates of 18 percent for Title II and 34 percent for Title VI.

The placement record of Titles II and VI of CETA does not measure up to pre-CETA PEP experience. Under the PEP program, transition of enrollees to unsubsidized public or private positions had been given top priority. Whether because of pressure from Washington or because the economy had begun to improve in 1972 and 1973, a high percentage of former participants found employment. More than half of PEP enrollees transferred directly from PEP jobs to other public or private sector jobs in fiscal years 1972 and 1973. A follow-up study of a national sample showed that, 1 month after they had left PEP, 71 percent were employed. A sample study of persons who enrolled in CETA public service employment programs from January to June 1975 showed that, of those who terminated, 58 percent were employed after 1 month, 28 percent were unemployed, and 15 percent were out of the labor force—either in school, training, or some other activity.[9]

The lower placement rate for public service employment under CETA is partly due to changes in overall labor market conditions but also to the relaxation of emphasis on transition. It seems odd that job entry rates for Titles II and VI are lower than for Title I, although public service employment participants are better educated, less disadvantaged, and more job-ready than those in Title I. Nearly all sponsors interviewed acknowledged that the placement of enrollees either in the private or the public sector is a primary objective but thought that, in the unfavorable economic climate, it was impractical to expect them to find jobs for PSE participants in the private or public sector. Some jurisdictions had imposed hiring freezes or were laying off regular local government workers; they found it hard to justify moving CETA participants into regular public service slots. Others avoided the commitment by putting CETA employees in less essential activities that could more readily be terminated without affecting normal government operations or by assigning them to private nonprofit organizations or state government jobs.

[9]PEP data from U.S. Department of Labor, Employment and Training Administration, *Longitudinal Evaluation of the Public Employment Program and Validation of the PEP Data Bank*, PB-242 779-SET/ST, Prepared by Westat, Inc., Rockville, Md. and cited in *Manpower Report of the President*, April 1974, p. 155. CETA public service employment data from the Continuous Longitudinal Manpower Survey, prepared by Westat, Inc., "Post-Program Experience and Pre-Post Comparisons for Terminees Who Entered CETA in January–June 1975."

Seldom were there placement strategies or mechanisms, such as reserving a portion of regular vacancies for CETA participants, giving the participants training for regular jobs, or preparing individual employability plans. According to DOL reports, prime sponsors spent only a negligible amount for training and supportive services to enhance the employability of PSE participants.

Only a third of the sponsors in the sample were taking positive job development steps. In one county, the sponsor required municipalities to sign an agreement to absorb CETA participants as a condition for acquiring them. Prime sponsors often do not directly control what happens to participants. When positions are assigned to program agents within the sponsor's jurisdiction, their transition responsibilities are delegated to that level.

In addition to economic and budgetary constraints, there are formal and informal barriers that hinder the transfer of CETA participants to regular public service jobs. In a minority of jurisdictions, civil service tests are required for some (usually police or fire fighters) or all positions; only those who qualify may transfer to regular posts. In other cases, more subtle barriers tend to keep out those who do not have the education or training to meet customary standards.

The percentage of terminees who obtain jobs is strikingly low for city sponsors compared with other types of sponsors (see Table 45). The lower placement rates in cities may be due to greater fiscal stringencies in cities, which affect employment opportunities in the public sector. For example, in New York City, only a handful of the approximately 20,000 CETA public service workers entered unsubsidized employment in fiscal 1976. Counties, which have less fiscal pressure, tend to have higher placement rates. The city–county differential in placement rates is also related to the higher proportions in cities of blacks, persons with less

TABLE 45   CETA Title VI Job Entry Rates by Type of Sponsor, Fiscal 1976 (cumulative to third quarter)

Rates	City	County	Consortium	Balance of State
Percent of terminations				
Entered employment	22.8	36.1	33.5	34.3
Direct placement	0.1	1.4	3.3	1.1
Indirect placement	16.5	21.8	19.0	17.9
Obtained employment	6.2	12.9	11.2	15.3

SOURCE: Computed from Employment and Training Administration, U.S. Department of Labor, unpublished data.

TABLE 46   Pre-Enrollment and Post-Enrollment Median Wage of CETA Terminees Who Entered Employment, Fiscal 1976 and 1977 (amounts in dollars)

Title	Median Hourly Wage Pre-Enrollment		Median Hourly Wage Post-Enrollment		Percent Wage Gain	
	FY 1976	FY 1977	FY 1976	FY 1977	FY 1976	FY 1977
Title I	2.66	2.73	2.84	3.10	7	14
Title II	2.95	2.96	3.39	3.63	15	23
Title VI	2.94	3.07	3.44	3.78	17	23

SOURCE: Computed from Employment and Training Administration, U.S. Department of Labor data.

than twelfth grade education, and the economically disadvantaged—groups that have fewer opportunities to get unsubsidized jobs.

THE QUALITY OF PLACEMENTS

There is very little information on the kind of employment obtained by those terminating from CETA. In the areas in the survey, few sponsors paid serious attention to the quality or duration of jobs obtained, wages, job security, the work environment, or prospects for upward mobility. Several sponsors indicated that they planned to follow up on enrollees to find out more about the nature and stability of jobs, but little actual follow-up has occurred.

DOL statistics record the expected duration of employment for enrollees placed by sponsors, but these data are incomplete and of dubious validity. They show that about 90 percent of jobs obtained by CETA participants were expected to last 150 days or more.

Another measure of the quality of placement is the wage level of enrollees who enter employment. DOL national summaries show only a marginal increase in average hourly wages compared with pre-CETA earnings for those moving into jobs from Title I, and a substantially larger gain for those who terminated from Titles II and VI[10] (see Table 46).

It is fairly obvious that wage gains of enrollees are influenced by the general upward drift in wage levels from year to year and the normal incremental wage rises over time of young workers. Differences in placement policies among CETA sponsors also have an effect; wage

[10]In computing median wages, the Department of Labor omits the class of workers whose wages were less than $1.00 per hour before and after enrollment. Thus the medians reflect wage change for only those workers who had jobs before and after CETA.

changes are likely to be minimal if participants are placed in low-wage, secondary labor market jobs and greater if employment occurs in the primary labor market.

Wage changes alone are not a satisfactory measure of increased earnings capacity unless accompanied by information on duration of employment. But studies of long-term benefits are not available yet.

JOB ENTRY EXPERIENCE BY CHARACTERISTICS OF CLIENTS

The differential results by type of clients are important in assessing CETA. For all CETA programs, persons with post-high-school education and those who are white have the best opportunity to obtain employment. To a lesser degree, those of prime working age and those who are not economically disadvantaged have better job prospects than other enrollees. Title I data are difficult to analyze because of the large percentage of people who are school youth not available for placement, but the pattern is clear for Title II and Title VI (see Table 47). Blacks were about one-fourth of Title VI enrollees in fiscal 1977 and about one-fifth of those who terminated, but only one-sixth of those who obtained jobs. Similarly, 21 percent of Title VI particpants who entered employment had 11 years or less of schooling, compared with 27 percent of those who terminated during the year.

There were variations among the areas studied, but for the most part the pattern was the same: a better placement record for those clients who were white, had good education, were of prime working age, and were not in the poverty class. Variations depended in part on the client selected and services offered. For example, in one county, a high proportion of placements were made for females because the Title I courses offered were in occupations in which female workers predominate. Among the reasons given by sponsors to explain differences in hiring patterns were employer preferences for persons with good education and stable work histories and differences among participants in motivation and initiative in seeking jobs.

One of the groups singled out by Congress for preferred consideration in public service jobs is Vietnam veterans. But there is little evidence from official statistics that sponsors were making a special effort to place veterans. The percentage of those placed was about in line with the proportion of Vietnam veterans in all three titles in fiscal years 1976 and 1977. With the present reporting system, there is no way to tell whether other groups designated by Congress for special consideration are in fact being given extra consideration in terms of job placements.

TABLE 47 Percentage Distribution of Individuals Served, Terminations, and Job Entries by Selected Characteristics, CETA Titles II and VI, Fiscal 1977

Characteristics	Title II				Title VI			
	Individuals Served	Terminations	Job Entries	Ratio Job Entries to Terminations	Individuals Served	Terminations	Job Entries	Ratio Job Entries to Terminations
Age:								
21 and under	20	20	19	0.95	20	24	19	0.79
22-44	64	65	68	1.05	65	64	69	1.08
45 and over	16	15	13	0.87	15	12	12	1.00
Education:								
11 years or less	23	23	19	0.83	27	27	21	0.78
12 years	43	44	44	1.00	42	42	44	1.05
Over 12 years	34	33	37	1.12	31	31	35	1.13
Economically disadvantaged	49	47	45	0.96	67	62	55	0.89
Race:								
White	71	72	77	1.07	66	70	78	1.11
Black	23	23	18	0.78	26	21	16	0.76

SOURCE: Computed from Employment and Training Administration, U.S. Department of Labor data.

TABLE 48 Comparison of Man-Year Cost, CETA Title I,
Fiscal 1976, and Pre-CETA Programs, Fiscal 1974 (dollars)

Program and Activity	FY 1976	FY 1974[a]
Title I, individuals served	3,252	–
Title I, enrolled in activities	3,715	3,498
Classroom training	4,861	5,614
On-the-job training	4,209	3,662
Public service employment	8,236	NA
Work experience	3,299	2,224
Other activities	1,024	NA

SOURCE: Employment and Training Administration, U.S. Department of Labor (unpublished data).
[a]Includes MDTA institutional, JOP/OJT, NYC in-school, Operation Mainstream, CEP, and JOBS.

UNIT COSTS

Omitting 1975 as a start-up year, estimated costs per man-year for fiscal 1976 were $3,300 for Title I, $7,200 for Title II, and $8,100 for Title VI, according to the Department of Labor. These estimates are generally comparable with pre-CETA programs if changes in salary levels and in program components are taken into account (see Table 48).

The man-year cost of $3,300 for Title I enrollees in fiscal 1976 is lower than the estimated $3,500 for comparable programs in fiscal 1974, but both figures are affected by the way the estimates were calculated. The Title I figures include the relatively low costs for persons who register but receive only minimal services. Excluding this group, the man-year cost was $3,700 in fiscal 1976. On the other hand, the Department of Labor 1974 figures exclude Public Service Careers and NYC out-of-school youth activities, both relatively high-cost programs. On balance, it appears that the costs are about comparable, but the blend of services offered is somewhat different, with a proportion of CETA funds going to public service employment (not part of the pre-CETA mix), and manpower services.

The emphasis on meeting costs and outcome standards under CETA has several side effects. Sponsors may select combinations of programs with a view toward keeping costs low, thereby giving most emphasis to programs that contribute the least to improved employability. The desire to hold costs down could also lead to creaming or to the use of ineffective, low-cost program operators.

Before CETA, there was less stress on unit cost in assessing perfor-

TABLE 49   Man-Year Cost, CETA Titles I, II, and VI by
Type of Sponsor, Fiscal 1976 (dollars)[a]

Type of Sponsor	Title I	Title II	Title VI
City	3,483	8,614	9,393
County	3,454	8,319	8,952
Consortium	3,378	7,586	8,683
Balance of state	3,332	6,597	7,915
TOTAL	3,419	7,905	8,778

SOURCE: Employment and Training Administration, U.S. Department of Labor (unpublished data).
[a]Man-year costs computed from cumulated data for July 1975 through March 1976.

mance, and it is impossible to say from cost data whether or not the public is getting more for its dollar under CETA programs than previously without considering the appropriateness of the services provided and the results, in terms of employability as well as in finding employment for participants. For example, the decline in the man-year cost of the classroom training component of Title I, compared with MDTA classroom training, may reflect shorter duration of courses under CETA and greater reliance on individual referral rather than class-size training. It is not apparent from the cost figures alone whether the lower man-year cost means more efficiency under CETA or lower quality of service.

The average man-year cost of $7,900 in fiscal 1976 for Titles II and VI combined is lower than the corresponding figure of about $8,100 per man-year for the PEP program in 1973, but the 1977 cost estimate of $8,400 is higher. Apparently the lower wage ceiling ($12,000 under PEP and $10,000 under CETA) had the effect of offsetting wage increases that might have resulted from upward pressure on wages. That a considerable proportion of expenditures (about 12 percent) was for work experience programs, which usually pay minimum wages, also tends to lower the man-year costs for CETA public service employment. Under the 1976 amendments, unit costs for public service employees were expected to be kept down by emphasis on project-type jobs.

There is only a slight difference in man-year costs by type of sponsor under Title I, with highest costs in the cities and lowest in balance-of-state areas (see Table 49). Variations in the blend of programs could account for the difference. The variation by type of sponsor has sharper focus under Titles II and VI; public service employment costs are higher in cities because of higher wage structures and more fringe benefits.

SUMMARY

Although there are serious shortcomings in available data, some broad conclusions as to the short-run outcomes of CETA programs can be drawn. Assessment of the long-term effects awaits the results of the Department of Labor's longitudinal study.

• A total of 2.5 million persons were served by CETA programs in fiscal 1976—more than twice the number reached in corresponding pre-CETA programs. There was a similar increase in expenditures for manpower programs.

• The average length of stay is 4 months in Title I programs and 8 months in public service employment, according to Department of Labor estimates.

• CETA costs per man-year are in line with those of earlier programs, but the content and quality of the Title I programs may be somewhat different.

• Omitting programs that are not expected to result in placements, job entry rates were low under all three titles compared with pre-CETA programs. The composite job entry rate for all three titles was 28 percent in 1976. It rose to 35 percent in 1977. While the economic downturn is often cited as the reason, other factors, including service strategy, may have been equally or more significant. The deemphasis on transition of Title II and VI participants is a case in point.

• Only about half of those who entered employment from Titles I, II, and VI in fiscal 1976 and 60 percent in fiscal 1977 were placed after having been enrolled either in a substantive training or employment program. The remainder were either placed without having participated in such programs or found jobs on their own. A substantial proportion of terminees were nonpositive. The nonpositive rate may reflect the characteristics of those selected, the quality of service, or the placement effort.

• CETA programs have been least successful in finding unsubsidized jobs for the hard-core unemployed—minority participants, persons with less than a high school education, younger workers, and the poor.

• While Congress identified specific groups for special consideration (e.g., the long-term unemployed, unemployment insurance exhaustees, etc.), little is known about their enrollment or postprogram experience because of limitations in the data collection system.

• The DOL reporting system produces little information about the quality of jobs obtained by CETA enrollees, retention of jobs, or changes in long-range earnings capacity. Reports show only negligible gains in the hourly earnings of participants in post-CETA jobs compared with pre-CETA programs.

While the record is mixed, there are significant benefits that should not be overlooked. CETA has provided access to public service jobs to large numbers of minority group members and other disadvantaged persons who might not otherwise have had an opportunity for employment. There are also noneconomic advantages for participants, in terms of improved morale, health, and ability to function in the labor market, that cannot be evaluated by statistics.

10 Findings and Recommendations

This chapter presents the recommendations of the Committee on Evaluation of Employment and Training Programs, which was established to assess the impact of CETA on manpower programs. The Committee was concerned not only with the extent to which the congressional intent was fulfilled, but also with broader social, economic, and institutional issues relating to manpower programs.

Government assistance in developing human resources through employment and training programs is an expression of social policy directed to persons who lack skills or are otherwise at a disadvantage in the competitive job market. Since funds are limited, the central social issue is whether the CETA allocation formulas, eligibility requirements, and the practices of prime sponsors in selecting participants are serving people and places with the greatest needs.

The institutional issue that concerned the Committee was the relationships among the federal, state, and local levels of government in the administration of CETA. The heart of the issue is the locus of decision making and accountability: Who decides among alternative places, programs, and people? Inherent in this set of relationships is the question of whether congruence can be achieved between national policies and local prime sponsor practices. The decentralization of manpower programs has also affected networks of institutions that traditionally have provided training and employment programs. The unsettled relationship between the Employment Service and prime sponsors is particularly troublesome. The question is whether CETA has indeed

241

created a better organized system for administering manpower programs, one of the objectives that led to manpower reform. Another issue is whether the CETA programs are being used for local political purposes rather than for improving employability or creating jobs.

Finally, the Committee was interested in whether CETA was achieving its basic economic objectives. Do the structurally oriented programs provide the skills, experience, and services that enable the disadvantaged to function more effectively in a complex and imperfect labor market or have they become a disguised form of income maintenance? Do the countercyclical public service employment programs reduce unemployment or substitute federal for local resources? The Committee was concerned with the kinds and quality of services, the balance of resources between structural and countercyclical programs, and the placement outcomes. A crucial question is how to protect programs to enhance employability during periods of high unemployment.

Although based on findings of the study, the recommendations also draw on the knowledge and experience of Committee members. In addition, the Committee examined other sources including materials from the National Council on Employment Policy and the National Commission on Manpower Policy. The specific findings and recommendations that follow are grouped in four categories: allocation of resources, substantive aspects of CETA programs, administrative processes, and institutional relationships.

ALLOCATION OF RESOURCES

ISSUES

Funds for manpower programs, which began as a trickle in the early 1960s, have grown to be a sizable share of federal and local government budgets in recent years. The amounts appropriated and the distribution pattern define the scope of manpower programs and set limits on the kinds of activities that can be undertaken. There are four principal issues associated with funding: the level of appropriations necessary to deal with manpower problems; the appropriate balance between subsidized public employment and other measures, particularly unemployment insurance, to alleviate countercyclical joblessness; the proportion of CETA funds that should be devoted to structural objectives vis-a-vis the proportion for countercyclical job creation; and the suitability of the allocation formulas for the specific objectives of each title.

FINDINGS

- Funds for CETA rose from $2.3 billion before CETA to $5.7 billion in fiscal 1976 and to more than $8 billion in both 1977 and 1978, as the CETA public service jobs program became one of the chief cornerstones of economic stimulus policies. But CETA is only one of the measures dealing with cyclical unemployment. In fiscal 1976, nearly four times as much was spent for unemployment insurance as for CETA, and there were also special appropriations for local public works and for countercyclical revenue-sharing. The amount of funds devoted to manpower training and employment compared with alternative approaches for dealing with the economic downturn has been a controversial issue.[1]

- CETA originally emphasized human capital development (Titles I, III, and IV), with a minor job creation component for areas of substantial unemployment (Title II). Most of the increases in CETA funds, however, have been for public service employment (Title VI), signifying a shift to countercyclical job creation. Even Title I, which was intended to address structural problems, has been used in some areas to support public service jobs for the unemployed. The enactment of the Emergency Jobs Programs Extension Act and the economic stimulus appropriation of 1977 greatly increased the scale of the PSE programs, but also targeted them to the long-term, low-income unemployed and to welfare recipients. The increase in funds for national training programs and the passage of a youth employment act in 1977 also represent a return to emphasis on those unemployed for structural reasons.

- Although allocating funds by formula is more predictable than methods used before CETA, the formulas themselves have had unanticipated results. Under Title I, the amounts going to major cities, where problems of unemployment and poverty are concentrated, have declined year by year, despite the mitigating effect of a "hold-harmless" adjustment that maintains funds for each area at 90 percent of the previous year's level. The hold-harmless adjustment has not been effective in preventing the erosion of funds for some areas at a time when inflation is chipping away at the purchasing power of CETA allotments.

---

[1]See, for example, U.S. Congress, Congressional Budget Office, *Temporary Measures to Stimulate Employment—An Evaluation of Some Alternatives*, Prepared by Nancy S. Barrett and George Iden, Washington, D.C.: Congressional Budget Office, September 1975; "Inflation and Unemployment," *Economic Report of the President 1978*, Washington, D.C.: U.S. Government Printing Office, 1978, Ch. 4; National Commission for Manpower Policy, "Commissioned Papers," Volume III of *Job Creation Through Public Service Employment*, An Interim Report to the Congress, Washington, D.C.: National Commission for Manpower Policy, 1978.

Moreover, there are serious questions about the formula elements that are supposed to measure economic hardship. The formula is weighted by the unemployment factor and does not adequately reflect other labor market dysfunctions, such as low labor force participation rates or underemployment, that may also be important.

• The NRC study found deficiencies in the Title II formula, which is designed to channel funds for public service jobs to areas of substantial unemployment. With a national rate hovering around 7 percent, the unemployment rate criterion for Title II areas (6.5 percent) has been too low to identify those areas suffering the most. Using unemployment data for a 3-month period to qualify areas and to allocate funds results in inequities due to seasonal and temporary factors. The allocation formula is based exclusively on the number of unemployed people and does not give extra weight to areas with the most severe unemployment, as reflected in unusually high unemployment rates.

• All of the allocation formulas rely on unemployment estimates for local areas. Unemployment is estimated from a combination of unemployment insurance data and the Census Bureau's monthly survey of the labor force. The other element in the Title I formula, the number of adults in low-income families, is also a derived figure. There are serious measurement problems involved in estimating both unemployment and poverty; both rely on derived techniques that are not sensitive enough to yield precise estimates for small geographic areas—in the case of unemployment figures, as small as neighborhoods with 10,000 population. A more serious question is whether the conventional measures of unemployment and poverty are appropriate for identifying the kinds of economic hardship and labor market disadvantage that Title I of CETA was intended to address. This problem was recognized in CETA itself. The act directed the Secretary of Labor to develop an annual statistical measure of economic hardship in the nation. Among the factors to be considered, in addition to unemployment, were: labor force participation, involuntary part-time employment, and full-time employment at less than poverty wages. The Department of Labor has not as yet developed and refined the kind of hardship measure envisioned by Congress. This subject is being studied by the National Commission on Employment and Unemployment Statistics, established under a 1976 amendment to CETA.

• Another question raised by the study relates to the timing of allocations. One of the most pervasive administrative problems has been uncertainty of funding. Since the economic conditions addressed by Titles I and II tend to persist from year to year, it would be preferable to have a longer funding cycle to eliminate year-to-year changes.

RECOMMENDATIONS

1. *While unemployment insurance should continue to be the major means of dealing with short-term unemployment, the Committee recommends that emphasis be given to more constructive measures than income maintenance for the long-term unemployed.*

The Committee believes that training or public service employment programs should be the primary vehicle for assisting those who have exhausted their unemployment insurance and other long-term unemployed people. Unemployment insurance should be used primarily to provide short-term income support. CETA and, more particularly, its training programs are geared toward retraining and employability development. In that sense, they may have more lasting benefits for persons who have little prospect of returning to previous jobs or who require remedial services.

Congress should determine the appropriate balance between the structural and countercyclical objectives of the different CETA titles. The Committee suggests that, for significant impact, the structural components of CETA (Titles I, III, IV, and VIII) should be supported at a level equal to 2 percent of the labor force (exclusive of summer employment programs for youth), and countercyclical public service employment programs should be supported at a level equivalent to 25 percent of the average number of persons unemployed 15 weeks or longer. In 1975, at the trough of the recession, the number of people unemployed for 15 or more weeks averaged 2.5 million. By 1977, it had fallen to 1.9 million. The structural and countercyclical programs of CETA would have provided 2.5 million opportunities, or about one-fifth of the number in need of employment or training assistance.

2. *The formulas for allocating Titles I, II, and VI and summer funds for youth should be revised.*

a. *Congress should discontinue the 90-percent hold-harmless adjustment under Title I. Instead the minimum amount for each area should be pegged at the amount received in 1978, with adjustments whenever the total amount of Title I funds is changed.*

The hold-harmless adjustment (90 percent of prior year's funds) was intended to prevent major disruptions in area fund levels, but it has only delayed them. Most of the major cities have received less Title I funds year by year, despite the 90-percent minimum. With more funds available for Title I, it is anomalous that any city or other CETA prime sponsor should now receive less money than it did in 1974. A hold-harmless adjustment based on 100 percent of the 1978 Title I allotment for each area would end the downward spiral in funds for major cities and other sponsors.

b. *The Department of Labor should continue to explore the development of an index of economic hardship and labor market disadvantage on a local basis to replace the unemployment and low-income factors in the Title I formula.*

The Title I formula relies on unemployment estimates; it does not consider measures of other labor market dysfunctions—intermittent employment, low income, and discouraged jobseekers. An index reflecting a combination of unemployment and low income may be a more appropriate measure of economic hardship, if the data for small areas can be derived from unemployment and poverty statistics.[2] The index might also be designed to take into account other relevant factors, such as the duration of unemployment and the educational attainment of the unemployed. A study should be made not only of the feasibility of an index of economic hardship, but also of its distributional effects. If the present concept of "adults in low-income families" as a proxy for various labor market problems is retained, the Department of Labor should adjust the figures for regional and urban–rural differentials in living costs.

c. *The 6.5 percent unemployment rate criterion used to identify areas of substantial unemployment under Title II should be changed to a rate that is a fixed percentage above the national unemployment rate.*

The 6.5 percent unemployment rate to qualify for Title II funds was adopted when the national unemployment rate was about 5 percent. When the national rate was more than 7 percent and practically all prime sponsor areas qualified for Title II funds, it was obviously inappropriate. A sliding "trigger" would more effectively direct funds to areas with the most severe unemployment. The local trigger, for example, might be set at an unemployment rate of 35 percent above the national unemployment rate, or 6 percent, whichever is higher.

d. *Annual, rather than 3-month average, unemployment figures should be used to qualify areas of substantial unemployment and to allocate Title II funds.*

A 3-month eligibility period, prescribed for identifying areas of substantial unemployment, is designed for quick response to sudden

---

[2] The National Commission on Employment and Unemployment Statistics is studying various alternatives.

changes in unemployment levels. However, it is not appropriate for Title II, which is meant for areas with chronic unemployment problems. Moreover, the 3-month average creates inequities in distribution of funds due to the influence of temporary and seasonal factors. Areas with volatile unemployment fare better than those where unemployment is high but seasonal fluctuations are less sharp.

e. *A uniform method of identifying subareas of substantial unemployment should be adopted.*

The geographic unit for Title II eligibility—an area of substantial unemployment—may be a relatively small section of a city or county. Such areas are sometimes gerrymandered: Sections with relatively low unemployment rates may become eligible for funds by being combined with adjoining high unemployment neighborhoods.[3] The results are funding inequities. A uniform method should be adopted for delineation of areas, based on standard and objective data, that are not subject to manipulation.

f. *Congress should include a "severity" factor in the Title II formula to give extra funds to areas of high unemployment.*

The Title II formula allocates funds on the basis of the total number of unemployed persons. It does not differentiate among eligible areas on the basis of severity of unemployment. For example, if two areas have the same number of unemployed, but one has an unemployment rate of 10 percent while the other has a rate of 6.5 percent, both receive the same allotment although the labor market conditions are much worse in the first area. A two-part formula should be used for Title II, with the second part distributing additional funds to areas of extremely high unemployment where prospects of obtaining jobs are not favorable. Part of the Title II funds could be distributed on the basis of the number of unemployed in each eligible area and part on the basis of the number of unemployed above 6.5 percent (or whatever rate is used as a criterion for identifying areas of substantial unemployment).

g. *Title VI should be a standby public service employment program that becomes operational when the national unemployment rate reaches a level that signifies the onset of a recession and remains at that level for at least 3 months.*

To avoid delay in getting a countercyclical public service employment

[3]*Progress and Problems in Allocating Funds under Titles I and II—Comprehensive Employment and Training Act,* General Accounting Office, Jan. 1977.

program under way, Title VI should be retained on a standby basis, actuated automatically by a national unemployment rate trigger. The amount of funds might be graduated, based on the number or proportion of unemployed people out of work 15 weeks or longer. In order for Title VI to have greater effect, areas with low unemployment rates (less than 3 percent) should be excluded.

h. *The Title VI formula should be revised to take into account new eligibility criteria.*

The Emergency Jobs Programs Extension Act of 1976 changed eligibility requirements for Title VI to reserve new openings for low-income, long-term unemployed persons and for welfare recipients. The allocation formula should be reviewed to see how it can be made more relevant in terms of these new eligibility requirements. Factors based on income and/or duration of unemployment might be included.

i. *The Department of Labor should revise the formula for the summer employment program for youth to include youth unemployment factors.*

The formula for the summer program for economically disadvantaged youth is essentially the same as the Title I formula. It should be made more responsive, subject to the development of necessary data, to the population to be served, particularly minority youth in large cities. The Department of Labor should explore with the Census Bureau the possibility of deriving area estimates of disadvantaged unemployed youth from special national family income surveys. The 1975 *Survey of Income and Education* provides state data on the number of youth in poverty families which may be used as a basis for deriving estimates, but the information does not include age or unemployment status.

3. *Biennial apportionment should be used for Title I funding.*

Since Title I addresses long-term, intractable problems, it may be unnecessary to recompute the proportional share for each area every year. The share could be established every 2 years and the amount adjusted each year according to changes in the Title I appropriations. A longer cycle would make planning more meaningful and contribute to more effective administration.

SUBSTANTIVE ASPECTS OF CETA PROGRAMS

While CETA has shifted the locus of responsibility for administering manpower programs, the underlying policy remains the same—to improve opportunities for individuals faced with chronic barriers to employment, that is, those unemployed for structural reasons. During periods of economic sluggishness, manpower policy objectives are extended to those unemployed for cyclical reasons. Although there is consensus as to these general goals, there is less agreement on the specific questions of who should be served, what assistance should be provided, and what results should be expected. The Committee has reviewed these issues against the backdrop of the recession, which enlarged the demand for services and reduced the potential for successful outcomes.

WHO SHOULD BE SERVED

Issues

The competition for limited resources between those who were the focus of federal assistance in the 1960s—the poor and minorities—and the rising numbers of less disadvantaged, cyclically unemployed persons in the 1970s has emerged as a basic issue affecting manpower legislation and program operations.

Findings

• The preamble to CETA that identifies persons to be served—the economically disadvantaged, unemployed, and underemployed—is broad and ambiguous. The individual titles are more specific. Under Title I, for example, prime sponsors are to serve persons "most in need," including low-income persons and those who have limited English-speaking ability. Title II requires prime sponsors to give consideration to the long-term unemployed, Vietnam veterans, former manpower trainees, and to the "significant segments" of the unemployed population that are in particular need of assistance. Under the original Title VI, enacted in 1974, preferred consideration was to be given to persons who had exhausted unemployment insurance benefits or who were not eligible for UI, but those preferences stopped short of being either priorities or eligibiity criteria for entrance into Title VI PSE programs. Sponsors were free to choose target groups, based upon their analysis of the local job markets.

• In addition to the statutory language, other factors have contributed to broadening the client base: the allocation formulas, which spread funds into relatively affluent suburban areas; decisions by local officials in response to community pressure; and built-in incentives to select those most likely to succeed.

• During the first 2 years of CETA, there was a large increase in the number of persons served, due to substantially greater resources, and there were some significant changes in the types of clients.

With a large proportion of CETA enrollees in public sector employment, the characteristics of enrollees changed. CETA clients as a whole are relatively older, better educated, and less disadvantaged than those in corresponding manpower programs in fiscal 1974.

Title I training and employability programs continue to be oriented primarily toward the young, minorities, and the economically disadvantaged. However, the proportions of youth, of persons who have not finished high school, and of poor persons are smaller than in corresponding pre-CETA programs. The decline in the proportion of clients who have not completed high school is related to the decline in the proportion of youth.

Participants in PSE programs (Titles II and VI), are better educated, less disadvantaged, and less likely to come from minority groups than those enrolled in Title I activities. The percentage of AFDC and other public welfare beneficiaries was much lower in PSE than in Title I programs: 13 percent under Title II and 18 percent under Title VI in 1977, compared with 26 percent under Title I. The percentage of females was also significantly lower: 40 percent for Title II and 36 percent for Title VI, compared with 48 percent for Title I. While Titles II and VI were not meant specifically for the disadvantaged groups, the difference in socioeconomic level between their participants and those in Title I raises a question of social policy.

• In the 1976 extension of Title VI, Congress directed additional resources to the low-income, long-term unemployed. This change, when added to existing programs, may result in a three-part system: employability programs largely for the disadvantaged under Title I; employment in regular public service activities under Title II and the original Title VI for those higher on the socioeconomic ladder; and a new type of public service employment for the low-income person in special projects in the public sector, the new Title VI.

Recommendations

1. *Congress should reconcile the eligibility requirements among the various titles of the act.*

Under Title I, an enrollee may be any unemployed, underemployed, or economically disadvantaged person. Title II states that enrollees must have been unemployed for 30 days or more and must live in an area of substantial unemployment. Originally, Title VI required 30 days of unemployment. The 1976 amendments to Title VI tightened eligibility criteria: Most new participants under Title VI must be long-term (15 weeks or more), low-income unemployed people or welfare recipients.[4] Thus eligibility standards for Title VI, a countercyclical measure, are more stringent than for Title I, which was intended to deal with structural unemployment. These anomalous requirements should be reconciled so that the criteria for participation in a CETA program are related to the type of client to be served under each of the CETA titles.

The Committee recommends that:

• Titles I and II be restricted either to the economically disadvantaged or to those in the low-income group (including welfare recipients).
• Title VI be limited to (a) economically disadvantaged or low-income individuals, or (b) the long-term unemployed, with representation of the unemployed poor (including welfare recipients) in proportion to their numbers among all eligible persons.

These eligibility restrictions would not only result in more consistency but, more importantly, assure that limited resources are spent on those most in need. Alternative (b) would maintain the countercyclical nature of the PSE program, permit some flexibility in selecting applicants for PSE openings, but still ensure that the unemployed poor participate in the program.

2. *Congress should establish a limited number of client groups to be given priority under Titles I, II, and VI.*

The act at present identifies a number of groups for consideration within eligible categories: those "most in need," including low-income persons and persons of limited English-speaking ability in Title I; Vietnam-era veterans, former manpower trainees, and the disadvantaged long-term unemployed (Titles II and VI); and unemployed persons who have exhausted UI benefits, persons not eligible for UI, persons unemployed for 15 or more weeks, and welfare recipients (Title VI). Moreover, sponsors are to serve equitably the "significant segments" of the unemployed population in PSE programs. This patchwork system of priorities needs to be reconciled. The attainment of one objective is often

[4]Economically disadvantaged persons are defined as members of families whose annual income is less than the poverty criteria—$5,800 for an urban family of four in 1976. A low-income person is one whose family income is less than 70 percent of the Bureau of Labor Statistics lower income family budget—about $6,700 for a family of four in 1976.

made at the expense of others. The problem arises in particular between Vietnam veterans and the low-income population, since veterans do not necessarily fall in the low-income category. A similar problem exists in trying to reconcile the priorities between persons who have exhausted UI or those not eligible for UI with the income criterion. The Committee believes that the family income criterion should take precedence.

3. *Prime sponsors should exercise more control over the client selection process to ensure that priorities set forth in the act are observed.*

Selection of participants for public service employment is typically left to employing agencies, which tend to choose those whom they consider the most qualified from among the applicants referred rather than those most in need. Moreover, sponsors exercise little control over the selection process of Title I programs. Sponsors should tighten control over intake and selection systems either by direct operation of manpower centers or, where other agencies do the selection, by requiring that applicants be rated by a point system related to the eligibility and preference criteria in the act.

TITLE I PROGRAM MIX

Issues

Two major types of program changes were anticipated with the decategorization of Title I. The distribution of funds among major programs was expected to change as sponsors began to adapt categorical programs to the specific needs of their clients and their labor markets. And it was expected that the elimination of categorical restraints would generate ideas that would refashion program design. The issue is the extent to which local program changes have been made and the implication of such changes for clients.

Findings

• Department of Labor (DOL) reports indicate a relative shift from programs that stress preparation for economic self-sufficiency to those providing temporary employment. Although the absolute amount spent for classroom and on-the-job training has risen under CETA, the proportion of Title I funds spent for these activities declined from 60 percent in fiscal 1974 to 42 percent in fiscal 1976 and 50 percent in 1977. There have been relative increases in public sector employment and in manpower services to participants—including assessment, counseling, and supportive services. More than 80 percent of combined expenditures under Titles I, II, and VI in fiscal 1976 were for work experience or public service jobs.

• Although the balance among programs has changed, there has been little change in basic program design. Sponsors were inclined to continue the kinds of programs they inherited. Few of the sponsors had the necessary expertise to improve existing models. Moreover, during the first 2 years of CETA, both the Department of Labor and the sponsors were occupied with administrative matters and pressures arising from the recession.

• There are indications that the quality of Title I services has been diluted. Some sponsors pursued strategies involving low-cost, short-duration courses and began to emphasize direct placement of persons who are ready for jobs.

Recommendations

1. *The type and quality of training programs should be upgraded and made more relevant to demands of the labor market.*

Approval of plans for training should rest upon evidence of specific standards for skill acquisition that are relevant to occupational requirements and that contribute to a significant improvement in the employability of enrollees. Insofar as practicable, training should be directed to occupations that offer stable employment.

DOL regional offices and prime sponsors should emphasize greater involvement of private employers in the training process in order to tailor skill training to the demand for workers. They should foster employer/union advisory groups to contribute to the design, implementation, and evaluation of classroom training in specific occupations, as well as to assist in the placement of trainees. Greater efforts should be made to develop on-the-job training programs and apprenticeship openings in the private sector.

2. *The Department of Labor should emphasize more strongly substantive manpower programs that contribute to the enhancement of human capital.*

Title I resources should be focused more heavily on education and skill training for clients who need assistance to become readily employable. A higher proportion of Title I funds should be devoted to classroom and on-the-job training and a smaller proportion to work experience (unless accompanied by substantive basic education and skills training) and to job market services that result in short-term employment in secondary labor markets.

3. *The Department of Labor should do more to encourage sponsors to develop creative program approaches.*

The Department recently set aside funds for skill training and improvement projects and has encouraged experimentation with new approaches under the Youth Employment and Training Act of 1977. Continued emphasis should be given to such experiments and to the development of models for both youth and adults that combine work experience with training to improve the skills and employability of clients. For example, work and training projects leading to occupational credentials should be developed in cooperation with community colleges. Combining work experience in the public or private sector with formal training might be considered as a means of enriching work experience and making it more relevant to the job market. The Department should also encourage innovation by offering incentive funds or by subsidizing some of the risk. State manpower services funds might also be used to foster new approaches.

PROGRAM RESULTS

Issues

The prime measure of CETA's effectiveness is the extent to which persons completing manpower programs are successful in obtaining and retaining jobs both in the short and long term. The NRC study considered only the short-range effects, although it is recognized that enhancement of employability and long-term earnings potential are important objectives.[5] The issue is whether CETA programs are effective in obtaining unsubsidized employment for participants after termination.

Findings

• In fiscal 1976, 0.5 million of the 1.7 million persons who terminated from Title I, II, and VI programs found employment (see table below). And even despite some tendency to enroll those most likely to succeed, the ratio of persons who obtained jobs to the number who terminated was lower than for corresponding pre-CETA training and public service employment programs. Lower placement ratios are partly due to generally looser labor market conditions, but other factors, including placement strategy and deemphasis on transition of Title II and Title VI

[5] A longitudinal study conducted by the Census Bureau and by Westat, Inc., for the Department of Labor will have information on the long-range effect of the earnings potential of enrollees.

participants to unsubsidized employment, may be equally significant. Placement rates rose from 29 percent in 1976 to 35 percent in fiscal 1977.

	FY 1976		FY 1977	
	Number (in thousands)	Percent	Number (in thousands)	Percent
Enrolled in Titles I, II, and VI	2,482	–	2,361	–
Terminated	1,677	100	1,471	100
Entered employment	486	29	510	35
Direct placements[a]	117	7	70	5
Indirect placements[b]	261	16	320	22
Obtained employment	109	6	120	8
Other positive terminations[c]	648	39	533	36
Nonpositive terminations[d]	543	32	428	29

SOURCE: Computed from Employment and Training Administration, U.S. Department of Labor data.
NOTE: Details may not add to totals due to rounding.
[a]Individuals placed after receiving only intake, assessment, and/or job referral service.
[b]Individuals placed after participation in training, employment, or supportive services.
[c]Entered armed forces or enrolled in school or in other manpower programs.
[d]Did not obtain employment, enter armed forces, or enroll in school or in other manpower programs.

• About one-half of those who entered employment went through a CETA training course or other substantive activity (indirect placements); the rest were placed directly, without participating in a program, or they found jobs on their own. Job opportunities were better for white than for nonwhite persons. Persons with a high school or post-high-school education and those who were not economically disadvantaged appeared to have better job opportunities.

• About one-third of the terminations were "nonpositive," that is, CETA participants who did not enter employment or return to school; this high percentage is indicative of underlying problems either in selection of enrollees or in program activities.

• Little reliable information is available at this time as to the quality of placements, job duration, or long-term earnings gains. Information on the noneconomic benefits of CETA in terms of the human resource development is no better. Finally, little is known about possible negative effects of the CETA experience.

Recommendations

1. *Placement of participants in unsubsidized employment should be recognized as the primary objective and should receive more attention at all levels of* CETA *administration.*

Although the possibilities for enrollees to obtain jobs are limited in a loose labor market, the study finds that the decline in placement ratios compared with pre-CETA programs is in part related to less effective job development efforts under CETA. Assignment of more resources to job development and staff training in this function should improve the employment prospects of enrollees. However, increased job placement rates should not be accomplished through placements in low-wage, temporary jobs; the goal should be placements in long-term, stable employment.

The original CETA legislation emphasized the need to find openings for PSE program participants in regular unsubsidized employment, but Congress explicitly downgraded this objective in an effort to hasten the implementation of the program. A 1974 CETA amendment stipulated that placement should not be required as a condition for receiving funds, but considered a goal, and that waivers would be permitted when the goal was infeasible. It is recommended that Congress restore the transition objective for Titles II and VI. Quotas or other administrative measures should be used to spur efforts to place participants in nonsubsidized jobs. For example, employing agencies should be required to fill a specified percentage of their regular vacancies with CETA employees.

Moreover, Congress should limit the duration of employment of any participant to 1 year. Under the Emergency Jobs Programs Extension Act, projects are limited to a year, but a participant may be kept on the rolls indefinitely. Limiting tenure would create pressure to find unsubsidized jobs. Sponsors should be urged to use either Title II or Title VI administrative funds or Title I funds for auxiliary training that will enable participants to qualify for unsubsidized employment.

2. Research should be undertaken to assess the economic and noneconomic effects of CETA.

The national longitudinal study sponsored by the Department of Labor is expected to provide insights into the effect of CETA on subsequent earnings of participants. However, sponsors should also conduct follow-up studies on terminated participants to ascertain the kinds of employment obtained, earnings, stability of employment, and relationship of jobs to training or experience in CETA programs. Special efforts should be made to determine the reasons for terminations to obtain clues on how to improve program design and effectiveness.

Research should be undertaken to measure the offsetting savings of CETA programs in welfare and unemployment insurance payments and tax revenues from earnings, as well as the noneconomic effects of CETA in terms of improving morale, family stability, etc. Possible counterproductive aspects of CETA, such as disincentives to seek nonsubsidized employment, development of poor work habits in CETA programs, and any negative effects of CETA on the quality of public service should also be explored. Further research is needed on the effect of targeting, project requirements, and limited duration of projects on the effectiveness of PSE in meeting economic objectives.

PUBLIC SERVICE EMPLOYMENT

Issues

The objective of Title II in the original CETA legislation was to provide federally subsidized public sector jobs in areas of substantial unemployment. With the onset of the recession, Congress enacted Title VI, which provided for public service employment programs in all areas and authorized a sixfold increase in resources. Two of the large issues associated with public service employment programs are substitution, the use of CETA funds to support jobs that would otherwise be financed from local resources, and the targeting of public service employment to specific client groups. Other matters of concern are the relationship between the Title II and Title VI programs, the usefulness of PSE activities, and the placement of participants in unsubsidized jobs.

Findings

• With the authorization of Title VI, the focus as well as the scale of PSE programs changed radically. Although Congress intended that Titles II and VI have different objectives, the differences between the two in terms of geographic coverage, eligibility, and target groups were soon obscured. Most areas qualified for both programs, and participants were often switched from one title to the other.

• Most PSE jobs were in public works, transportation, parks and recreation, law enforcement, education, and social services. It was the opinion of most respondents that PSE workers were engaged in useful public service activities. In fiscal 1976, Title II and Title VI employees represented 2.3 percent of all state and local government employees. (By early 1978, with the expansion under the economic stimulus program, Titles II and VI accounted for over 5 percent of all state and local employees.) In some areas the percentage was much higher, and sponsors were becoming dependent on CETA employees to provide essential services.

• The common objective of Titles II and VI is to reduce unemployment by creating public sector jobs that would not otherwise have existed. Experience under the Emergency Employment Act and other federal grant programs indicated that there is a strong incentive for local governments to substitute federal for local funds. Congress sought to prevent substitution by requiring sponsors to maintain the level of public service employment they would have had without CETA.

This study classified prime sponsors according to the extent of job creation with Title II and Title VI funds from July 1974 to October 1975. The classifications were based on observations of local field associates, trends in local government employment, the fiscal position of the principal governmental units, perceptions of local officials as to the objectives of CETA public service employment programs, types of positions held by participants, extent to which nonprofit agencies were the employing units, and overt instances of maintenance-of-effort violations.

Based on this information, 14 of the 24 local prime sponsors were found to have had substantial job creation in the first six quarters of CETA, 5 had moderate job gains, and 5 had litle gain. Most of the areas with substantial gains were small- or medium-sized areas with moderate or little fiscal pressure. Larger urban areas were difficult to classify because they may have used some CETA positions to prevent cutbacks in employment.

• Based on an econometric model, the net job creation ratio nationally was estimated to have ranged from 0.82 in the second quarter after the program began to 0.54 after 10 quarters, averaging 0.65. That is, for every 100 CETA positions, 65 represented positions that would not otherwise have existed, and 35 may have been substituted for regular jobs. Economists have noted, however, that even where substitution occurs, federal grants for public service employment, like other federal grants, are likely to have stimulative effects on local economies, either through public or private spending. A selective PSE program has the added advantage of being able to address structral problems by targeting assistance to specific groups.

• Congress addressed substitution in the 1976 CETA amendments by requiring that new enrollees above the number necessary to sustain existing levels of PSE employment must be in limited-duration projects and that most new PSE enrollees must have been unemployed for 15 weeks or more and must be from low-income or welfare families. By limiting the expansion of PSE to special projects outside of regular governmental functions, it was anticipated that substitution would be held down. Indeed, the original DOL interpretation of the statute did preclude projects that were merely incremental to ongoing governmental activities. But in the face of prime sponsor opposition and in the interest of speedy implementation of the enlarged PSE program, projects were defined very loosely in the final DOL regulations.

Recommendations

1. *The Committee recommends a three-part public service employment program aimed at both structural and countercyclical objectives.*

Public service employment programs can embrace several objectives: opening employment opportunities for the disadvantaged, providing additional assistance to chronically depressed areas, and combating cyclical unemployment. A design incorporating these objectives should include:

• A continuing PSE program restricted to the low-income, long-term unemployed and welfare recipients. This program should include a built-in training component to increase the employability of participants while giving them an opportunity to acquire useful experience.

• Supplemental funds for areas of substantial unemployment, also limited to those unemployed for structural reasons.

• Countercyclical funds that would trigger on automatically as the national unemployment rate rises. The countercyclical component could either be targeted to the disadvantaged or partially targeted, for example, by setting aside an amount for the disadvantaged in proportion to their number among the eligible group in the prime sponsor's area.

In all three of the above, areas with low unemployment rates should be excluded on the grounds that the unemployed there have a better opportunity to be absorbed in the private sector in areas with a favorable labor market. The advantage of the above three-part formulation is that it establishes the principle that the government has a responsibility to create jobs in the public sector, as an alternative to welfare, for the hard-to-employ. It also retains the principle that special efforts are needed to stimulate the economy in areas of high unemployment. (See Appendix C, which summarizes the recommendations of the National Commission for Manpower Policy on job creation in the public sector.)

2. *Congress and the Department of Labor should ensure that Title II and Title VI funds are used for net job creation.*

Several methods are recommended:

• Congress should continue to provide countercyclical revenue-sharing funds as needed to sustain the regular public service work force. Title II of the Public Works Employment Act of 1976 authorized funds for state and local governments to maintain public services and prevent layoffs despite fiscal difficulties. Congress should extend this legislation in some form beyond the present termination date of September 1978 if the economy has not recovered sufficiently by then. This will indirectly help to avoid substitution by giving hard-pressed local governments alternative support.

• The likelihood of substitution would be reduced by establishing useful projects outside the regular activities of local government. But the Department of Labor should revise its regulations to preclude projects that are merely an extension of existing services. The development of such projects may be hindered by lack of equipment and supplies, particularly in jurisdictions that are hard-pressed financially. Sponsors should, therefore, attempt to develop projects linked with economic development or other subsidized programs to obtain the necessary capital from other sources.

• The Department of Labor should continue to require that a proportion of all Title VI project funds be used for jobs in the private nonprofit sector as an additional means of creating new employment opportunities.

• Congress should amend CETA to permit the setting of quotas on rehired staff. This would permit the Department of Labor to restrict the percentage of laid-off local public service employees rehired under CETA. It would tend to constrain overt substitution and would allow other unemployed people to have the same opportunity as former local government employees to fill CETA openings.

• The Department of Labor review and auditing capability should be strengthened to assure compliance with maintenance of effort rules. General Accounting Office reports indicate that detailed studies of local government tax efforts and employment patterns are necessary to ascertain the extent of substitution. DOL auditing should be intensified to make the systematic reviews that are needed. A specific percentage of PSE funds should be earmarked for auditing and monitoring.

• The DOL should set up a task force to review and establish methods to deal with maintenance-of-effort problems. The task force should: develop methods for identifying direct and indirect substitution; devise means of ensuring compliance of program agents, nonprofit institutions, and subjurisdictions of prime sponsor areas; examine the relationship between the capacity of local governments to expand their work force in productive activities and the substitution problem; and explore the relationship between length of stay of participants and substitution.

The task force should consider other administrative means of ensuring that local governments maintain normal hiring as a condition for obtaining PSE participants. One proposal would be to establish a ratio of CETA employees to regular employees for each prime sponsor (or for each employing agency within a sponsor's jurisdiction) and require the sponsor to maintain the same ratio in hiring replacements.

ADMINISTRATIVE PROCESSES

When the management of manpower programs was decentralized, it was assumed that local officials would develop a comprehensive plan in consultation with local advisory groups and would be able to put together a program tailor-made for the local labor market. This section deals with the planning, administration, and organization of a local delivery system. The central question is how well did local officials, most of whom had little or no experience with manpower activities, assume and carry out these new responsibilities during the first 2 years of CETA.

PLANNING

Issues

Decentralization was expected to result in planning for the distribution and use of federal resources that would be more responsive to community needs than was the case under the earlier centralized, categorical manpower system. The issue is whether the concepts of planning are being applied or whether planning is merely a ritual for obtaining federal grants.

Findings

In fiscal 1976, prime sponsor planning was in transition from a purely mechanical exercise to a useful strategic process. On the whole, sponsors were better able to analyze their needs and to prepare planning documents than in fiscal 1975, the first year of CETA, but weaknesses remain. Some are rooted in federal practices, such as preoccupation with procedure instead of program substance. Other problems, such as perfunctory attention to the planning process, are local in character.

• Decentralization has not yet resulted in a clear perception of the nature of local planning; few local sponsors have developed long-range goals as a framework for year-to-year planning. There is still a need to improve management information systems to provide a basis for analysis, to upgrade planning skills, and to develop effective evaluation techniques.

• Planning for Titles II and VI is not integrally related to that for Title I; nor do plans adequately take into consideration other related programs in the community.

• Few sponsors have involved private industry effectively in the planning process. Yet links to the private sector are vital to the central objective of CETA—employment in nonsubsidized jobs.

• Balance-of-state sponsors, consortia, and large counties that encompass smaller units of government tend to decentralize planning responsibility. When the subunits are small, opportunities for job placement may be limited. Fragmented planning may also lead to unnecessary duplication in training facilities and other manpower services.

Recommendations

1. *Local plans should be made more comprehensive by integrating planning for Titles I, II, and VI, and by incorporating information on related programs in the community.*

Department of Labor regional offices should disseminate information on CETA national programs (Title III) and other manpower programs to local sponsors so they have a more comprehensive picture of activities in their areas. Sponsors should obtain information on other federal programs that are available to local governments (community development, housing, health, law enforcement, social services, etc.) to assist in linking CETA with programs that could provide related services or employment opportunities. State and local elected officials should establish mechanisms to coordinate planning for these related activities. The Department of Labor should provide planning grants for experimental models of coordinated planning.

Most planning under CETA is for small geographic areas. Even in consortia and balance of states, there is a tendency to decentralize and fragment plans. The Department of Labor should encourage planning on a labor market area basis wherever it is feasible to do so. This would provide a broader analysis of occupational demand and training opportunities within commuting range. In consortia and balance of states, consideration should be given to multicounty planning to make the plans more comprehensive.

2. *The Department of Labor should require evidence of participation of*

private employers in Title I planning as a condition for approval of Title I programs.

It is important that private employers be drawn into the planning process at an early stage to ensure that training programs are relevant to occupational demand and to advise on specific elements of skill training programs. Private employers can be particularly helpful in planning for on-the-job training. Since almost all CETA participants must eventually find employment in the private sector, local planners should also consult private employers about job development.

LOCAL MANAGEMENT

Issues

Decentralization conferred on state and local governments the responsibility for managing a complex array of manpower programs. The capability of local governments to handle these programs efficiently is a central element in assessing the CETA block-grant approach. Of particular concern are management problems in counties, consortia, and balance of states, where sponsors must deal with other subunits of government. The extent to which administration of public service employment is integrated with Title I programs presents another management issue.

Findings

Prior to CETA, employment and training programs were managed by the Manpower Administration directly or through state employment service and education agencies. One of the most notable achievements of CETA has been the successful transfer of this responsibility to state and local units of government, most of which had only minimal prior contact with manpower programs. Now, for the first time, the administration of manpower programs is an accepted responsibility of local government.

• The first year of CETA was spent in setting up the administrative machinery for planning, budgeting, supervising contracts, reporting, and establishing fiscal control. Considerable progress was made in the second year; some expertise was developed and many of the problems of integrating manpower programs into the structure of local government were resolved. However, local staffs still lack technical knowledge of the substance of manpower programs, a serious weakness that also applies to federal staff assigned to supervise local programs.

• The framers of CETA contemplated a close relationship between PSE programs and the employability development activities of Title I. Titles II and VI require that former manpower trainees be given consideration for PSE slots. The NRC study found that administrative units handling PSE are indeed generally lodged in the same organizational office that handles Title I, but functional coordination is usually minimal. Planning, grant management, subcontracting, and supervision are handled separately, and there is little interchange among clients.

• Consortia and balance-of-state areas must grapple with administrative problems inherent in joint ventures. Delegation of responsibilities to constituent jurisdictions often means less control by the sponsor and fragmentation of administration. Balance-of-state sponsors administering programs over broad geographic areas have unique problems, especially where administrative substructures are lacking. Councils of government and other multicounty structures that are now administering CETA were initially planning organizations without experience in program management. There is still a need for developing administrative capability in subareas of balance of states.

Recommendations

1. *The Department of Labor should encourage integration of public service employment and training programs.*

The planning, administration, and evaluation of Title I, II, and VI programs should be coordinated. Bringing these programs closer together should make it possible to integrate the procedures for selecting participants, to expose clients to a broad range of program options, to arrange combinations of training and employment, and to improve the effectiveness of job development and placement.

2. *Management studies should be undertaken to explore administrative problems that occur among overlapping jurisdictions.*

More information is needed on administrative relationships between sponsors and subunits in counties, consortia, and balance of states. The Department of Labor should initiate studies of administrative problems such as the effects of administrative layers on processes, divided accountability, and the trade-offs between centralized and decentralized contracting and supervision of operations. Problems of fragmented administration and the effects of using planning organizations to administer programs in balance of states also need further exploration.

MANAGEMENT DATA

Issues

In implementing CETA, the Employment and Training Administration restructured its reporting system to unify the data systems of numerous separate programs. While this resulted in integrated reporting, it does raise several questions: Does the new system serve the program and information needs at all levels of government—local as well as national? Does it provide Congress and policymakers with information necessary to determine whether CETA's objectives have been met? Is it responsive to information needs arising from the Emergency Jobs Programs Extension Act?

Findings

The study finds that the data system does not provide adequate information for national policy purposes or for local management.

• One of the most serious gaps in the data system that limits its usefulness for program evaluation at the national and local levels is the lack of an accurate count of individuals enrolled. A participant may be counted more than once if he or she is transferred among programs or terminates and reenrolls. Another problem results from aggregation of data for youth and adults, which makes it difficult to assess program results, since the expected and actual outcomes for youth are quite different from those for adults. In addition, the CETA data system has not yet been expanded to cover the new target groups that have been added by the CETA amendments.

• There are also gaps in the information needed for planning. Data on the number and characteristics of persons in need of assistance, occupations in demand, and alternative services in the community are generally unavailable in sufficient geographic detail or on a current basis.

• Some sponsors have gone beyond the DOL data requirements and have established local management information systems flexible enough to generate information for local program planning and evaluation. For the most part, however, sponsors do not have satisfactory systems for evaluating the performance of subcontractors or for assessing the relative costs and effectiveness of program activities. As a consequence the data system cannot adequately serve the needs of the sponsors themselves.

• Information about public service employment programs is sparse, particularly with respect to occupations and earnings, activity of the employing unit, duration of employment, and the number of former public service workers rehired under CETA.

Recommendations

1. *The Department of Labor should establish a task force of federal and local personnel to design a more useful data base for planning, management, and evaluation.*
The task force should consider revisions in data elements and processing to:

Differentiate data for youth and adults. The high incidence of youths in many CETA programs tends to obscure information about services to adults, particularly their placement rates.

Relate data to the requirements of the act. For program control and accountability to Congress, the reporting system should include service and outcome data on target groups listed in the act—those who have exhausted UI benefits, persons not eligible for UI, those unemployed for 15 weeks or more, the long-term low-income unemployed, former manpower trainees, etc.

Refine data elements. Data items that need to be defined more clearly and validated to be useful include the count of participants, the identification of the economically disadvantaged, the labor force status of participants prior to entry in the program, and "direct" versus "indirect" placements.

Develop evaluation data. Local management information systems require, at a minimum, outcome data by type of program and by program operator, information on targeting, costs by service components, and more flexibility in cross-tabulation of program and targeting data.

Develop better follow-up data. For evaluation purposes, the data system should furnish more information on post-program labor force experience—retention in jobs, duration of employment, earnings, and whether employment is in a training-related occupation.

These suggestions may increase the reporting workload, but offsetting savings could be achieved by other means, such as a regional computerized system with coded entries from individual record cards. This could reduce processing time, provide needed flexibiity, and free local staff for validation of reports and for analysis of data.

Alternative approaches to the present reporting system that might be considered are: periodic surveys of a nationally representative sample of sponsors to obtain more detailed information, special reports from all sponsors on a less frequent basis than the normal quarterly cycle covering selected items not in the regular reporting system, or expansion of the longitudinal survey being conducted for the Department of Labor to include specific items that could be extracted quickly and fed back to sponsors and the national office.

2. *The Department of Labor and state governments should assist prime sponsors in installing management information systems.*

Efforts of the Department of Labor to improve management information systems should be increased. Exchange of information among sponsors and assistance from specialists trained in operations research would strengthen local information and evaluation systems. Such exchanges would be an appropriate activity for state governments to undertake with the state manpower services fund. The states could arrange for consultants, training of local staffs, or for a central management information system to serve all prime sponsors within the state.

Technical assistance is especially necessary to make the evaluation process more comprehensive. Broadly conceived, evaluation should deal with program results in relation to needs and the relative effectiveness of alternative program strategies and various deliverers of service.

3. *Methods of measuring the quality of programs should be studied.*

One of the most serious gaps is the lack of information on the quality of the services offered under Title I of CETA. National and state technical staff should explore methods of systematically measuring the quality of training and work experience programs. This would include assessing curriculum, the duration of courses, proficiency standards, and the adequacy of the equipment for skill training, as well as the training and supervision components of youth work experience programs. (See also p. 253.)

THE DELIVERY SYSTEM

Issue

The fragmented nature of the delivery system was one of the most heavily criticized aspects of pre-CETA manpower programs. One purpose of CETA was to bring about a better integration of various programs for training and employment and a closer coordination among agencies providing those services. At issue is the extent to which local delivery systems are being made more rational and whether this results in better service to clients.

Findings

The NRC study noted a trend toward consolidation of services to enhance employability. Of the local sponsors surveyed, about 33 percent have adopted a comprehensive delivery system for Title I programs—one in which intake is coordinated, a wide range of services is available according to individual need, and each client is followed through a sequence of activities from initial assessment to training and eventually to placement. Forty percent retained a categorical delivery system, and the remaining sponsors in the study sample had mixed systems.

In a number of places manpower centers are being established as a focal point for bringing clients and services together. There has also been some movement toward centralized exit activities, particularly job development and placement. The trend toward a comprehensive system is more evident in smaller areas than in large cities and consortia, which tend to use established program deliverers.

Although there is a trend toward comprehensive delivery of employability services (Title I), there is little indication that PSE programs are being integrated with them.

Recommendations

1. *Prime sponsors should arrange for combinations of training and public service employment programs leading to career opportunities.*

Participants in structurally oriented programs should have access to public service jobs, particularly those that offer career potential. Title II or Title VI openings could provide useful experience for clients trained initially under Title I. This neglected concept of CETA should be implemented. Congress should provide additional Title I funds specifically to encourage combinations with PSE training.

2. *The Department of Labor should arrange for research to determine how client convenience and quality of services are related to various Title I delivery patterns.*

Studies should analyze the client flow and availability of program options under comprehensive, mixed, and categorical systems. Centralized versus decentralized arrangements for service in balance-of-state programs should be compared. Delivery models should be developed that expose clients to a spectrum of services and ensure continuity of responsibility as clients move from intake to placement.

CONTINUING RESEARCH AND EVALUATION

Issues

The growth and complexity of CETA makes it increasingly important to assess the degree to which the purposes of the legislation are met. The act provides for research and evaluation activity and the passage of the Youth Employment and Training Act adds a significant new experimental and demonstration dimension. At issue is the need for greater in-house and independent research and evaluation capabilities to provide to Congress and government agencies information necessary for the development of national policy and to provide experimental models for local programs.

Findings

The NRC study, as well as other research activity, has identified numerous problems requiring further exploration, experimentation, and evaluation. There is a clear need for further study of the content and quality of training and work experience programs, the relevance of CETA programs to job market demands, the participation of the private sector in employment and training, substitution of federal for local funds in PSE programs, alternative patterns for delivery of manpower services, intergovernmental roles, the Employment Service/CETA relationship, linkages between CETA and other manpower programs, and, in particular, the effects of CETA on clients.

Recommendations

1. *Congress should provide for a continuous research, evaluation, and demonstration program both within government agencies and by outside, independent research organizations. Approximately 1 percent of CETA funds should be earmarked for this purpose.*

The Committee is aware of the valuable research activities of the Department of Labor, the National Commission for Manpower Policy, and the National Commission on Employment and Unemployment Statistics. State and local governments and private nonprofit research organizations have also undertaken useful studies. However, the magnitude and complexities of the problems associated with CETA programs in a changing economic environment are so great that a more systematic and comprehensive program should be underwritten by Congress. The Committee believes that this would be a wise investment that would pay dividends in contributions to national policy and improvement of local programs. An allotment of 1 percent of federal appropriations for this purpose would not be excessive, considering that much of the money would be used for payment of allowances in experimental and demonstration programs. In elementary and secondary education research, approximately 5 percent of the federal education budget is devoted to research (this does not include allowances for student support).

INSTITUTIONAL RELATIONSHIPS

The original CETA legislation enacted not so much a new program as a new set of relationships. A system of checks and balances among federal, state, and local units of government was designed to permit local flexibility within a framework of national objectives. Sponsor autonomy was to be balanced by federal oversight. States were made responsible for conducting programs in the balance-of-state areas and for providing assistance to all sponsors within a state. Within the sponsor's jurisdiction, diverse elements in the community were to participate in the decision-making process. Sponsors were free to choose institutions to deliver services, subject to giving due consideration to established programs of "demonstrated effectiveness."

THE FEDERAL ROLE

Issues

The relationship between federal and local units of government lies at the heart of decentralization. CETA represents an uneasy compromise between a commitment to local determination and a recognition of the need for federal oversight in the furtherance of national objectives. The act is ambiguous in defining the federal role. It leaves the bounds of the federal presence to be worked out in the interaction between the Department of Labor and prime sponsors.

Findings

• CETA assigns to the Department of Labor responsibility for making sure that the requirements of the legislation are met, but at the same time it cautions the DOL not to second-guess decisions of local officials on program. Since the original act, Congress has added several categorical programs—public service employment, summer activities for youth, and youth employment demonstration projects—that tend to circumscribe local autonomy, but the basic federal–local relationship has not been clarified.

• The Department of Labor has outlined four functions for itself in addition to allocation of funds: establishment of national objectives, priorities, and standards; provision of technical assistance; review and approval of plans; and assessment of prime sponsor performance against plans. During the first year there was a general feeling of uncertainty in federal–local relations, reflecting the gray area between local autonomy and federal oversight. Federal involvement increased the second year as a consequence of the demands of new legislation and the awareness of weaknesses in program implementation.

• DOL regional office review of prime sponsor plans has focused largely on procedure. Assessments emphasized meeting goals in plans, the rate at which funds were spent, administrative costs, financial management, and reporting. Regional office staff intervened from time to time in such program matters as placement policies and maintenance-of-effort and rehire problems, but not on a regular basis.

• Tension between regional offices and sponsors centered around repeated requests for modifying plans, lack of uniformity in interpreting regulations, irregular and unpredictable funding, and the use of rigid performance standards. Sponsors felt that the performance standards tended to constrain the kinds of programs and services they could choose and placed a premium on low-cost strategies. They also resented DOL pressure to use the employment service agencies.

Recommendations

1. *The Department of Labor should interpret national policies and issue annual statements of priorities for prime sponsor guidance.*

The Department of Labor has responsibility to interpret the objectives of the act. In addition, it should have explicit authority to set national goals and priorities. These could be issued in an annual statement of current objectives and priorities prior to the planning cycle. The statement should deal with such matters as types of clientele to be served, mix of programs, and patterns of delivery. To achieve harmony of local programs with national policies, the regional offices of the Department of Labor should then interpret evolving national objectives and goals in the context of local social and economic conditions. The purpose is not to replace local with national goals but to provide additional and broader perspective to local planners.

2. *Federal oversight should emphasize program content and quality in addition to placement goals and other quantitative measures.*

Program assessment should be broadened to encompass the content and quality of work experience and training programs. Technical assistance has tended to focus on procedure, but it is equally important to help local staff gain an understanding of the substantive aspects of training and employment programs so that they can supervise and monitor the performance of program contractors. Regional offices should have a core of trained specialists to assist field representatives in working with sponsors.

3. *The Department of Labor should promote intergovernmental cooperation to assist local sponsors.*

The Department of Labor should reinforce present interagency agreements or establish new ones with agencies that have manpower-related responsibilities (the Departments of Health, Education, and Welfare and of Housing and Urban Development and the Economic Development Administration of the Department of Commerce) to foster cooperation at the local level. Concerted action can improve the quality and relevance of local training and open up new possibilities for unsubsidized jobs.

THE STATE ROLE

Issues

CETA has given state governments multiple responsibilities. In addition to sponsoring balance-of-state programs, they are responsible for maintaining a manpower services council, administering the state manpower services fund and the state vocational education fund, and coordinating the services of state agencies with local prime sponsors. State manpower services councils (SMSCs) are charged with reviewing local plans and monitoring local programs. There are questions, however, as to whether the state role is properly defined in the legislation, as well as to whether the current role is being carried out effectively.

Findings

• During the first year of CETA, the NRC survey found that SMSCs had virtually no impact on local manpower programs. Some councils were not organized in time to review plans, and there was little monitoring of local activities. In the second year, plan review was still perfunctory, there was some monitoring, but for the most part SMSCs still had little influence on local programs.

• Although there were some attempts at the state level to coordinate the services of various agencies with CETA, most states did not systematically establish such arrangements.

• The act intended that the state manpower services fund (4 percent of the Title I appropriation each year) would enable states to provide services to areas and groups not adequately covered by local programs and would ensure the support of state agencies. The NRC study found that these funds are being used mainly for miscellaneous projects rather than for supportive services to local sponsors, such as labor market information and program evaluation.

Recommendations

1. *Congress should strengthen the coordinating responsibilities of the State Manpower Services Councils.*

Congress should give the SMSCs responsibility for the comprehensive state manpower plan, increase their authority and responsibility for coordinating manpower-related activities at the state level, and end their responsibility to monitor local programs.

A SMSC is too unwieldy an organization to monitor local programs. Moreover, in a federal–local system, state monitoring is redundant, especially since the state's authority to influence local programs is minimal. SMSCs should continue to review local plans with a view to identifying areas in which the state can be helpful to local sponsors.

The state may be most helpful in coordinating state social services, vocational education, employment services, and economic development activities with the CETA programs. The governor is in an advantageous position to accomplish this coordination through the use of the state grant funds, authority over state governmental units, and the overall influence of the office.

2. *State manpower services grants should be used primarily to support activities beneficial to all prime sponsors.*

In addition to funding projects, the state should use its manpower services funds for activities that assist local sponsors and promote coordination. The state could use the fund to provide current data on labor supply and demand for sponsor planning, to establish residential training facilities beyond the capability of individual sponsors, to organize statewide on-the-job training programs with major employers, or to arrange with universities or research organizations to provide technical assistance to local sponsors in installing management information and evaluation systems.

LOCAL PLANNING COUNCILS

Issues

In an effort to ensure community participation in decisions affecting local programs, Congress mandated the establishment of local advisory councils. Membership was to include those who delivered manpower services, those who received them, and others who might be directly affected by the quality and substance of programs offered. It was presumed that suppliers and consumers would operate as a check on each other and that members of the general public would exercise a moderating influence. Under the recent extension of Title VI, the purview of the planning councils was extended to include review of public service employment projects. At issue is whether advisory councils have played the active role contemplated by the legislation.

Findings

• The advisory councils in the first year of CETA fell short of fulfilling the legislative intent. There was a quickening of interest in manpower planning on the part of local officials, but the community was not drawn into the decision-making process to any significant extent. Lack of time was partly responsible; councils were being established as Title I decisions were being made. By the second year, about a third of the planning councils in the NRC sample were rated as having a significant influence in Title I planning, usually through a subcommittee structure.

• Influence on the councils from the various sectors of the community has been uneven; client groups and private employers have had the least weight. Securing adequate participation by employers has been difficult, although that link is critical for effective planning. Community organizations, as program operators, have interests that do not always coincide with those of the client groups whom they represent.

• Conflict of interest continues to be a problem where program operators participate in decisions affecting contract awards. To avoid such conflicts, some prime sponsors exclude service deliverers from council membership although permitting them to form a technical council to advise the CETA administrator. Others permit service deliverers to be members of planning councils but do not allow them to vote on renewal of their own contracts.

Recommendations

1. *The prime sponsors, with the support of the Department of Labor, should increase the effectiveness and independence of local planning councils.*

If planning councils are to be effective their members need to be well informed and capable of taking independent positions. Prime sponsors should assign staff to ensure that the council is fully informed. Councils should be drawn into the planning process for Titles II and VI and for youth programs, as well as for Title I. (The act calls for separate local councils for youth employment.) DOL regional offices and prime sponsors should arrange for periodic training of council members. Councils should actively participate in the evaluation process through special subcommittees or other means.

The legislation should require that all Title I program proposals be subject to council consideration and recommendations. Prime sponsor decisions that are contrary to council recommendations should be explained in writing.

2. *Service deliverers that are members of planning or technical councils should be prohibited from voting on contracts.*

The participation of service deliverers is desirable to keep councils informed of issues and practical problems in service delivery, but their presence may lead to conflicts of interest. Present regulations do not permit them to vote on their own contracts, but do permit them to vote on other contracts. It is recommended that service deliverers work with planning councils, but not vote on any contract decisions.

3. *The Department of Labor should encourage prime sponsors to broaden council representation and public awareness of CETA.*

The DOL should foster increased representation and participation of employers, client representatives, and citizen groups on local councils and in related planning and monitoring activities.

REALIGNMENT OF SERVICE DELIVERERS

Issues

The ambiguity of CETA with respect to the selection of local organizations to provide manpower programs and services has been a source of concern. Respecting the decentralization objective, CETA gave prime sponsors the option of using existing program deliverers or selecting new ones. Yet in deference to established institutions, CETA stipulated that existing agencies of demonstrated effectiveness must be considered to the extent feasible. The issue is how to reconcile these two principles and, more importantly, whether the organizations selected are the best available to serve the needs of clients, particularly minority groups and the poor, formerly served by ethnic-oriented, community-based organizations.

The employment service/prime sponsor relationship is particularlly troublesome. In its effort to eliminate duplication among manpower programs, Congress created, through CETA, a federal–local manpower system that parallels in many respects the Wagner–Peyser network of local employment service offices. At issue is the structuring of a relationship between the two systems that identifies (or merges) the separate roles of each and uses the strengths of each.

Findings

The selection of service deliverers has been accompanied by a struggle over turf. Pre-CETA agencies sought to retain their influence and their funding; others sought entry into the system.

• Congress expected that prime sponsors would choose the best program deliverers. However, with new responsibilities facing them, there was neither the time nor the capability to assess the relative performance of competing agencies in the first year. Decisions were based largely on general impressions, political considerations, agency influence, and cost. Initially, existing program deliverers were continued, although in many cases their activities were changed to fit sponsors' plans.

• One of the most striking and unexpected results of decentralization is the appearance of prime sponsors as direct deliverers of services. Within the NRC sample, 17 of 24 local sponsors were directly operating some programs. This development has far-reaching implications for the relationship between the prime sponsor and other agencies providing manpower services and needs further study.

• Community-based organizations such as the Opportunities Industrialization Centers (OICs), Jobs for Progress (SER), and the Urban League have been receiving more funds than previously, but their roles and their autonomy have diminished. The rise of these kinds of community organizations in the 1960s was part of the "Great Society" thrust to ensure attention and service to minorities. They are now concerned about whether the service and attention they were able to gain for their constituencies will continue under the decentralized CETA system.

• Under CETA, the proportion of funds going to public educational institutions has been sustained, but their influence has declined. Sponsors are using larger numbers of training agencies and have shifted to the use of individual referrals of enrollees to established skill-training programs rather than organizing classes of CETA particpants.

• The Employment Service (ES), which had a leading role under the Manpower Development and Training Act and other pre-CETA programs, lost its key position as well as funds and staff in the first year of CETA. Its responsibilities in many areas, particularly large metropolitan cities, were taken over by prime sponsors or other agencies. These losses were attributed by sponsors to cost considerations, effectiveness, and degree of rapport with the disadvantaged. There was some recovery in the second year as the Employment Service was used more extensively in implementing the Title II and VI programs.

The Emergency Jobs Programs Extension Act and the expansion of PSE programs resulted in a larger role for the ES. The impact was felt in several ways. First, the legislation specified UI beneficiaries and welfare clients as people eligible for Title VI programs. This fostered the use of the ES in developing pools of applicants since these groups are already registered in local ES offices. In addition, the policy of the DOL to relieve prime sponsors of responsibility for enrolling ineligible participants, provided the eligibility determination is made by the ES, encouraged the use of that agency. Finally, the large and rapid expansion of PSE programs led sponsors to rely more heavily on the ES.

Recommendations

1. *Objective standards should be established by prime sponsors for rating program deliverers.*

Sponsors now have sufficient experience to enable them to assess "demonstrated effectiveness" in selecting program operators. The criteria for selecting Title I contractors should be stipulated and the ratings of competing organizations should be available to the planning councils.

2. *Several alternatives for structuring* ES/CETA *responsibilities should be considered.*

Earmarked funds for ES. One alternative is to earmark a proportion of Title I CETA funds for state ES agencies to be used to provide services to prime sponsors. This would parallel the existing 5 percent fund for state vocational education agencies. The employment service and prime sponsors would negotiate nonfinancial agreements stipulating the services to be provided.

"Laissez faire." Under this approach, each sponsor and ES local office would work out their own arrangements, based on local needs, capabilities, and relationships. The present effort of the DOL to experiment with different types of ES/CETA relationships is a step in this direction.

A two-part system. This alternative would differentiate between job-ready clients and those needing services to develop employability. The employment service would be responsible for the job-ready and CETA would concentrate on supplying developmental services and PSE programs.

Employment Service as presumptive deliverer. CETA could be amended to reintroduce the employment service as the exclusive deliverer of all manpower functions stipulated in the Wagner–Peyser Act. These services could be provided to the prime sponsor without cost if provision were made to defray the ES cost.

Merger. The most fundamental (and the most difficult) resolution would combine the Wagner–Peyser and the CETA systems through legislation and create a single "super" manpower system. This alternative would require a reexamination of the state role in the manpower system and the restructuring of federal–state–local relationships.

Congress should mandate an independent study that would examine the manpower functions now being performed by both the ES *and* CETA *organizations, assess existing* ES/CETA *relations, and explore the merits and problems associated with each of the alternatives.* Basic legislative changes should be based upon the findings of such a report.

SUMMARY

During the 4 years since CETA became operational, employment and training programs have become institutionalized as an integral part of local and state government activities and structures. Federally funded manpower programs, previously administered by the federal establishment, are now the responsibility of local units of government and are conducted under the direction of state and local officials.

The NRC study has focused both on the processes and the product of manpower programs. It has found that local control of programs has resulted in tighter program management, greater accountability, and more rational delivery systems. Local manpower planning, though still weak, is more meaningful than in the pre-CETA period, and grass roots participation in the planning process is greater. However the shift of program control scrambled the relationships among goverment jurisdictions and among the local institutions that deliver manpower services. The role of the Employment Service was particularly affected.

The study identified several major areas of concern, including: the choice of participants to be served, the processes for providing services, the kind and quality of programs, and their outcomes in terms of the adjustment of clients to the labor market. There are also serious questions as to the extent of new job creation under public service employment programs—now the bulk of manpower activities.

The recommendations of the Committee on Evaluation of Employment and Training Programs are directed to these issues and are summarized below under two categories: processes and institutional aspects of CETA, and program substance and outcomes.

PROCESSES AND INSTITUTIONAL ASPECTS OF CETA

• Revise formulas for allocating Title I, II, VI, and summer youth employment funds so that resources are distributed among areas on the basis of the specific groups to be served under each title.

• Integrate Title I, II, and VI plans and incorporate information on related programs in the community.

• Require evidence of private sector participation in Title I planning as a condition for the approval of plans.

• Increase the effectiveness and independence of local advisory councils; strengthen the coordinating authority of State Manpower Services Councils and eliminate their monitoring responsibilities.

• Establish a federal–local task force to design a more useful data base for planning, management, and evaluation; provide assistance to prime sponsors in developing management information systems.

• Conduct research to illuminate such issues as: the Employment Service/CETA relationship; linkages between CETA and other manpower programs; and the effectiveness of various systems for delivering client services.

PROGRAM SUBSTANCE AND OUTCOMES

• Rely on unemployment insurance as the major means of dealing with short-term unemployment, but rely on training and public service employment programs as the primary vehicles for assisting the long-term unemployed.

• Restrict Titles I and II to persons who are economically disadvantaged or members of low-income families. Limit Title VI to the same groups or, alternatively, to the long-term unemployed, with representation of the economically disadvantaged in proportion to their numbers among all eligible persons.

• Stress greater control by prime sponsors over client selection to assure that the priorities in the act are observed.

• Give priority to Title I programs that enhance human capital over those that are primarily income maintenance programs.

• Give greater emphasis, at all levels of administration, on upgrading the program content and quality of training programs.

• Greater emphasis should be given to job development and placement of program participants in unsubsidized employment; with more follow-up to determine whether CETA participants are able to obtain stable employment.

• Integrate PSE and employability development programs to improve the effectiveness of both training and placement outcomes.

• Redesign the PSE program to provide a three-part system aimed at both structural and countercyclical objectives: (a) continuing program for low-income, long-term unemployed and welfare recipients; (b) supplemental funds for areas of substantial and chronic unemployment, also limited to those unemployed for structural reasons; and (c) countercyclical program triggered automatically by changes in the national unemployment rate.

• Constrain the substitution of PSE funds for local resources by: (a) providing countercyclical revenue-sharing funds to substain the regular work force of state and local governments; (b) limit PSE projects to those that are outside of the regular activities of local government; (c) require that a proportion of all Title VI projects be used for jobs in the private nonprofit sector; (d) amend CETA to permit limitations on rehires; and (e) strengthen the DOL review and auditing capabilities.

A Manpower Acronyms

LEGISLATION

AFDC	Aid to Families with Dependent Children
CETA	Comprehensive Employment and Training Act of 1973
EEA	Emergency Employment Act of 1971
EJPEA	Emergency Jobs Programs Extension Act of 1976
EJUAA	Emergency Jobs and Unemployment Assistance Act of 1974
EOA	Economic Opportunity Act of 1964
MDTA	Manpower Development and Training Act of 1962
PWEA	Public Works Employment Act of 1976
PWEDA	Public Works and Economic Development Act of 1965
YEDPA	Youth Employment and Demonstration Projects Act of 1977

PLANNING SYSTEMS

AMPB	Ancillary Manpower Planning Board (pre-CETA)
BOS/MPC	Balance of State Manpower Planning Council
CAMPS	Cooperative Area Manpower Planning System (pre-CETA)
MAPC	Manpower Area Planning Council (pre-CETA)
MPC	Local Manpower Planning Council
SMPC	State Manpower Planning Council (pre-CETA)
SMSC	State Manpower Services Council

PROGRAMS

CEP	Concentrated Employment Program
FSB	Federal Supplemental Benefits (extended UI)
JOBS	Job Opportunities in the Business Sector—National Alliance of Businessmen
JOP	Jobs Optional Program (MDTA–OJT)
NYC	Neighborhood Youth Corps
OJT	On-the-Job Training
PEP	Public Employment Program (EEA)
PSC	Public Service Careers Program (includes New Careers)
PSE	Public Service Employment (CETA or EEA)
SUA	Special Unemployment Assistance Program
UI	Unemployment Insurance
WE	Work Experience
WIN	Work Incentive Program (for welfare recipients)

ORGANIZATIONS AND AGENCIES

BOS	Balance of State
CAA	Community Action Agency
CBO	Community Based Organization
COG	Council of Governments
CSA	Community Services Administration
DHEW	U.S. Department of Health, Education and Welfare
DOL	U.S. Department of Labor
ES	Employment Service (state agency)
ETA	Employment and Training Administration (DOL) (formerly Manpower Administration)
NPO	Nonprofit Organization
OEO	Office of Economic Opportunity (now Community Services Administration)
OIC	Opportunities Industrialization Center
SER	Services, Employment, Redevelopment (also Jobs for Progress)
SESA	State Employment Security Agency (includes ES, UI, and WIN)
UIS	Unemployment Insurance Service (state agency)
UL	Urban League
VOED	Vocational Education Agency (state or local)

B The Calculation of the Job Creation Ratio

The net job creation ratio of CETA was calculated as the level of actual state and local government employment minus the level of employment predicted in the absence of CETA, divided by the number of state and local CETA employees:

$$\text{NJCR} = \frac{\begin{array}{l}\text{Actual State and Local Government Employment} \\ - \text{ Predicted State and Local Government Employment} \\ \text{in the Absence of CETA}\end{array}}{\text{Number of CETA State and Local Government Employees}}$$

This ratio will take on a value of 1 if all CETA employees represent net additions to the aggregate state and local government work force; it will equal 0 if all CETA employees are substituted for employees that would have been funded by state and local governments if CETA funds had not been available. Thus, the rate of substitution is measured as 1 minus the net job creation ratio:

$$S = 1 - \text{NJCR}$$

The primary difficulty in estimating the net job creation rate arises from the necessity to predict what state and local government employment would have been in the absence of CETA. The approach used was to estimate the association between aggregate state and local government employment and a number of variables thought to

283

determine the level of that employment. A regression equation provided a series of parameters that described the historical relationship between the determinants, or explanatory variables, and employment. The actual values of the explanatory variables during the CETA program were used in this regression equation to obtain a predicted level of employment in the absence of CETA. The model used to obtain these predictions is:

$$E = f(R,W,t)$$

The dependent variable, E, is aggregate state and local government employment minus instructional personnel in the education sector minus net new jobs under PEP. Instructional personnel were removed from aggregate employment for two reasons: (1) relatively few CETA personnel were employed in an instructional capacity, thus the possibility of substitution was not relevant to these jobs; and (2) by removing instructional personnel, the problems of modeling changes in educational employment due to shifts in demographic characteristics of the population were avoided.

The number of net new jobs under PEP was subtracted from aggregate employment to remove the effect of PEP during the estimation period. In making this adjustment, the level of displacement under PEP was assumed to be 0.5, a rate consistent with the mid-duration findings of Johnson and Tomola. However, alternative rates, ranging from 0.3 to 0.7, were tested. These changes in the assumed level of displacement under PEP had an insignificant effect on the job creation rate estimated under CETA. (In general, an increase of 0.2 in the assumed displacement rate under PEP lowered the estimated job creation effect of CETA by 0.02).

The model utilized three explanatory variables. R represents state and local government receipts. It measures the resources from all sources (including federal grants) that state and local governments have available to purchase labor and indirectly reflects society's taste for public sector goods and services. The wage variable in the model, W, is the average compensation of government employees. The early 1970s saw fairly large increases in compensation paid to government employees. This variable was included to pick up whatever dampening effects these wage changes may have had on state and local government employment. The final variable, t, takes on the value of the observation number and was included due to the strong upward trend in state and local government employment. In addition, it helps to capture the effect of any variables omitted from the model.

The revenue and wage variables were measured in real terms (deflated by the implicit gross national product price deflator for state and local purchases of goods and services) and the equation was specified in log linear form. The log linear form was found to fit the data better than the linear equation. Moreover, a log linear equation is a first-order approximation to any functional form and hence more general than a linear equation.

Time is measured by its log, since we have assumed that the taste for governmental goods and services has increased at a decreasing rate over the estimation period. This might be expected, since the rapid rate of expansion of the public sector that occurred in the 1960s should continue at a decreasing rate in the early 1970s. If time were measured in units, the implicit assumption would be that the taste for state and local services was growing at a constant rate. This latter assumption seemed unreasonable given some of the institutional readings in recent years, e.g., tax revolts, defeats of bond issues, tax referendums, etc. Table 1 provides an indication of the magnitudes of the variables and their components over the estimation period.

The model was estimated for 54 quarters from 1961 I to 1974 II using the Cochrane–Orcutt technique for adjusting for autocorrelated residuals. Predictions were then made from 1974 III to 1976 IV. The results were:

$$\ln E_t = 7.851 + 0.032 \ln R_t - 0.237 \ln W_t + 0.366 \ln t$$
$$\quad (0.230) \quad (0.044) \qquad (0.119) \qquad\quad (0.020)$$

$$R^2 = 0.9994 \qquad\qquad\qquad F_{(3,50)} = 24{,}641$$

$$\text{rho} = 0.8281 \qquad\qquad\qquad \text{D.W.} = 1.92$$

standard error of the regression = 0.0043

The net job creation ratios based on the predictions obtained from this equation appear in Table 2. In every quarter the job creation estimates fall between 0 and 1, and in the tenth quarter it was 0.54. Furthermore, this result is obtained without constraints or wide confidence intervals. We can be 95 percent sure that in the tenth quarter the job creation ratio will fall between 0.29 and 0.78.

There are two major limitations to this approach. First, the results are influenced by the way the trend is measured. This instability may stem from the omission of a variable measuring the cost of nonlabor inputs into the state and local production function. Also, the model requires that the taste for government services, and hence government employ-

TABLE 1 Changes in State and Local Government Employment, Receipts, and Compensation, 1961–1976

Year	Quarter	Number of State and Local Government Employees (thousands)	Number of State and Local Government Instructional Personnel (thousands)	State and Local Government Receipts ($ billions)	Average Compensation of Employees ($ thousands)
1961	1st	6,439	1,835	91.1	7,280
1966	2nd	8,247	2,432	123.4	7,732
1971	3rd	10,196	2,967	162.0	8,192
1976	4th	12,295	3,565	197.2	7,677

SOURCE: Computed from U.S. Department of Commerce Survey of Current Business and Public Employment, GE Series No. 1.
NOTE: State and local government receipts and average compensation of employees are seasonally adjusted annual rates, expressed in constant dollars (1972 = 100). Number of state and local government employees is seasonally adjusted. Average annual percent change in employment and in receipts covers the period from the preceding date.

TABLE 2 Job Creation Ratio of CETA Public Service Employment, United States, June 1974 through December 1976

| | | State and Local Government Employment (Less Instructional Personnel) | | Actual Minus Estimated | CETA PSE (Less Nonprofit) | Job Creation Ratio (Column 3 ÷ Column 4) |
Year	Quarter	Actual	Estimated[a]			
		(1)	(2)	(3)	(4)	(5)
1974	3rd	8,121	8,110	11	40	0.27
	4th	8,236	8,178	58	71	0.82
1975	1st	8,400	8,233	167	206	0.81
	2nd	8,496	8,288	208	275	0.76
	3rd	8,532	8,342	190	272	0.70
	4th	8,571	8,393	178	299	0.59
1976	1st	8,612	8,443	169	306	0.55
	2nd	8,661	8,490	171	298	0.57
	3rd	8,685	8,540	145	264	0.55
	4th	8,730	8,598	132	246	0.54

SOURCE: Computed from U.S. Bureau of Labor Statistics and Employment and Training Administration data.
[a] Estimate of state and local government employment, less instructional personnel, excluding CETA employment, derived from regression analysis.

ment, increase at a decreasing rate. As noted earlier, this is not an unreasonable assumption.

Secondly, if CETA had an effect on state and local government revenue or wages, then predicted employment will reflect this effect, because these variables are included on the explanatory side of the model. For example, if CETA causes state and local governments to put off tax increases because needed services can be provided through substitution, then the revenue variable will be lower than it would have been in the absence of CETA. This would lead to a predicted employment figure lower than what actually would have occurred in the absence of CETA. As a result, the job creation ratio would be overstated.

While these limitations call for caution in the interpretation of the job creation estimates, there are several factors that suggest that the estimates are reliable. First, the confidence intervals are narrow, as mentioned above. Second, an alternative model designed to avoid the limitations of the above procedure resulted in a similar long-run job creation estimate of 0.44. This model took the form:

$$E = f(Yn,W,PSE)$$

where E is total aggregate state and local government employment minus the number of PSE slots under PEP and CETA. As suggested by Roger Bolton in his studies of the Brookings Model, net income, Yn, is defined as personal income plus indirect state and local business taxes minus federal personal taxes. In addition, federal grants-in-aid to state and local governments were added because these grants are becoming an increasingly large portion of state and local government resources. W is the same wage variable used earlier and PSE is the sum of PSE slots created under PEP and CETA, adjusted for PEP summer youth employment and nongovernmental CETA positions.

All of the variables were expressed in real per capita terms. This procedure removes much of the trend from the variables, reducing the chances of getting a good fit due merely to growth of population and inflation in the dependent and independent variables. In addition, it seems to be a correct procedure on purely theoretical grounds, as state and local government decision makers must operate in these terms.

This equation was estimated from 1961 I to 1977 IV again using the Cochrane–Orcutt technique to adjust for autocorrelated residuals. The following results were obtained:

The parameter on the PSE variable (0.56) reflects the average long-run (14 quarters) rate of substitution, under the PEP and CETA programs. It is similar to the long-run (10 quarters) rate of substitution estimated from the first model, 0.46. Furthermore, we can be 95 percent sure that the rate of substitution will fall between 0.26 and 0.86. The estimate obtained

$$E_t - PSE_t = \underset{(0.005)}{0.079} + \underset{(0.661)}{2.686} \ Yn_t - \underset{(0.0005)}{0.004} \ W_t - \underset{(0.155)}{0.564} \ PSE_t$$

$R^2 = 0.9990$ $F = 24{,}138$

rho = 0.978   D.W. = 1.287

standard error of the regression = 0.00022

from the second model, while not as statistically precise as the previous one, does not suffer from some of the limitations of the first model. The results are not dependent on a trend variable or nonlinear functional forms. The equation tends to exhibit a greater degree of stability, and by using net income rather than revenue the second model will not be influenced by any revenue effects CETA might have had.

The second model appears to be reliable and correct for some of the problems in previous estimates.

C National Commission for Manpower Policy: Job Creation Through Public Service Employment

The National Commission for Manpower Policy issued an interim report to Congress with recommendations relating to the public service employment programs under CETA. Because of their relevance to the CETP recommendations, the highlights of the commission's proposals and recommendations are reproduced below:

1. That PSE be used as a major instrument of national manpower policy and programming primarily for the purpose of providing interim employment opportunities for structurally unemployed persons and that Congress adopt the amended eligibility criteria established in the Emergency Jobs Programs Extension Act (PL 94-444) for all PSE positions.

2. The establishment of a policy of automatic increases and decreases in the number of PSE jobs in response to changes in the national level of unemployment but with the same eligibility criteria enumerated in recommendation 1 above.

3. That Congress fund the recently expanded PSE program at the level fo 725,000 jobs through fiscal 1979, which will provide additional time for assessing the optimal size of such a program under the CETA system.

4. That local sponsors be required to provide remedial education and skill training to enrollees in need of such assistance, and that they be directed to involve local employers more actively in the planning of local PSE programs so that they can contribute to designs aimed at improving transition.

5. That the wage structure emphasize the following components:

• Wages be set at levels which will not discourage enrollees from seeking alternative employment or from suffering wage decreases when they move into regular jobs.

• Consideration be given to providing some wage increases when a person is on PSE, especially if he or she is assigned increased responsibilities.

• The ceiling of $10,000 of federal subsidy for a PSE job, as in the current legislation, to be continued, and the scope for local supplementation above that sum be limited to no more than 15 percent of all funds to provide elasticity for adjustments where this is necessary to take into account regional wage differences.

6. The forward funding of PSE on the ground that such action will enable local sponsors and their program managers to improve their design of PSE programs, improve their selection of enrollees, and strengthen their management procedures with the aim of contributing to the employability of their clients, increasing their productivity, and containing the costs of the projects.

7. That Congress seek to increase and improve the program information that is available by stipulating the types of information that it requires for overseeing the program and for gauging its effectiveness; by making the requisite resources available to the Department of Labor and to the prime sponsors for the collection and analysis of the required data; by prescribing, as a condition of continued funding, that federal grantees furnish the required information, including data on their regular budget and employment, on a timely basis; and by establishing procedures for the periodic review of the assessments and evaluations prepared by the Department of Labor and other responsible federal agencies, such as the General Accounting Office.

Statistical
Tables

TABLE 1   Appropriations and Expenditures, Department of Labor: Manpower Development and Training Act, Economic Opportunity Act, Emergency Employment Act, and Comprehensive Employment and Training Act, Fiscal Years 1963-1978 (millions of dollars)

| Fiscal Year | DOL Manpower Appropriations | | | | | Expenditures |
	MDTA	EOA	EEA	CETA	Total	
	(1)	(2)	(3)	(4)	(5)	(6)
1963	69.9				69.9	51.8
1964	130.0				130.0	110.0
1965	396.9	132.5			529.4	280.3
1966	399.6	577.8[1]			977.4	754.8
1967	390.0	667.1			1,057.1	857.6
1968	398.5	745.7			1,144.2	1,087.7
1969	407.5	907.8			1,315.3	1,081.1
1970	705.8	753.7			1,459.5	1,065.4
1971	867.2	761.8			1,629.0	1,356.5
1972	905.3	776.8	1,000.0		2,682.1	2,154.9
1973	719.6	831.6	1,250.0		2,801.2	2,392.6
1974			250.0	2,015.6[2]	2,265.6	2,058.5
1975				3,742.8	3,742.8	3,175.0
1976				5,741.8	5,741.8	5,045.0
1976TQ[3]				597.6	597.6	1,577.0
1977				8,052.8[4]	8,052.8[4]	5,631.3
1978				8,061.9[5]	8,061.9	NA

Source: Employment and Training Administration, U.S. Department of Labor
[1] Figures for 1966-1969 include amounts for Job Corps, administered by the OEO during those years, as follows (million $)—FY 1966 - 306.3; 1977 - 209.2; 1978 - 282.3; 1979 - 278.4.
[2] Combined funds for MDTA, EOA, and Title II of CETA.
[3] Transition quarter, July-Sept. 1976.
[4] Excludes amounts forward funded for fiscal 1978 in the fiscal 1977 supplemental appropriations.
[5] House and Senate Conference approved $3,377.9 for fiscal 1978; $4,684.0 forward funded from fiscal 1977.

TABLE 2 Federal Obligations for Work and Training Programs Administered by the Department of Labor, Selected Fiscal Years 1963–1974 (amounts in thousands)

Manpower Programs	FY 1974 (1)	FY 1972 (2)	FY 1970 (3)	FY 1968 (4)	FY 1966 (5)	FY 1963–1964 (6)
Total	$2,143,613[1]	$2,696,940	$1,418,552	$802,173	$628,407	$198,181
Manpower Development & Training Act	398,462	424,553	336,580	296,418	339,649	198,181
Institutional Training	307,896	355,708	287,031	221,847	281,710	190,744
JOP-OJT[2]	90,566	68,845	49,549	74,571	57,939	7,437
Neighborhood Youth Corps	661,712	517,244	356,589	281,864	263,337[3]	—
In School	88,570	74,897	59,242	58,908	[3]	—
Out of School	113,651	121,962	97,923	96,279	[3]	—
Summer	459,491	320,385	199,424	126,677	[3]	—
Operation Mainstream	114,664	85,164	51,043	22,319	—	—
Public Service Careers	28,334	58,301	89,366	7,557	—	—
Special Impact[4]	—	—	—	2,038	—	—
Concentrated Employment Program	146,489[5]	154,602	187,592	93,057	25,421	—
Jobs (Federally Financed)	64,026	118,224	148,820	89,920	—	—
Work Incentive Program	250,127	174,788	78,780	9,000	—	—
Job Corps	149,551	202,185	169,782	—	—	—
Public Employment Program	281,120[6]	961,879	—	—	—	—

Source: Manpower Reports of the President, 1970-75
[1] Includes $39,127,612 obligated for the Migrants Program and $10 million for Title IX, National Older Workers Program, which are not shown separately.
[2] Includes the JOBS-Optional Program (JOP), which began in fiscal 1971, and the MDTA on-the-job (OJT) program, which ended in fiscal 1970 except for national contracts. Also includes Construction Outreach.
[3] Data are not available for NYC components prior to fiscal 1967.
[4] Transferred to the Office of Economic Opportunity, July 1, 1969.
[5] Total includes $36,775,542 in Comprehensive Manpower Program allocations for FY 1974 only.
[6] Includes $44,010,000 under Title II and $237,110,000 under Title III-A of CETA (extension of Emergency Employment Act).
(Details may not add to totals due to rounding.)

TABLE 3 CETA Appropriations, Fiscal Years 1974-1978 (millions of dollars)

| Title | Fiscal Year 1974[1] | Fiscal Year 1975 | Fiscal Year 1976 | | Fiscal Year 1977 | | Fiscal Year 1978 |
			July 1975-June 1976	Transition Quarter[2]	Initial	Final[3]	
	(1)	(2)	(3)	(4)	(5)	(6)	(7)
I	1,010.0	1,580.0	1,580.0[4]	395.4	1,880.0	1,880.0	1,880.0
II	370.0	400.0	1,600.0[4]	100.0	400.0	524.0	1,016.0[7]
III	180.0[5]	239.4	268.4	58.4	239.3	1,600.7[6]	387.9
IV	150.0	175.0	140.0	43.8	197.5	274.1	417.0
VI	250.0	875.0	1,625.0	—	1,384.0	3,179.0	3,668.0[7]
Summer Youth	305.6[5]	473.4	528.4	—	595.0	595.0	693.0
Total	2,265.6	3,742.8	5,741.8	597.6	4,695.8	8,052.8	8,061.9

Source: Employment and Training Administration, U.S. Department of Labor
[1] Appropriations for Department of Labor manpower programs corresponding with Title I, II, and for the Emergency Employment Act.
[2] July-Sept. 1976.
[3] Includes supplemental appropriations as part of the Economic Stimulus Act.
[4] $1,200 million authorized under Title II for both Title II and VI.
[5] Excludes $91 million in summer youth funds and $33 million in funds for national programs carried forward from fiscal 1973.
[6] Includes $233.3 million for Young Adult Conservation Corp., Title VIII of CETA; also funds for veterans programs (HIRE), skill training improvement (STIP), and other youth programs.
[7] Forward funded from 1977 appropriation.

TABLE 4 Federal Funds for Manpower Programs, Total and Department of Labor, Compared with Gross National Product Fiscal Years 1972-1978 (amounts in millions of dollars)

| Fiscal Year | Obligations | | | Gross National Product (GNP) | Total Obligations as Percent of GNP |
| | Total All Agencies | Department of Labor | | | |
		Amount	Percent of Total		
	(1)	(2)	(3)	(4)	(5)
1972	4,941	3,348	67.8	1,110,500	0.44
1973	5,252	3,432	65.3	1,237,500	0.42
1974	4,641	2,817	60.7	1,359,200	0.34
1975	6,931	4,797	69.2	1,454,600	0.48
1976[1]	8,670	5,876	67.8	1,625,400	0.53
1977	12,628	10,393	82.3	1,838,000	0.69
1978 (est.)	10,894	8,613	79.1	2,043,200	0.53

Source: Office of Management and Budget, Special Analyses, Budget of the United States
[1] Excludes transition quarter.

TABLE 5 CETA Allocations by Title, Sample Prime Sponsors, Fiscal Years 1974-1977 (thousands of dollars)

Prime Sponsor	Fiscal Year	Title I[1]	Public Service Employment				Summer Youth Program[2]	Total Allocation[3]
			EEA	Title II	Title VI	Total		
	(1)	(2)	(3)	(4)	(5)	(6)	(7)	(8)
CITIES								
Gary, Ind.	1974	5,625.7	148.1	403.5	–	551.6	–	6,177.3
	1975	5,063.1	–	437.7	786.6	1,224.3	2,946.9	9,234.3
	1976	4,556.8	–	1,592.8	1,496.1	3,088.9	3,229.1	10,874.8
	1977	4,101.1	–	1,536.7	6,695.0	8,231.7	3,229.0	15,561.8
Long Beach, Ca.	1974	3,025.1	690.0	974.2	–	1,664.2	–	4,689.3
	1975	2,722.6	–	1,015.0	2,286.9	3,301.9	888.9	6,913.4
	1976	2,457.2	–	3,764.6	3,141.8	6,816.4	1,012.7	10,286.3
	1977	2,786.3	–	2,937.7	12,661.9	15,599.6	1,163.2	19,549.1
New York, NY	1974	70,074.4	11,171.0	19,540.2	–	30,711.2	–	100,785.6
	1975	63,067.0	–	18,873.0	47,844.7	66,717.7	26,579.5	156,364.2
	1976	56,760.3	–	93,707.0	79,214.4	72,921.4	29,124.9	158,806.6
	1977	67,584.0	–	68,820.6	301,391.7	370,212.3	29,196.0	466,992.3
Philadelphia, Pa.	1974	15,479.6	3,658.7	6,327.2	–	9,985.9	–	25,465.5
	1975	13,931.6	–	6,247.6	12,402.0	18,649.6	4,687.2	37,268.4
	1976	12,538.5	–	16,947.2	14,788.9	31,746.1	5,136.1	49,420.7
	1977	14,650.4	–	17,292.6	72,069.1	89,361.7	5,550.3	109,562.4
St. Paul, Minn.	1974	2,597.9	294.4	718.1	–	1,012.5	–	3,610.4

COUNTIES

Place	Year							
Topeka, Ks.[4]	1975	2,338.1	102.5	628.5	1,301.8	1,930.3	560.9	4,829.3
	1976	2,104.3	—	2,578.9	2,577.0	5,157.9	674.1	7,936.3
	1977	2,196.5	—	2,918.1	11,363.0	14,281.1	805.5	17,283.1
Calhoun, Mich.	1974	1,083.5	167.2	134.8	—	273.3	—	1,356.8
	1975	975.2	—	118.0	337.9	455.9	298.6	1,729.7
	1976	1,072.6	—	1,102.2	823.0	1,925.2	330.2	3,328.0
	1977	1,051.8	—	381.2	2,458.0	2,839.2	358.5	4,249.5
Chester, Pa.	1974	849.3	101.2	509.5	—	676.7	—	1,526.0
	1975	853.7	—	421.4	799.9	1,221.3	233.5	2,308.5
	1976	892.1	—	1,421.2	1,522.5	2,943.7	295.1	4,130.9
	1977	1,096.7	—	1,502.3	6,405.4	7,907.7	414.6	9,419.0
	1974	1,052.6	—	—	—	101.2	—	1,153.8
	1975	1,028.4	—	—	411.3	411.3	311.7	1,751.4
	1976	983.1	—	752.5	979.8	1,732.3	391.5	3,106.9
	1977	1,153.5	—	983.6	4,781.6	5,765.2	473.2	7,392.0
*Cook, Ill.	1974	4,823.4	848.6	664.4	—	1,513.0	—	6,336.4
	1975	6,665.6	—	941.6	3,777.9	4,719.5	1,535.6	12,920.7
	1976	7,180.9	—	3,419.2	7,877.4	11,296.6	1,942.7	20,420.2
	1977	9,132.1	—	7,789.6	40,772.0	48,561.6	2,879.1	60,572.8
Lorain, O.	1974	648.0	133.0	173.4	—	306.4	—	954.4
	1975	841.0	—	151.7	697.9	849.6	356.2	2,046.8
	1976	992.4	—	1,783.9	1,847.7	3,631.6	450.8	5,074.8
	1977	1,455.1	—	1,832.7	7,305.9	9,138.6	628.8	11,222.5

TABLE 5 (Continued)

Prime Sponsor	Fiscal Year	Title I[1]	Public Service Employment				Summer Youth Program[2]	Total Allocation[3]
			EEA	Title II	Title VI	Total		
	(1)	(2)	(3)	(4)	(5)	(6)	(7)	(8)
COUNTIES (continued)								
Middlesex, NJ	1974	2,468.0	797.5	1,217.8	–	2,015.3	–	4,483.3
	1975	2,947.5	–	1,420.4	3,531.7	4,952.1	850.0	8,749.6
	1976	2,970.4	–	4,910.0	4,267.8	9,177.8	1,075.2	13,223.4
	1977	3,781.1	–	5,723.2	25,190.0	30,913.2	1,487.6	36,181.9
Pasco, Fla.	1974	253.6	171.5	222.3	–	393.8	–	647.4
	1975	380.4	–	–	382.7	382.7	85.2	848.3
	1976	523.7	–	616.6	648.3	1,264.9	107.7	1,896.3
	1977	785.5	–	1,150.1	5,252.6	6,402.7	168.2	7,356.4
*Ramsey, Minn.	1974	313.7	71.4	–	–	71.4	–	385.1
	1975	470.6	–	–	253.5	253.5	80.4	804.5
	1976	529.9	–	710.6	691.2	1,401.8	101.7	2,033.4
	1977	671.6	–	819.6	3,422.2	4,241.8	150.7	5,064.2
Stanislaus, Ca.	1974	1,346.1	1,246.6	1,704.6	–	2,951.2	–	4,297.3
	1975	1,972.4	–	1,459.5	1,686.4	3,145.9	476.7	5,595.0
	1976	2,166.2	–	4,719.0	4,448.9	9,167.9	603.3	11,937.4
	1977	2,459.2	–	3,767.9	17,013.3	20,781.2	857.1	24,097.5
*Union, NJ	1974	1,388.2	191.0	221.1	–	412.1	–	1,800.3
	1975	1,590.2	–	245.0	1,026.9	1,271.9	368.7	3,230.8

	Year	(7)	(6)	(5)	(4)	(3)	(2)	(1)
	1976	1,803.0	–	2,517.2	2,481.3	4,998.5	466.5	7,268.0
	1977	2,346.3	–	3,325.5	14,142.5	17,468.0	691.3	20,505.6
CONSORTIA								
Austin, Tex.	1974	2,669.8	100.3	–	–	100.3	–	2,770.1
	1975	2,714.4	–	–	490.6	490.6	736.3	3,941.3
	1976	2,552.5	–	326.1	861.1	1,187.2	880.6	4,620.3
	1977	2,784.8	–	1,027.1	6,038.1	7,065.2	1,013.4	10,863.4
Cleveland, O.[5]	1974	15,031.1	(1,738.4)	3,321.1	–	5,059.5	–	20,090.6
	1975	15,581.0	–	3,220.8	7,608.6	10,829.4	5,493.6	31,904.0
	1976	14,960.3	–	11,256.8	10,377.3	21,634.1	6,118.4	42,712.8
	1977	13,893.1	–	11,428.8	46,988.7	58,417.5	5,788.2	78,098.8
Kansas City, Ks.	1974	1,804.3	124.3	89.2	–	213.5	–	2,017.8
	1975	1,623.9	–	78.1	523.1	601.2	424.6	2,649.7
	1976	1,467.3	–	1,340.7	1,388.8	2,729.5	465.3	4,662.1
	1977	1,488.0	–	1,474.9	5,786.7	7,261.6	541.0	9,290.6
Lansing, Mich.	1974	1,917.9	183.7	1,451.9	–	1,635.6	–	3,553.5
	1975	2,177.8	–	1,367.6	1,647.8	3,015.4	549.0	5,742.2
	1976	2,557.1	–	3,869.8	4,072.1	7,941.9	693.8	11,192.8
	1977	3,105.2	–	3,414.3	14,709.7	18,124.0	1,022.1	22,251.3
Phoenix/Maricopa, Ar.[6]	1974	8,279.4	724.6	763.3	–	1,487.9	–	9,767.3
	1975	8,196.6	–	792.7	5,710.8	6,503.5	2,536.3	17,236.4
	1976	7,690.8	–	9,340.4	9,898.0	19,238.4	2,914.3	29,843.5
	1977	5,663.3	–	8,387.6	35,000.0	43,387.6	2,193.2	51,244.1

TABLE 5 (Continued)

Prime Sponsor	Fiscal Year (1)	Title I[1] (2)	Public Service Employment				Summer Youth Program[2] (7)	Total Allocation[3] (8)
			EEA (3)	Title II (4)	Title VI (5)	Total (6)		
CONSORTIA (continued)								
Orange Co., Ca.	1974	5,648.7	1,503.9	1,769.8	—	3,273.7	—	8,922.4
	1975	7,732.4	—	1,637.1	7,126.0	8,763.1	1,456.9	17,952.4
	1976	8,364.9	—	10,934.2	10,234.3	21,168.5	1,842.7	31,376.1
	1977	10,180.9	—	10,322.0	40,319.7	50,641.7	2,731.0	63,553.6
Raleigh, NC[7]	1974	2,075.6	(106.7)	—	—	106.7	—	2,182.3
	1975	2,234.9	—	—	771.0	771.0	678.9	3,684.8
	1976	1,574.7	—	2,116.7	2,104.4	4,221.1	730.6	6,526.4
	1977	1,799.9	—	1,098.0	5,517.3	6,615.3	799.1	9,214.3
Pinellas/St. Petersburg, Fla.	1974	2,194.3	153.7	118.3	—	272.0	—	2,466.3
	1975	2,521.0	—	32.2	1,507.8	1,540.0	738.4	4,799.4
	1976	3,164.7	—	3,963.9	3,981.8	7,945.7	934.2	12,044.6
	1977	4,717.6	—	4,390.9	19,096.7	23,487.6	1,384.4	29,589.6
San Joaquin, Ca.	1974	2,517.9	1,028.8	1,346.3	—	2,375.1	—	4,893.0
	1975	2,883.9	—	1,130.3	1,401.3	2,531.6	1,009.4	6,424.9
	1976	2,782.6	—	3,141.3	3,174.9	6,316.2	1,151.3	10,250.1
	1977	2,876.1	—	3,277.7	14,540.5	17,818.2	1,157.4	21,851.7
STATES								
*Maine[8]	1974	7,879.0	1,500.0	2,771.1	—	4,271.1	—	12,150.1
	1975	7,091.1	—	2,675.1	4,797.6	7,472.7	1,841.8	16,405.6

	1974						
	1976	4,884.8	–	7,978.9	6,653.4	14,632.3	2,124.2	21,641.3
	1977	4,637.3	–	5,350.2	23,896.1	29,246.3	1,999.8	35,883.4
*Arizona	1974	5,735.5	572.9	140.5	–	713.4	–	6,448.9
	1975	5,162.0	–	400.5	1,812.6	2,213.1	2,536.3	9,911.4
	1976	4,645.8	–	2,952.7	3,034.3	5,987.0	1,373.3	12,006.1
	1977	4,507.9	–	4,885.0	21,322.2	26,207.2	1,571.4	32,286.5
*North Carolina	1974	24,524.4	NA	–	–	–	–	24,524.4[9]
	1975	22,108.7	–	98.7	14,091.7	14,190.4	658.1	36,957.2
	1976	20,117.3	–	33,497.0	37,047.3	70,544.3	9,101.2	99,762.8
	1977	24,662.0	–	20,613.9	82,501.5	103,115.4	10,714.0	138,491.4
*Texas	1974	21,797.9	NA	914.0	–	914.0	–	22,711.9[9]
	1975	19,764.3	–	636.6	8,840.4	9,477.0	6,617.6	35,868.9
	1976	16,309.3	–	5,840.8	9,091.7	14,932.5	7,301.9	38,543.7
	1977	15,876.3	–	5,991.4	37,351.8	43,343.2	6,961.5	66,181.0

Source: Employment and Training Administration, U.S. Department of Labor

[1] Fiscal Year 1974 figures are obligations for manpower programs corresponding with Title I.

[2] Summer youth employment funds for 1974 included in Title I figures.

[3] Excludes allotments from State vocational education, manpower services, and planning funds.

[4] Topeka became Topeka-Shawnee Consortium in fiscal 1976.

[5] Lake County withdrew from Cleveland Consortium in fiscal 1976.

[6] Phoenix and Maricopa County disbanded consortium in fiscal 1977. Figures for 1977 are for Phoenix only.

[7] Balance of Wake County withdrew from consortium in fiscal 1976.

[8] Cumberland and Penobscot Counties withdrew from balance of state in fiscal 1976; Kenebec and Hancock Counties withdrew in fiscal 1977.

[9] Does not include EEA funds for fiscal 1974.

*Balance of county or state.

( ) Estimated.

Note: Details may not add to totals due to rounding. Fiscal 1976 figures exclude transition quarter.

TABLE 6 CETA Public Service Employment, Titles II and VI, Sample Prime Sponsors, Fiscal Years 1975 and 1976

Prime Sponsors	Title	Fiscal Year 1975				Fiscal Year 1976				Transition Quarter[1]
		Sept. 30	Dec. 31	Mar. 31	June 30	Sept. 30	Dec. 31	Mar. 31	June 30	
	(1)	(2)	(3)	(4)	(5)	(6)	(7)	(8)	(9)	(10)
CITIES										
Gary, Ind.	II	1	110	189	206	71	67	60	61	185
	VI	–	–	43	55	212	233	228	243	71
	Total	1	110	232	261	283	300	288	304	256
Long Beach, Ca.	II	9	68	327	440	93	90	97	66	305
	VI	–	–	214	222	514	476	318	241	–
	Total	9	68	541	662	607	566	415	307	305
New York, NY	II	NA	1,981	6,707	13,105	3,112	2,745	2,401	13,318	12,502
	VI	–	–	4,141	6,802	14,653	13,811	13,171	1,034	918
	Total	NA	1,981	10,848	19,907	17,765	16,556	15,571	14,352	13,420
Philadelphia, Pa.	II	–	1,262	1,596	1,599	739	–	–	2,740	2,642
	VI	–	–	897	1,162	2,138	2,808	2,023	–	–
	Total	–	1,262	2,493	2,761	2,877	2,808	2,023	2,740	2,642

St. Paul, Minn.									
II	NA	14	199	362	129	125	127	129	529
VI	NA	—	293	174	268	338	485	514	—
Total	NA	14	492	536	397	463	612	643	529
Topeka, Ks.[2]									
II	13	21	60	70	NA	NA	NA	NA	NA
VI	—	—	64	68	NA	NA	NA	NA	NA
Total	13	21	124	138	NA	NA	NA	NA	NA
COUNTIES									
Calhoun, Mich.									
II	32	94	191	198	124	19	19	19	175
VI	—	—	56	111	122	167	325	299	64
Total	32	94	247	309	246	186	344	318	239
Chester, Pa.									
II	—	—	—	—	—	—	—	—	—
VI	—	—	33	48	77	123	178	142	76
Total	—	—	33	48	77	123	178	142	76
*Cook, Ill.									
II	54	117	330	342	268	5	8	—	—
VI	—	—	395	407	478	863	1,001	1,030	972
Total	54	117	725	749	746	868	1,009	1,030	972
Lorain, O.									
II	NA	12	64	68	57	80	30	25	226
VI	—	—	63	117	106	161	327	418	91
Total	NA	12	127	185	163	241	357	443	317

TABLE 6 (Continued)

Prime Sponsors	Title	Fiscal Year 1975				Fiscal Year 1976				Transition Quarter[1]
		Sept. 30	Dec. 31	Mar. 31	June 30	Sept. 30	Dec. 31	Mar. 31	June 30	
COUNTIES (continued)	(1)	(2)	(3)	(4)	(5)	(6)	(7)	(8)	(9)	(10)
Middlesex, NJ	II	62	175	584	583	165	130	130	651	734
	VI	–	–	399	427	770	747	666	96	–
	Total	62	175	983	1,010	935	877	796	747	734
Pasco, Fla.	II	10	36	50	40	31	26	16	18	132
	VI	–	–	47	52	96	106	119	120	–
	Total	10	36	97	92	127	132	135	138	132
*Ramsey, Minn.	II	–	–	–	–	–	–	–	–	–
	VI	–	–	23	29	63	69	73	90	35
	Total	–	–	23	29	63	69	73	90	35
Stanislaus, Ca.	II	88	333	712	497	160	165	160	572	582
	VI	–	–	149	204	510	550	554	89	32
	Total	88	333	861	701	670	715	714	661	614

*Union, NJ	II	–	10	NA	97	108	105	69	63	277
	VI	–	–	NA	190	198	295	461	525	189
	Total	–	10	NA	287	306	400	530	588	466
CONSORTIA										
Austin, Tex.	II	–	–	–	–	–	–	–	–	–
	VI	–	–	100	74	44	156	142	135	NA
	Total	–	–	100	74	44	156	142	135	NA
Cleveland, O.[3]	II	409	596	648	714	857	245	77	98	1,311
	VI	–	–	364	553	799	1,541	1,878	924	180
	Total	409	596	1,012	1,267	1,656	1,786	1,955	1,022	1,491
Kansas City, Ks.	II	2	18	42	50	44	43	44	71	238
	VI	–	–	49	67	111	172	304	374	–
	Total	2	18	91	117	155	215	348	445	238
Lansing, Mich.	II	72	245	429	487	93	99	97	95	505
	VI	–	–	56	89	491	521	529	324	–
	Total	72	245	485	576	584	620	626	419	505
Phoenix/Maricopa, Ar.	II	45	142	224	204	226	337	324	289	NA
	VI	–	–	647	771	830	1,405	1,929	1,873	NA
	Total	45	142	871	975	1,056	1,742	2,253	2,162	NA

TABLE 6 (Continued)

Prime Sponsors	Title	Fiscal Year 1975				Fiscal Year 1976				Transition Quarter[1]
		Sept. 30	Dec. 31	Mar. 31	June 30	Sept. 30	Dec. 31	Mar. 31	June 30	
(1)		(2)	(3)	(4)	(5)	(6)	(7)	(8)	(9)	(10)
CONSORTIA (continued)										
Orange Co., Ca.	II	76	278	562	536	295	291	254	433	920
	VI	–	–	641	703	1,178	1,266	1,308	958	514
	Total	76	278	1,203	1,239	1,473	1,557	1,562	1,391	1,434
Raleigh, NC[4]	II	–	–	–	–	NA	94	89	79	355
	VI	–	–	98	121	393	403	429	402	4
	Total	–	–	98	121	393	497	518	481	359
Pinellas/ St. Petersburg, Fla.	II	NA	NA	26	47	144	164	183	173	867
	VI	–	–	191	232	734	802	875	742	–
	Total	NA	NA	217	279	878	966	1,058	915	867
San Joaquin, Ca.	II	63	216	410	397	126	208	169	156	494
	VI	–	–	190	171	377	392	396	264	1
	Total	63	216	600	568	503	600	565	420	495

STATES

*Maine[5]	II	147	388	1,346	1,319	1,269	NA	NA	443	NA
	VI	–	–	679	783	894	1,600	1,268	NA	NA
	Total	147	388	2,025	2,102	2,163	NA	NA	NA	NA
*Arizona	II	10	44	150	99	70	120	196	79	580
	VI	–	–	251	248	305	489	682	441	NA
	Total	10	44	401	347	375	609	878	520	NA
*North Carolina	II	NA	NA	45	43	137	1,058	1,308	1,427	3,346
	VI	–	–	5,887	4,621	5,946	5,269	6,858	6,095	3,245
	Total	NA	NA	5,932	4,664	6,083	6,327	8,166	7,522	6,591
*Texas	II	96	397	476	461	36	151	221	217	1,196
	VI	–	–	947	1,534	2,002	2,360	2,446	2,190	261
	Total	96	397	1,423	1,995	2,038	2,511	2,667	2,407	1,457

Source: Employment and Training Administration, U.S. Department of Labor

[1] July-Sept. 1976
[2] Topeka became Topeka-Shawnee Consortium in fiscal 1976.
[3] Lake County withdrew from the Cleveland Consortium in fiscal 1976.
[4] Balance of Wake County withdrew from the Raleigh Consortium in fiscal 1976.
[5] Cumberland and Penobscot Counties withdrew from balance of state in fiscal 1976.
*Balance of county or state.

309

TABLE 7 Characteristics of CETA Participants, U.S. Total for Fiscal Years 1975, 1976, and 1977, Compared with Participants in Comparable Fiscal Year 1974 Programs (Percentages)

Characteristics	Manpower[1] Programs FY 1974	PEP[2] Program FY 1974	CETA Title I			CETA Title II			CETA Title VI		
			FY 1975	FY 1976	FY 1977	FY 1975	FY 1976	FY 1977	FY 1975	FY 1976	FY 1977
	(1)	(2)	(3)	(4)	(5)	(6)	(7)	(8)	(9)	(10)	(11)
Total Number	549,700	66,200	1,126,000	1,731,500	1,449,400	227,100	255,700	336,200	157,000	495,200	575,500
Sex: Male	58	66	54	54	52	66	64	60	70	65	64
Female	42	34	46	46	48	34	36	40	30	35	36
Age: Under 22	63	23	62	57	52	24	22	20	21	22	20
22-44	31	67	32	36	41	63	64	64	65	64	65
45 and over	6	11	6	7	8	13	14	15	14	14	15
Years of School:											
8 or less	15	} 23	13	12	10	9	8	7	8	8	8
9-11	51		48	43	40	18	18	15	18	18	19
12 and over	34	77	39	45	50	72	74	78	73	74	73
AFDC	} 23	10	16	15	16	7	6	6	6	6	10
Public Assistance			11	11	10	9	9	7	8	7	8
Economically Disadvantaged	87	34	77	76	78	48	47	48	44	44	66

310

Race: White	55	69	55	55	57	65	61	71	71	68	66
Black	37	23	39	37	35	22	27	23	23	23	26
Spanish Speaking	15	13	13	14	14	16	12	8	13	10	8
Veteran:[3]											
Recently Separated	NA	NA	NA	2	3	NA	4	5	NA	5	7
Special	15	39	5	4	3	11	10	7	13	9	6
Other	{	{	4	5	0	13	11	1	15	12	1
Full-Time Student	NA	NA	33	31	25	3	2	2	3	2	2
Labor Force Status:											
Unemployed	76[5]	90	62	70	74	84	77	74	88	82	81
Underemployed	9[5]	10	4	5	5	8	7	6	6	6	3
Other[4]	16[5]		34	25	21	8	16	21	5	12	16
Receiving Unemployment Insurance	5	7	4	6	6	12	13	14	15	14	16

Source: Employment and Training Administration, U.S. Department of Labor

[1] Includes MDTA-Institutional, JOP-OJT, NYC in-school, NYC out-of-school, Operation Mainstream, CEP, and JOBS. Excludes OIC, SER, CMP, Urban League, and Public Service Careers.

[2] Excludes enrollees in PEP (Emergency Employment Act) Summer Youth Program.

[3] May be duplication between recently separated and special (Vietnam era) veterans.

[4] Employed or not in the labor force.

[5] Excludes NYC in-school and JOBS enrollees for whom data were not available.

Note: Fiscal 1976 figures exclude the transition quarter, July-Sept. 1976.

TABLE 8 Characteristics of Participants in CETA, Titles I, II, and VI, Sample Prime Sponsors, Fiscal Year 1976 (percentages)

| Prime Sponsors | Title | Participants (Cumulative)[1] | Percent of Total | | | | | | | | | | Veterans | |
| | | | Female | Age 21 and Under | Age 45 and Over | 8 Years or Less of School | 12 Years or More of School | Economically Disadvantaged | Public Assistance | White | Black | Spanish American | Special Veteran | Other[2] |
		(1)	(2)	(3)	(4)	(5)	(6)	(7)	(8)	(9)	(10)	(11)	(12)	(13)
CITIES														
Gary, Ind.	I	4,485	54.6	64.7	3.2	7.0	35.4	97.0	50.4	10.8	88.4	7.6	2.1	0.9
	II	235	34.9	22.6	14.1	6.8	67.2	98.7	21.3	6.8	85.1	6.8	6.8	6.4
	VI	488	14.3	25.6	11.8	8.0	63.3	98.8	26.0	5.7	86.3	7.8	6.4	9.8
Long Beach, Ca.	I	2,588	44.2	44.5	7.2	5.5	60.8	98.4	25.3	46.3	34.8	15.2	4.3	3.8
	II	248	46.4	19.4	9.3	0.4	92.8	5.2	9.7	58.1	31.9	7.7	20.2	3.6
	VI	629	34.8	12.3	13.5	1.4	89.4	25.0	20.2	65.5	26.7	11.9	11.8	14.0
New York, NY	I	81,605	48.0	62.7	6.1	10.6	42.1	80.5	25.7	34.2	47.0	30.3	3.2	1.4
	II	24,253	38.9	20.7	11.2	6.5	65.6	41.4	25.6	20.8	57.2	16.7	18.4	10.9
	VI	17,946	37.2	19.4	11.3	6.2	66.4	40.3	20.1	23.3	56.6	16.0	14.8	12.8
Philadelphia, Pa.	I	17,194	47.7	65.2	2.2	7.1	36.0	76.0	44.3	12.5	80.2	6.5	2.8	3.3
	II	4,493	21.1	13.5	11.6	4.2	66.0	65.9	24.5	27.9	66.4	5.0	35.1	16.8
	VI	3,960	19.4	14.9	8.0	3.6	63.7	68.0	28.1	22.7	70.4	6.0	33.2	12.9
St. Paul, Minn.	I	5,772	40.5	36.6	7.7	2.9	73.2	65.5	19.0	75.4	19.0	2.9	4.3	5.2
	II	213	41.3	22.1	9.0	0.9	96.3	35.2	9.4	85.7	11.0	4.2	8.9	8.0
	VI	678	39.8	19.5	11.4	2.5	88.0	42.5	11.2	76.1	18.1	8.8	1.3	8.1
Topeka, Ks.[3]	I	1,262	39.9	55.9	5.0	3.6	51.7	78.7	21.4	51.8	36.3	9.0	6.4	5.8
	II	94	42.6	17.0	8.5	1.1	80.9	26.6	15.9	55.3	34.0	5.3	10.6	13.8
	VI	313	40.3	25.3	5.4	3.2	77.9	57.2	14.0	48.6	38.7	8.9	4.8	6.4
COUNTIES														
Calhoun, Mich.	I	1,600	45.3	38.2	7.0	4.4	68.0	68.1	31.7	48.4	45.3	4.1	5.2	4.4
	II	174	40.8	13.7	20.1	5.2	86.8	75.3	24.7	72.4	24.1	3.4	7.5	12.1
	VI	477	37.1	16.1	12.1	5.9	78.2	70.6	24.3	69.2	23.5	4.0	8.8	11.3

		Count												
Chester, Pa.	I	1,704	43.7	62.6	4.5	9.6	46.9	63.9	33.5	48.8	47.5	11.2	4.7	2.3
	II	51	37.3	13.7	15.7	3.9	84.3	47.1	21.5	74.5	23.5	5.9	9.8	11.8
	VI	279	41.2	19.7	7.9	2.2	84.2	42.3	16.2	68.8	30.8	4.7	11.1	5.7
*Cook, Ill.	I	5,081	46.9	50.4	14.9	7.4	50.4	53.3	14.8	54.4	44.3	6.2	2.4	6.8
	II	468	34.8	23.5	19.0	6.8	70.9	33.1	16.5	40.2	59.8	3.0	8.1	9.8
	VI	1,528	36.5	24.1	20.1	3.9	81.2	38.9	7.1	66.4	33.0	1.8	7.3	7.5
Lorain, O.	I	1,014	46.3	40.6	7.4	6.5	60.3	62.7	32.3	49.3	36.1	13.7	5.3	5.8
	II	145	57.9	23.4	12.4	4.8	80.0	46.2	20.7	55.9	31.0	13.1	9.7	3.4
	VI	574	38.9	30.3	25.9	6.3	72.3	53.8	14.9	61.8	28.7	9.1	6.3	9.9
Middlesex, NJ	I	2,246	54.4	47.6	4.8	15.3	40.9	86.1	33.0	36.6	46.1	30.9	1.6	1.8
	II	780	38.7	17.7	19.8	5.5	80.1	27.8	6.9	81.5	18.2	3.7	7.9	6.4
	VI	1,068	35.0	19.0	18.3	5.6	80.0	24.3	7.1	82.7	17.0	4.9	9.4	10.5
Pasco, Fla.	I	3,511	46.6	31.6	17.2	10.9	56.4	53.2	21.6	82.7	14.5	2.5	3.8	11.8
	II	64	56.6	20.3	21.9	1.6	90.6	14.1	11.0	95.3	1.6	3.1	12.5	14.1
	VI	211	47.4	16.6	20.4	3.3	86.3	28.9	9.5	88.2	10.0	1.4	9.5	19.9
*Ramsey, Minn.	I	962	50.3	70.1	2.8	15.1	44.3	83.6	55.2	93.9	1.7	1.6	3.3	2.3
	II	30	50.0	6.7	0.0	0.0	93.3	50.0	3.3	93.3	6.7	0.0	6.7	6.7
	VI	201	45.8	16.4	5.0	0.5	98.0	47.8	11.0	95.5	1.5	2.0	8.0	6.0
Stanislaus, Ca.	I	3,627	42.8	67.5	8.9	6.9	36.9	61.5	25.3	89.0	6.5	24.8	2.4	3.6
	II	280	66.1	25.4	6.0	2.1	93.2	63.2	25.0	88.9	6.1	13.6	5.7	8.2
	VI	840	40.8	24.4	7.8	5.4	80.7	65.2	39.3	86.5	9.9	21.8	9.8	8.6
*Union, NJ	I	1,962	44.1	70.6	4.4	6.7	40.9	61.5	10.7	27.7	63.4	6.3	1.5	1.0
	II	142	31.7	14.1	11.3	4.2	78.8	31.7	2.1	31.7	59.2	8.5	15.5	10.6
	VI	659	46.9	31.7	13.2	2.0	78.3	39.5	4.1	43.9	49.3	4.6	4.4	5.0
CONSORTIA Austin, Texas	I	2,048	57.2	57.0	3.6	14.1	36.8	89.8	24.0	64.6	33.7	43.1	1.8	0.8
	II	–	–	–	–	–	–	–	–	–	–	–	–	–
	VI	350	49.1	20.0	10.3	8.6	74.3	55.7	12.2	82.9	16.6	28.6	6.6	2.9

313

TABLE 8 (Continued)

Prime Sponsors	Title	Participants (Cumulative)[1]	Female	Age 21 and Under	Age 45 and Over	8 Years or Less of School	12 Years or More of School	Economically Disadvantaged	Public Assistance	White	Black	Spanish American	Veterans	
													Special Veteran	Other[2]
		(1)	(2)	(3)	(4)	(5)	(6)	(7)	(8)	(9)	(10)	(11)	(12)	(13)
CONSORTIA (continued)														
Cleveland, O.[4]	I	15,879	42.5	43.7	21.3	6.0	56.7	45.9	28.9	44.1	55.5	10.4	4.3	7.7
	II	1,641	15.4	19.0	20.9	6.8	67.9	33.9	18.7	52.8	46.7	1.7	5.1	10.0
	VI	2,100	23.4	19.4	25.7	6.7	71.5	20.7	16.6	60.9	38.7	1.0	7.8	18.0
Kansas City, Ks.	I	2,428	56.0	47.8	3.8	5.4	59.2	74.0	27.9	36.0	62.6	12.4	6.0	6.1
	II	104	22.1	26.0	35.6	12.5	53.8	54.8	16.3	32.7	66.3	4.8	6.7	17.3
	VI	492	32.9	27.1	19.7	7.9	75.4	32.7	11.8	62.8	36.4	3.9	7.3	14.2
Lansing, Mich.	I	8,526	36.1	42.4	2.2	8.5	55.2	63.7	39.5	66.0	25.5	11.7	4.5	4.8
	II	387	33.9	17.3	7.0	1.3	92.7	27.9	8.2	86.8	12.4	2.6	18.1	7.5
	VI	851	31.7	19.0	6.3	1.6	88.0	39.6	10.9	87.2	10.1	3.9	15.4	8.6
Phoenix/Maricopa, Ar.	I	8,026	48.1	50.5	5.0	12.8	41.0	84.2	18.0	68.8	25.4	39.1	3.8	4.2
	II	703	42.1	18.9	11.0	4.7	84.4	56.0	14.2	85.6	12.1	26.1	11.7	12.2
	VI	3,162	41.3	20.1	12.0	3.2	87.3	46.2	13.0	86.5	11.5	20.9	9.0	11.8
Orange Co., Ca.	I[5]	6,859	46.7	71.5	5.1	7.2	34.4	95.2	28.6	84.5	9.5	46.9	5.7	2.0
	II[6]	513	37.2	18.0	13.0	2.3	86.8	39.0	16.1	91.6	1.8	16.4	15.0	7.0
	VI[6]	1,964	37.5	15.3	14.3	1.2	89.9	34.5	19.3	90.4	5.2	14.4	15.1	9.1
Raleigh, NC[7]	I	1,887	49.0	64.7	3.8	10.8	36.6	80.8	28.3	30.3	68.6	0.2	2.8	3.0
	II	122	57.4	20.5	13.9	5.7	81.2	25.4	6.6	61.5	36.9	0.0	4.9	7.4
	VI	682	31.8	17.2	16.7	13.2	68.2	8.9	9.1	57.9	40.2	0.1	3.1	–
Pinellas/ St. Petersburg, Fla.	I	3,356	50.9	45.2	8.5	9.0	42.1	91.0	19.9	52.6	46.8	0.7	4.1	5.2
	II[6]	355	38.0	14.1	21.4	5.6	77.7	47.9	16.9	63.7	35.5	0.8	7.0	14.4
	VI[6]	1,338	23.4	20.5	17.0	6.6	72.2	33.6	15.4	69.0	30.1	0.7	6.8	17.6

San Joaquin, Ca.	I	8,759	36.7	39.7	16.4	31.8	38.8	76.6	21.7	73.3	12.9	56.8	2.4	2.3
	II	590	55.6	20.0	7.5	0.7	90.1	52.0	31.0	74.4	16.4	28.8	8.0	18.3
	VI	687	44.1	18.0	7.3	2.2	86.1	47.0	29.6	73.5	17.2	21.3	7.1	19.4
STATES Maine[8]	I	3,399	42.8	38.6	7.2	8.3	64.6	95.7	21.3	97.5	0.4	0.1	6.7	7.8
	II	2,207	35.2	13.3	19.5	9.4	74.5	99.0	6.3	99.1	0.2	0.0	7.2	20.1
	VI	2,663	34.7	11.4	18.0	9.0	76.7	93.3	8.5	98.8	0.2	0.0	7.1	16.4
*Arizona	I	5,793	47.6	63.6	6.7	12.4	41.2	78.2	17.5	58.0	5.4	21.9	2.9	3.7
	II	363	38.6	44.7	10.2	10.7	50.2	68.3	18.0	83.5	6.9	33.1	7.4	10.7
	VI	1,332	38.4	24.3	14.2	7.4	77.3	40.9	11.4	88.3	6.8	34.2	8.6	13.7
*North Carolina	I	15,285	54.1	63.1	5.1	16.6	34.8	61.7	20.1	43.6	53.7	0.2	1.3	4.9
	II	2,899	31.9	27.7	14.2	11.9	61.0	38.1	5.7	64.0	34.3	0.4	3.2	16.2
	VI	11,157	36.7	23.6	14.6	12.6	64.1	36.1	4.8	65.4	32.6	0.4	3.2	14.7
*Texas	I	26,231	45.6	67.0	6.2	18.6	28.0	90.8	19.8	65.2	34.0	28.0	2.9	2.5
	II	861	36.1	24.1	17.3	20.1	55.0	78.7	13.1	89.7	8.9	61.4	6.4	3.5
	VI	5,061	35.4	28.2	16.3	15.8	62.1	74.0	11.6	79.6	19.2	25.3	7.1	8.3

Source: Quarterly Summary of Client Characteristics, Employment and Training Administration, U.S. Department of Labor

[1] Through June 30, 1976.
[2] Recently separated veterans not included since figures partly overlap special veterans.
[3] Topeka became Topeka-Shawnee Consortium in fiscal 1976.
[4] Lake County withdrew from the Cleveland Consortium in fiscal 1976.
[5] Characteristics for the fourth quarter of fiscal 1975.
[6] Characteristics for the third quarter of fiscal 1976.
[7] Balance of Wake County withdrew from the Raleigh Consortium in fiscal 1976.
[8] Cumberland and Penobscot Counties withdrew from balance of state in fiscal 1976.
*Balance of county or state.

TABLE 9 Status of Terminated CETA Participants, Titles I, II, and VI, Sample Prime Sponsors, Fiscal Year 1976

Prime Sponsors	Title	Individuals Served[1]	Terminated	Percentage of Terminations[2]				Other Positive	Non-Positive
				Entered Employment					
				Total	Direct Placement	Indirect Placement	Obtained Employment		
		(1)	(2)	(3)	(4)	(5)	(6)	(7)	(8)
CITIES									
Gary, Ind.	I	4,485	3,504	17.1	4.8	12.1	0.2	30.1	52.9
	II	235	174	18.4	4.6	13.2	0.6	72.4	9.2
	VI	488	245	35.5	3.3	30.6	1.6	9.4	50.2
Long Beach, Ca.	I	2,588	1,956	49.5	—	43.9	5.6	31.2	19.3
	II	248	182	29.1	—	26.4	2.7	55.5	15.4
	VI	629	388	28.6	—	25.2	3.3	36.3	35.0
New York, NY	I	81,605	61,993	21.8	7.4	12.3	2.1	54.5	23.7
	II	24,253	10,935	0.7	—	—	0.7	77.2	22.1
	VI	17,946	16,912	4.4	—	3.1	1.3	64.5	31.0
Philadelphia, Pa.	I	17,194	14,958	31.8	20.8	9.0	1.9	37.3	30.9
	II	4,493	1,753	1.7	—	1.6	—	93.6	4.8
	VI	3,960	3,960	1.2	—	1.2	—	90.0	8.8

St. Paul, Minn.	I	5,772	2,905	47.0	8.5	18.2	20.3	33.8	19.1
	II	213	84	44.0	8.3	20.2	15.5	35.7	20.2
	VI	678	164	48.2	9.7	7.9	30.5	32.3	19.5
Topeka, Ks.[3]	I	1,262	1,105	55.1	23.7	14.0	17.2	8.7	36.3
	II	94	66	56.0	3.0	40.9	12.1	1.5	42.4
	VI	313	153	48.3	–	26.8	21.5	2.6	49.0
COUNTIES									
Calhoun, Mich.	I	1,600	1,280	38.3	12.2	23.3	2.7	13.0	48.7
	II	174	174	21.3	1.1	20.1	–	67.8	10.9
	VI	477	178	30.3	1.7	19.7	9.0	12.9	56.7
Chester, Pa.	I	1,764	1,455	9.6	0.6	2.9	6.0	72.8	17.7
	II	–	–	–	–	–	–	–	–
	VI	279	137	51.8	–	27.0	24.8	16.1	32.1
*Cook, Ill.	I	5,081	3,656	35.8	2.0	20.0	13.7	30.1	34.1
	II	468	468	8.8	–	3.2	5.5	73.1	18.2
	VI	1,528	498	40.2	–	13.0	27.1	8.8	51.0
Lorain, O.	I	1,014	325	33.8	8.0	8.6	17.2	52.0	14.1
	II	145	120	8.3	–	5.8	2.5	72.5	19.2
	VI	574	156	25.6	–	14.7	10.9	31.4	42.9

TABLE 9 (Continued)

Prime Sponsors	Title	Individuals Served[1]	Terminated	Percentage of Terminations[2]				Other Positive	Non-Positive
				Entered Employment					
				Total	Direct Placement	Indirect Placement	Obtained Employment		
		(1)	(2)	(3)	(4)	(5)	(6)	(7)	(8)
COUNTIES (continued)									
Middlesex, NJ	I	2,194	1,374	46.4	7.0	35.1	4.3	21.1	32.4
	II	780	129	31.0	–	12.4	18.6	40.3	28.7
	VI	1,068	972	19.7	–	9.0	10.6	59.4	21.0
Pasco, Fla.	I	3,511	2,263	41.5	17.2	2.8	21.4	11.1	47.4
	II	64	46	45.7	–	36.9	8.7	30.4	23.9
	VI	211	91	54.9	–	31.9	23.0	4.4	40.6
*Ramsey, Minn.	I	962	775	20.0	1.4	11.1	7.5	69.0	11.0
	II	–	–	–	–	–	–	–	–
	VI	201	111	36.0	–	17.1	18.9	42.3	21.6
Stanislaus, Ca.	I	3,627	2,780	23.8	–	18.9	4.9	31.5	44.7
	II	280	124	62.9	–	47.6	15.3	16.1	21.0
	VI	840	751	20.6	–	13.8	6.8	58.1	21.3

*Union, NJ	I	1,962	1,603	22.8	12.7	8.7	1.4	61.6	15.5
	II	142	79	8.9	—	5.1	3.8	49.4	41.8
	VI	659	134	38.1	—	32.8	5.2	14.9	47.0
CONSORTIA									
Austin, Tex.	I	2,048	1,703	37.9	15.0	15.4	7.4	31.5	30.6
	II	—	—	—	—	—	—	—	—
	VI	350	215	60.0	—	54.4	5.6	2.8	37.2
Cleveland, O.[4]	I	15,879	11,738	28.1	14.5	5.9	7.7	24.1	47.8
	II	1,609	1,511	8.1	0.1	6.0	2.0	76.0	15.9
	VI	2,110	1,186	27.8	0.1	23.9	3.8	59.0	13.1
Kansas City, Ks.	I	2,428	1,831	52.3	19.1	33.2	—	7.6	40.1
	II	104	33	42.4	—	26.3	15.1	12.1	45.4
	VI	492	118	22.9	—	15.2	7.6	1.7	75.4
Lansing, Mich.	I	8,526	5,331	29.2	10.9	6.6	11.7	24.8	45.9
	II	387	292	12.7	—	8.9	3.8	77.7	9.6
	VI	851	527	34.3	—	18.2	16.1	30.6	35.1
Phoenix/Maricopa, Ar.	I	8,026	6,134	44.1	16.2	27.9	—	29.4	26.5
	II	703	414	22.9	—	22.9	—	42.0	35.0
	VI	3,162	1,289	32.4	—	32.4	—	20.2	47.3

TABLE 9 (Continued)

Prime Sponsors	Title	Individuals Served[1] (1)	Terminated (2)	Percentage of Terminations[2]				Other Positive (7)	Non-Positive (8)
				Entered Employment					
				Total (3)	Direct Placement (4)	Indirect Placement (5)	Obtained Employment (6)		
CONSORTIA (continued)									
Orange Co., Ca.	I	7,717	6,515	58.2	31.5	24.9	1.7	20.6	21.2
	II	724	291	24.7	–	17.2	7.6	37.1	38.1
	VI	2,155	1,197	33.4	–	19.3	14.1	31.0	35.6
Raleigh, NC[5]	I	1,887	1,430	12.3	–	6.2	6.0	68.9	18.8
	II	122	43	34.9	–	9.3	25.6	4.6	60.5
	VI	682	280	36.1	–	15.0	21.1	6.4	57.5
Pinellas/St. Petersburg, Fla.	I	3,356	2,439	30.9	13.6	4.2	13.0	30.0	39.1
	II	355	182	44.5	–	26.9	17.6	4.9	50.5
	VI	1,411	669	45.7	–	29.6	16.1	4.0	50.2
San Joaquin, Ca.	I	8,759	6,860	31.4	14.6	5.8	10.9	12.1	56.5
	II	590	434	15.9	–	9.7	6.2	68.9	15.2
	VI	687	423	30.0	–	16.3	13.7	44.7	24.3

STATES

*Maine[6]	I	3,399	2,709	53.4	0.5	47.8	5.0	11.3	35.3
	II	2,207	1,764	25.2	–	19.4	5.7	51.5	23.4
	VI	2,663	2,663	14.9	–	6.8	8.1	44.9	40.2
*Arizona	I	5,793	4,733	24.5	5.6	12.0	6.9	41.0	34.5
	II	363	284	19.7	–	7.7	12.0	66.5	13.7
	VI	1,332	891	28.6	0.2	20.0	8.4	30.8	40.6
*North Carolina	I	15,285	7,565	23.4	0.2	6.8	14.5	9.4	67.3
	II	2,899	1,472	29.9	–	2.2	27.6	9.0	61.0
	VI	11,157	5,062	29.3	–	1.2	28.0	8.8	61.9
*Texas	I	26,231	22,853	24.9	9.2	10.6	5.0	61.8	13.3
	II	861	644	34.2	2.0	18.3	13.8	33.7	32.1
	VI	5,061	2,871	49.3	2.3	24.9	22.1	9.4	41.3

Source: Quarterly Progress Reports, Employment and Training Administration, U.S. Department of Labor

[1] Through June 30, 1976.

[2] Column heading definitions:

Direct Placement—placed in unsubsidized employment after receiving only outreach, intake, and referral services.

Indirect Placement—placed in unsubsidized employment after receiving training, employment, or other manpower services.

Obtained Employment—obtained employment through other means.

Other Positive—enrolled in school, entered armed forces, transferred to another manpower program or completed program objective but did not enter employment.

Non-Positive—left program for other reasons.

[3] Topeka became Topeka-Shawnee Consortium in fiscal 1976.

[4] Lake County withdrew from the Cleveland Consortium in fiscal 1976.

[5] Balance of Wake County withdrew from the Raleigh Consortium in fiscal 1976.

[6] Cumberland and Penobscot Counties withdrew from State program in fiscal 1976.

*Balance of county or state.

TABLE 10 Characteristics of Persons Served, Terminated, and Entered Employment, U.S. Titles I, II, and VI, Fiscal 1976 (Percentages)

Characteristics	Title I			Title II			Title VI		
	Individuals Served[1]	Terminations	Entered Employment	Individuals Served[1]	Terminations	Entered Employment	Individuals Served[1]	Terminations	Entered Employment
Sex: Male	54	55	56	64	64	63	65	67	67
Female	46	45	43	36	36	37	35	33	33
Age: 21 and under	57	59	40	22	22	20	22	22	21
22-44	36	35	51	64	65	68	64	65	68
45 and over	7	6	9	14	13	11	14	12	11
Education: 11 years or less	55	57	38	26	25	21	26	23	21
12 years	33	31	45	42	43	44	43	43	44
over 12 years	12	12	17	32	32	35	31	30	33

Family Income:									
AFDC	15	14	9	6	6	5	6	6	5
Economically Disadvantaged	76	75	66	47	45	43	44	45	38
Race: White	55	56	64	61	65	75	68	67	78
Black	37	37	29	27	26	18	23	23	17
Spanish Speaking	14	14	14	12	10	9	10	11	8
Veterans:									
Recently Separated	2	2	3	4	3	3	5	5	5
Special	4	3	5	10	10	10	9	9	10
Other	5	4	6	11	11	12	12	12	12
Labor Force Status:									
Unemployed	70	67	81	77	81	82	82	81	85
Underemployed and Other	30	32	19	23	19	17	18	18	15

Source: Employment and Training Administration, U.S. Department of Labor
[1] Through June 30, 1976.

Additional
References

Advisory Commission on Intergovernmental Relations. *Block Grants: A Roundtable Discussion.* A-51. Washington, D.C.: U.S. Government Printing Office.

Advisory Commission on Intergovernmental Relations. *The Comprehensive Employment and Training Act: Early Readings from a Hybrid Block Grant.* Prepared by Carl Stenberg. A-58. Washington, D.C.: U.S. Government Printing Office, June 1977.

Aronson, Robert L., ed. *The Localization of Federal Manpower Planning.* Manpower Research Program, New York State School of Industrial and Labor Relations. Ithaca: Cornell University, 1973.

Clague, Ewan, and Leo Kramer. *Manpower Policies and Programs—A Review, 1935–75.* Kalamazoo, Michigan: W. E. Upjohn Institute for Employment Research, 1976.

Fechter, Alan. *Public Employment Programs.* Evaluative Study 20. Washington, D.C.: American Enterprise Institute for Public Policy Research, May 1975.

Levitan, Sar A., and Garth L. Mangum. *Federal Training and Work Programs in the Sixties.* Ann Arbor: Institute of Labor and Industrial Relations of the University of Michigan and Wayne State University, 1969.

Levitan, Sar A., and Robert Taggart, eds. *Emergency Employment Act: The PEP Generation.* Salt Lake City: Olympus Publishing Company, 1974.

Nathan, Richard P., and Charles F. Adams, Jr. *Revenue Sharing: The Second Round.* Washington, D.C.: The Brookings Institution, 1977.

Nathan, Richard P., Robert F. Cook, Janet M. Galchik, and Richard W. Long. *Monitoring the Public Service Employment Program.* Volume II of *An Interim Report to the Congress of the National Commission for Manpower Policy, Job Creation through Public Service Employment.* Preliminary report from the Brookings Institution dated March 20, 1978. Washington, D.C.: National Commission for Manpower Policy, April 1978.

Nathan, Richard P., Allen D. Manvel, and Susannah E. Calkins. *Monitoring Revenue Sharing.* Washington, D.C.: The Brookings Institution, 1975.

325

326 Additional References

National Commission for Manpower Policy. *Addressing Continuing High Levels of Unemployment.* Interim Report to the President and Congress. Report No. 4. Available from National Commission for Manpower Policy, Washington, D.C., April 1976.

National Commission for Manpower Policy. *The Challenge of Rising Unemployment.* Interim Report to Congress. Report No. 1. Available from National Commission for Manpower Policy, Washington, D.C., February 1975.

National Commission for Manpower Policy. *An Employment Strategy for the United States: Next Steps.* Second Annual Report to the President and Congress. Report. No. 5. Available from National Commission for Manpower Policy, Washington, D.C., December 1976.

National Commission for Manpower Policy. *Public Service Employment and Other Responses to Continuing Unemployment.* Interim Report to Congress. Report No. 2. Available from National Commission for Manpower Policy, Washington, D.C., June 1975.

National Commission for Manpower Policy. *Toward a National Manpower Policy.* First Annual Report to the President and Congress. Report No. 3. Available from National Commission for Manpower Policy, Washington, D.C., October 1975.

National Council on Employment Policy. *The Case for CETA Reauthorization: Continued Decentralization and Decategorization.* Washington, D.C.: National Council on Employment Policy, January 1978.

National Council on Employment Policy. *The Impact of Employment and Training Programs.* A Policy Statement. Washington, D.C.: National Council on Employment Policy, Novemenber 1976.

National League of Cities/U.S. Conference of Mayors. *The Impact of CETA on Institutional Vocational Education.* Prepared by Robert Anderson and Rosa Rozansky. Washington, D.C.: National League of Cities/U.S. Conference of Mayors, 1974.

National League of Cities/U.S. Conference of Mayors. *The Impact of CETA on Institutional Vocational Education: Case Studies and Final Report 1977.* Prepared by Robert Anderson and Rosa Rozansky. Washington, D.C.: National League of Cities/U.S. Conference of Mayors, 1977.

National Research Council. *The Comprehensive Employment and Training Act: Impact on People, Places, Programs—An Interim Report.* Prepared by William Mirengoff and Lester Rindler. Washington, D.C.: Committee on Evaluation of Employment and Training Programs, National Academy of Sciences, 1976.

National Research Council. *The Comprehensive Employment and Training Act: Abstracts of Selected Studies.* Prepared by Claire K. Lipsman. Committee on Evaluation of Employment and Training Programs. Available from NTIS (PS-263 499/AS), Washington, D.C., 1976.

National Research Council. "Early Perceptions of the Comprehensive Employment and Training Act." Papers presented at the initial meeting of the Committee on Evaluation of Employment and Training Programs. Available from the Committee on Evaluation of Employment and Training Programs, National Research Council, Washington, D.C., 1974.

National Research Council. *Employment and Training Programs: The Local View.* William Mirengoff, ed. Washington, D.C.: Committee on Evaluation of Employment and Training Programs, National Academy of Sciences, 1978.

National Research Council. *Transition to Decentralized Manpower Programs: Eight Area Studies—An Interim Report.* Wiliam Mirengoff, ed. Committee on Evaluation of Employment and Training Programs. Available from NTIS (PB-263 499/AS), Washington, D.C., 1976.

SER/Jobs for Progress, Inc. *The Impact of the First Year Implementation of CETA on the Spanish Speaking.* Funded by Ford Foundation. Los Angeles: *ser*/Jobs for Progress, Inc. (9841 Airport Blvd., Suite 1020, Los Angeles, CA 90045), November 1975.

Snedeker, Bonnie B., and David M. Snedeker. *CETA: Decentralization on Trial.* Salt Lake City: Olympus Publishing Company, 1974.

Southern Regional Council. *The Job Ahead: Manpower Policies in the South.* Atlanta: Southern Regional Council, 1975.

U.S. Congress, House. *Authorization of Appropriations for Fiscal Year 1976 for Carrying Out Title VI of the Comprehensive Employment and Training Act of 1973.* Committee on Education and Labor. Hearings before the Subcommittee on Manpower, Compensation, and Health and Safety. 94th Congress, 1st Session, 1975.

U.S. Congress, House. *The Emergency Jobs Act of 1974.* Committeee on Education and Labor. Hearings before the Select Subcommittee on Labor. 93rd Congress, 2d Session, 1975.

U.S. Congress. Senate. *Emergency Jobs and Unemployment Assistance Amendments of 1975.* Committee on Labor and Public Welfare. Hearings before the Subcommittee on Employment, Poverty, and Migratory Labor. 94th Congress, 1st Session, 1975.

U.S. Congress. Senate. *Emergency Jobs and Unemployment Assistance Amendments, 1975–1976.* Part 2. Committee on Labor and Public Welfare. Hearings before the Subcommittee on Employment, Poverty, and Migratory Labor. 94th Congress, 2d Session, 1976.

U.S. Congress. Senate. *Implementing Comprehensive Manpower Legislation, 1974: Case Studies of Selected Manpower Programs.* Sar A. Levitan, ed. Committee print. Subcommittee on Employment, Poverty, and Migratory Labor. Committee on Labor and Public Welfare. 93d Congress, 2d Session, 1974.

U.S. Congress. Senate. *Public Service Employment Legislation, 1974.* Committee on Labor and Public Welfare. Hearings before the Subcommittee on Employment, Poverty, and Migratory Labor. 93d Congress, 2d Session, 1974.

U.S. Department of Labor. Manpower Administration. Office of Research and Development. *CETA Prime Sponsor Management Decisions and Program Goal Achievement.* Final Report, PB-268 387/8ST. Prepared by Randall B. Ripley. Ohio State University. Available from NTIS, Washington, D.C., June 30, 1977.

U.S. Department of Labor. Employment and Training Administration. Office of Research and Development. *The Implementation of CETA in Eastern Massachusetts and Boston.* R&D Monograph No. 57. Charles A. Myers, ed. Available from Inquiries Unit of the Employment and Training Administration (Room 10225, U.S. Department of Labor, 601 D Street, NW, Washington, D.C. 20213), 1978.

U.S. Department of Labor. Employment and Training Administration. *Public Service Employment in the Carolinas: Current Utilization and the Potential for Expansion in Selected Communities.* Prepared by Edward F. Dement of MDC, Inc. Available from MDC, Inc., Chapel Hill, North Carolina, June 15, 1976.

U.S. General Accounting Office. *Formulating Plans for Comprehensive Employment Services: A Highly Involved Process.* Washington, D.C.: U.S. General Accounting Office, July 23, 1976.

U.S. General Accounting Office. *Job Training Programs Need More Effective Management.* Washington, D.C.: U.S. General Accounting Office, July 7, 1978.

Urban Coalition of Minneapolis. *Comprehensive Employment and Training Act (CETA): Programs in the City of Minneapolis.* Prepared by Dana Schroeder, Percilla Paulson, and Keith Dennis. Minneapolis: Urban Coalition of Minneapolis, April 1976.